Sanyan Stories

ALSO AVAILABLE FROM
THE UNIVERSITY OF WASHINGTON PRESS

Compiled by Feng Menglong
Translated by Shuhui Yang and Yunqin Yang

Stories Old and New:
A Ming Dynasty Collection, volume 1

Stories to Caution the World:
A Ming Dynasty Collection, volume 2

Stories to Awaken the World:
A Ming Dynasty Collection, volume 3

Sanyan Stories

FAVORITES FROM A

MING DYNASTY COLLECTION

Collected by Feng Menglong

Translated by Shuhui Yang and Yunqin Yang

UNIVERSITY OF WASHINGTON PRESS

SEATTLE AND LONDON

University of Washington Press
www.washington.edu/uwpress

Library of Congress Cataloging-in-Publication Data
Sanyan stories : favorites from a Ming Dynasty collection / collected by Feng Menglong ;
translated by Shuhui Yang and Yunqin Yang.
     p.   cm.
   Includes bibliographical references.
   ISBN 978-0-295-99422-2 (pbk. : acid-free paper)
     1. Chinese fiction—Ming dynasty, 1368–1644.   I. Feng, Menglong, 1574–1646.
II. Yang, Shuhui (Translator).   III. Yang, Yunqin.
   PL2646.S28   2015
   895.13'408—dc23   2014026169

Contents

Introduction

The nine stories in this volume were selected from a three-volume set of celebrated stories from the Ming dynasty (1368–1644): *Stories Old and New* (Gujin xiaoshuo, 1620 or 1621), *Stories to Caution the World* (Jingshi tongyan, 1624; literally, *Comprehensive Words to Caution the World*), and *Stories to Awaken the World* (Xingshi hengyan, 1627; literally, *Constant Words to Awaken the World*). Each collection contains forty stories, and since *Stories Old and New* is also known as *Illustrious Words to Instruct the World* (Yushi mingyan), the three volumes are most often referred to collectively as the Sanyan (literally, "three words"), from the Chinese character *yan* at the end of each title.[1] The stories selected from the 120 in the Sanyan set to appear here were chosen on the basis of their popularity with American readers and their usefulness as texts in classes on Chinese and comparative literature.

The Sanyan collections were edited by Feng Menglong (1574–1646), the most knowledgeable connoisseur of popular literature of his time. He came from a well-to-do, educated family in the exceptionally prosperous Suzhou Prefecture, one of the great cultural centers of Ming China. Feng acquired the preliminary academic degree of *sheng yuan* when he was about twenty years old but apparently had no further luck in the civil service examinations, despite his erudition and great literary fame. Finally, in 1630, at the age of fifty-six or fifty-seven, he seems to have lost hope that he would pass the examinations and decided instead to take an alternative route to office by accepting the status of tribute student.[2] He then served one term as assistant instructor in Dantu County (about ninety miles northwest of Suzhou), probably from 1631 to 1634, before being promoted to a minor position as magistrate of Shouning County, Fujian.[3] He held this office for four years and proved to be an honest, caring, and efficient administrator, as is registered in the *County History of Shouning* (Shouning xian zhi), compiled in the early Qing period (1644–1911). The county history also tells us that Feng "venerated literary studies more than anything else" (*shou shang wenxue*) during his service.[4] Feng's last political involvement, toward the end of his life, was his association with the Southern Ming government in its desperate resistance against the crushing forces of the Manchus. He died in 1646 at the age of seventy-two.

Feng Menglong was one of the most prolific writers of his time. The books he published could literally be "piled up to reach his own height" (*zhuzuo dengshen*), a phrase traditionally used by critics to praise exceptionally productive writers,[5] and they covered such a wide range of interests and literary genres that Feng has been described as "presenting himself in two distinct personae, or . . . in a range of personae between two extremes."[6] At one extreme, he appears in some of his works as the wit, the ribald humorist, the bohemian, the drinker, and the romantic lover. This is the Feng Menglong who compiled *Treasury of Jokes* (Xiaofu) and published two volumes of folk songs (*Guazhir* and *Hill Songs*), mostly on erotic or ribald themes, and whose passionate love affair with the famous Suzhou courtesan Hou Huiqing is revealed in some of his poems. At the other extreme is Feng Menglong the patriot, orthodox scholar, and ardent examination candidate, who authored at least three handbooks on the Confucian classic *The Spring and Autumn Annals* (Chunqiu), wrote a similar handbook on the Four Books, and published many patriotic tracts as a consequence of his participation in Southern Ming resistance activities against the Manchus. These two personae may seem to be mutually exclusive, yet in his fiction as well as in his plays, Feng Menglong often reveals elements of both in a single text.[7]

Modern scholars generally agree, however, that Feng Menglong's greatest contribution to literature is in the field of vernacular fiction, particularly his collecting and editing of the three Sanyan books of 120 vernacular short stories. This genre, known as *huaben*, is believed to have developed, along with the vernacular novel, during the Song (960–1279) and Yuan (1260–1368) dynasties and reached maturity in the late Ming. As a passionate champion of popular literature, Feng managed to rescue from oblivion a significant proportion of the early *huaben* stories by making them available to the public again. But preservation of existing stories was by no means Feng Menglong's only concern—he was probably more interested in giving prestige to this new literary genre and establishing it socially. In the preface to *Stories Old and New*, he places vernacular fiction on a par with the highly esteemed classical tales of the Tang dynasty (618–907): "Literature and the arts have been so vigorously advanced by the imperial court of this Ming dynasty that each and every school is flourishing; in vernacular fiction alone, there is no lack of writings of a quality far above those of the Song. It is a mistake to believe, as some do, that such works lack the charm of those of the Tang. One who has a love for the peach need not forsake the apricot. Fine linen, silk gauze, plush, brocade—each has its proper occasion for wear."

In order to elevate the status of the vernacular story, Feng Menglong also claims, in the same preface, that the origin of all fiction is the grand tradition of historiography, and he ascribes more educational and moral power to the *huaben* story than to *The Analects of Confucius* (Lunyu).[8] With the aim of substantiating such claims, Feng is believed, not surprisingly, to have extensively modified some of the stories he had collected and to have incorporated many of his own stories and those of his friends into the Sanyan collections, although he does not acknowledge authorship in the preface.[9] According to Patrick Hanan, who applied rigorous stylistic criteria in his studies of the dating and authorship of Chinese vernacular stories, Feng Menglong is the probable author of nineteen stories in *Stories Old and New*, sixteen in the second collection, and one or two in the third.[10]

A less drastic but more obvious aspect of Feng's "editing" is his arrangement of the stories into pairs in each of the three collections. The thematically and grammatically parallel pairing of titles (which is evident in the complete volumes, although not in the current selection) may be an attempt to parody the parallelism of classical poetry and belles lettres prose (the two most honored literary genres of Feng's time) or may simply represent his effort to elevate the vernacular short story.[11] However, on the textual level, it is clear that the stories were composed with their pairings in mind.[12] The paired stories often share features of subject matter or plotline, and they occasionally contrast or comment on each other.

One of the most interesting and controversial characteristics of Chinese vernacular fiction is its "storyteller's rhetoric." This is part of what Patrick Hanan refers to as the "simulated context" or "the context of situation in which a piece of fiction claims to be transmitted."[13] In the Sanyan stories (and in other Chinese vernacular fiction), this simulacrum almost always takes the form of a professional storyteller addressing his audience. The storyteller-narrator asks questions of his simulated audience, converses with them, makes explicit references to his own stories, and intersperses his narrative with verses and poems. The narrator usually begins his talk with one or more prologue stories or poems, which supposedly allows time for his audience to gather before he presents the main piece in his performance.

Of course, in written literature, this storyteller's pose is only a pretense in which "the author and reader happily acquiesce in order that the fiction can be communicated."[14] It was a way to "naturalize, by reference to the familiar situation of hearing stories told in the vernacular by professional storytellers, the unfamiliar process of writing and reading fiction in vernacular Chinese."[15] But this formal feature, plus a misunderstanding of the term *huaben*, led many scholars of Chinese literature to subscribe, until the late twentieth century, to the "promptbook" theory, which held that the Chinese vernacular story developed directly from the promptbooks of marketplace storytellers in the Song dynasty and that the pre-Sanyan texts were genuine promptbooks written for performance in the Song and Yuan or early Ming periods.[16] W. L. Idema, however, argues that the storyteller's manner was developed deliberately in literati imitations by Feng Menglong and others. According to Idema, the conspicuous use of this rhetorical stance in the Sanyan collections was "a consequence mainly of Feng Menglong's reinterpretation of the genre and due to his overall rewritings."[17] In other words, Feng's editing of the collections included a systematic elaboration of the storyteller's rhetoric, which became a hallmark of the *huaben* story as he conceived of it.

This, however, is not to deny the presence of elements of oral folk literature in the Sanyan stories. Most contain anecdotes or episodes known even to the illiterate, which suggests that the editor looked to storytelling for raw materials as well as for rhetorical formulas. And we may assume that traces of the marketplace story-teller and the values he represented would unavoidably have remained in these *huaben* stories despite Feng Menglong's often meticulous editing. Idema argues that professional storytelling was but one of the many factors that helped to shape traditional Chinese fiction.[18] Small wonder that the Sanyan collections provide for us such a vivid panoramic view of the bustling world of imperial China before the end of the Ming; we see not only scholars, emperors, ministers, and generals but also a gallery of ordinary men and women in their everyday surroundings— merchants and artisans, prostitutes and courtesans, matchmakers and fortune-tellers, monks and nuns, servants and maids, thieves and impostors. We learn about their joys and sorrows, likes and dislikes, their views of life and death, and even their visions of the netherworld and the supernatural.

Thus, the Sanyan stories are necessarily overdetermined texts—historically, ideologically, and formally. They can justifiably be taken as an intersection of complex cultural determinations, with generic mixture and multiple voices making different and sometimes conflicting claims. In some of the previous translations of these stories, the storyteller's rhetoric, the verses, and the prologue stories were deleted.[19] The interlinear and marginal comments, generally believed to have been made by Feng Menglong himself, are omitted even in modern Chinese editions of the collection.[20] The unabridged translations presented here provide the English-language reader with a fuller picture of the complex social environment of imperial China and, more important, they show the intricate interactions among different voices in the texts, especially between the voice of the conventional storyteller-narrator and that of the literati editor Feng Menglong.[21]

Shuhui Yang

Translators' Note

In this translation, the interlinear and marginal comments in the original text appear in italic within parentheses in roman text and in roman within parentheses in italic text.

Chinese proper names are rendered in the pinyin system. For the convenience of those readers who are more accustomed to the Wade-Giles system of romanization, we have provided the following short list of difficult consonants:

c = ts'
q = ch'
x = hs
z = tz
zh = ch

Information about previous translations of stories in this collection (in varying degrees of completeness and accuracy) is provided in the endnotes for individual stories.

Frequently Encountered Chinese Terms

chi, a unit of measurement, translated as "foot"

jin, translated as "catty," equals half a kilogram

jinshi, one who passed the imperial civil service examinations at the national level

li, approximately one third of a mile

liang, translated as "tael," equals one sixteenth of a jin

mu, roughly one sixth of an acre

shi, a married woman known by her maiden name (e.g., Wang-shi)

xiucai, translated as "scholar," a successful candidate at the county level

zhuangyuan, a jinshi who ranked first in the palace examination, in which the emperor interviewed those who had passed the imperial civil service examination at the national level

zi, translated as "courtesy name," the name by which an educated person was addressed by people of his or her own generation, probably used more often than an official name

Chronology of Chinese Dynasties

Xia	ca. 2100–ca. 1600 B.C.E.
Shang (Yin)	ca. 1600–ca. 1028 B.C.E.
Zhou	ca. 1027–ca. 256 B.C.E.
Western Zhou	ca. 1027–771 B.C.E.
Eastern Zhou	770–256 B.C.E.
Spring and Autumn	770–476 B.C.E.
Warring States	475–221 B.C.E.
Qin	221–207 B.C.E.
Han	206 B.C.E.–220 C.E.
Western Han	206 B.C.E.–8 C.E.
Xin	9–25
Eastern Han	25–220
Three Kingdoms	220–80
Wei	220–65
Shu	221–63
Wu	222–80
Six Dynasties (Wu, Eastern Jin, Former Song, Southern Qi, Southern Liang, and Southern Chen)	222–589
Jin	265–420
Western Jin	265–316
Eastern Jin	317–420
Southern and Northern Dynasties	420–589
Southern Dynasties	
Former Song	420–79
Southern Qi	479–502
Southern Liang	502–57
Southern Chen	557–89
Northern Dynasties	
Northern Wei	386–534
Eastern Wei	534–50
Western Wei	535–56
Northern Qi	550–77
Northern Zhou	557–81

Sui	581–618
Tang	618–907
Five Dynasties and Ten Kingdoms	907–79
Five Dynasties	
Later Liang	907–23
Later Tang	923–36
Later Jin	936–46
Later Han	947–50
Later Zhou	951–60
Ten Kingdoms	907–79
Liao (Khitan)	916–1125
Song	960–1279
Northern Song	960–1126
Southern Song	1127–1279
Xixia (Tangut)	1038–1227
Jin (Jurchen)	1115–1234
Yuan (Mongol)	1260–1368
Ming	1368–1644
Qing (Manchu)	1644–1911

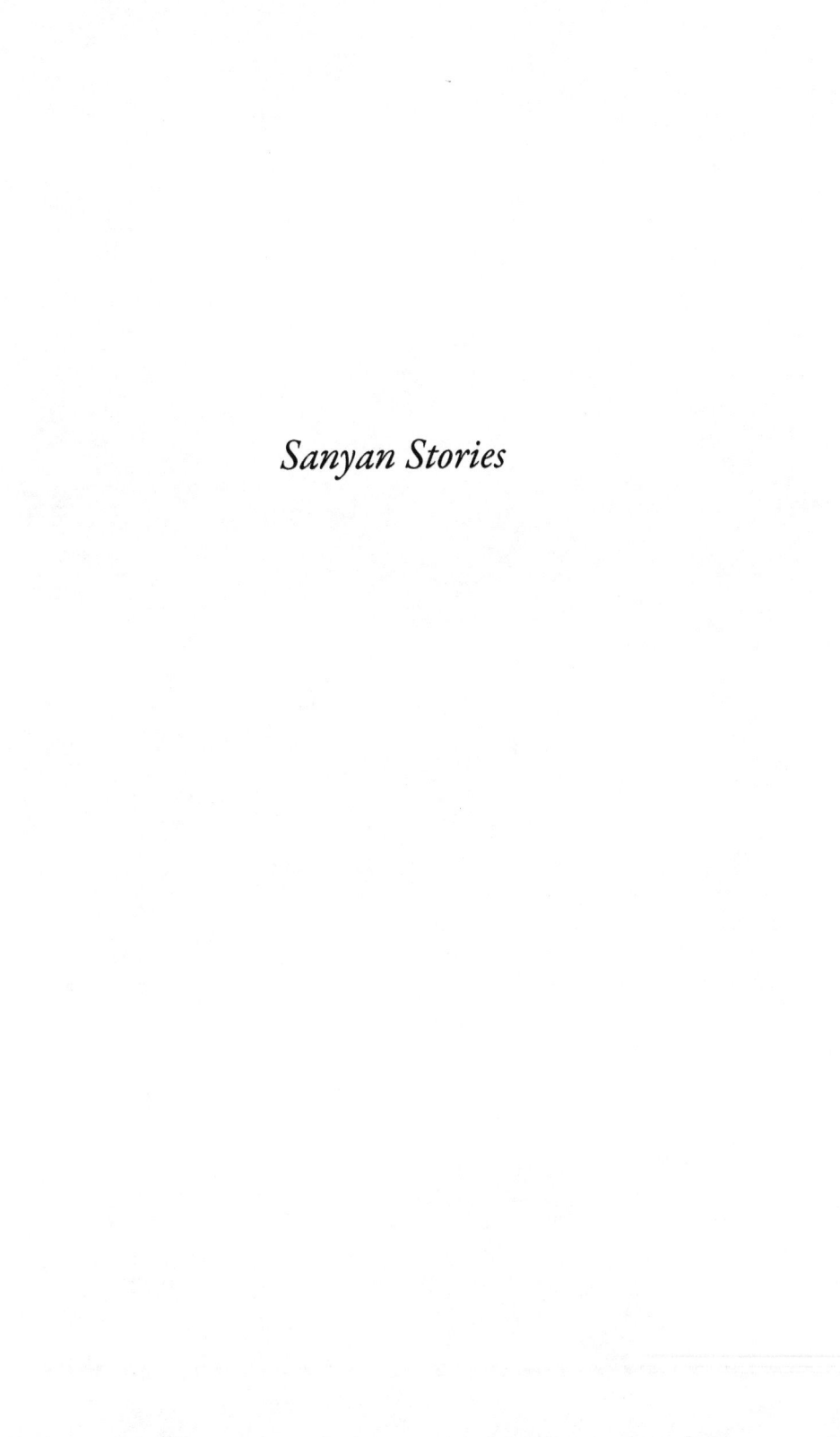

Sanyan Stories

Jiang Xingge Reencounters His Pearl Shirt

Wealth and rank are of no account,
And all too few live past seventy.
Can worldly fame last beyond the grave?
All in life is but an empty game.
Indulge not in youthful follies;
Nor with wine and women dally.
Break free from quarrels and worries;
Be content and enjoy a life of ease.

The above lyric poem to the tune of "The Moon over the West River" advises all to take life as it comes, to find delight in whatever lies in your lot, and not to let "drink," "lust," "wealth," and "wrath" consume your energies and compromise your integrity. Joy may turn out to be sorrow, and a gain may turn out to be a loss. But of the four vices cited above, "lust" is by far the most ruinous. The eyes are the go-between of love; the heart is the seed of desire. At the beginning, you will suffer from pangs of longing. By the end, your soul will take leave of your body. An occasional affair on the spur of the moment with some "wayside flower and willow" brings little harm, but never hatch deliberate plans against all sense of decency to seek some momentary gratification at the expense of the long-standing marriage of others. How would you feel if your own dear wife or beloved concubine were to fall a victim to another man's seduction? There is an ancient quatrain that puts it well:

The human heart may be blinded,
But the will of heaven never errs.
If I debauch not other men's wives,
Other men will not debauch mine.

Dear audience, now hear me tell the story of "The Pearl Shirt" as an illustration of the never-failing retribution of heaven to serve as a lesson for all young men.

The story is about a man named Jiang De, also known as Jiang Xingge, a native of Zaoyang County in Xiangyang Prefecture, Huguang.[1] His father, Jiang Shize, was a merchant who began traveling extensively in Guangdong at an early age. Shize's wife Luo-shi, now deceased, had left him with an only child, Xingge, who was nine years old at the time of her death. Jiang Shize could not bear the thought of parting with the child, yet neither could he afford to give up his Guangdong business as a means of livelihood. After giving much thought to the matter, he found no alternative but to take the nine-year-old along as a travel companion and teach the boy some worldly wisdom. Young as the boy was, he had

> Trim brows and bright eyes,
> White teeth and red lips.
> He moved with grace
> And spoke with ease.
> In intellect he surpassed the well-read.
> In cleverness he was equal to grown men.
> Everyone called him the darling boy;
> All praised him as a priceless gem.

Wary of stirring up envious feelings, Jiang Shize presented the boy, throughout their journeys, not as his son but as Young Master Luo, his wife's nephew. As a matter of fact, the Luo family was also engaged in business in the Guangdong region. Whereas the Jiang family had been in the Guangdong business for one generation only, the Luo family had been in it for three. The innkeepers and brokers there knew all three generations of the Luos and treated them as their own kith and kin. Indeed, it was through the initiation of his father-in-law, Mr. Luo, that Jiang Shize had first become a traveling merchant. However, due to straitened circumstances that resulted from a succession of unjust lawsuits against them, the Luos had not visited the area in the last several years. The innkeepers and brokers missed them so much that at the sight of Jiang Shize, everyone asked after the Luo family. When learning upon inquiry that the boy with him, with refined looks and a ready tongue, was from the Luo family, all rejoiced, for their friendship with the last three generations of the Luo family was now continuing into the fourth.

Not to encumber our story with unnecessary chatter, let us speak of Jiang Xingge, who, after traveling a few times with his father, learned, to his father's immense delight, to handle all business matters with adroitness and competence. It turned out, in a way no one would have expected, that when he was seventeen years old, his father died of a sudden illness. Luckily, he died at home instead of ending up a ghost on the road. After shedding some bitter tears, Xingge could not help but wipe his eyes dry and set about making arrangements for the funeral. Apart from the mortuary rites, he also had Buddhist prayers chanted to ensure that his father's spirit be spared the torments of hell, but that needs no more description here.

During the forty-nine days of mourning, all kith and kin on both sides of the family came to offer their condolences. A Mr. Wang of the same county, father of Xingge's newly betrothed fiancée, was among the visitors. Naturally, members of the Jiang clan engaged him in conversation as a courtesy. As the conversation turned to how mature Xingge was for his age in so ably handling such important matters all by himself, someone urged him, "Kinsman Wang, now that your daughter has come of age, why don't you marry them to offset the sadness of the occasion? Life will be easier for the couple when they have each other for company." That day Mr. Wang left without giving his consent.

After the burial rites were over, the relatives tried the proposition on Xingge. The young man also refused at first, but, after much persuasion, considerations about his lonely status prompted him to give in. The original matchmaker was sent to speak to the Wang family, but Mr. Wang declined, saying, "Our family needs to prepare a modest dowry, and it's not something to be had at a moment's notice. Moreover, to hold a wedding before the year of mourning is over would be against the rules of propriety. If there is to be a wedding, we'd better wait until after the first anniversary of the death." When the matchmaker brought back this reply, Xingge did not press the point, for he knew Mr. Wang to be right.

Time sped by like an arrow. Before they realized it, the anniversary was upon them. After offering oblations to his father's spirit tablet and taking off his garments of mourning made of coarse hemp, Xingge again asked the matchmaker to speak to the Wang family. This time, the proposal was accepted. Within several days, the six preliminaries[2] were completed, and the bride was brought over the threshold, as is attested by the following lyric poem to the tune of "The Moon over the West River":

> Red curtains replaced the white of mourning;
> Hemp gave way to colorful clothing.
> The festooned halls aglow with candles;
> The nuptial wine and wedding feast all set out.
> Why envy the splendor of a dowry?
> Harder to come by is beauty.
> Tonight, the pleasure of clouds and rain;[3]
> Tomorrow, visitors with wishes of joy.

The bride was Mr. Wang's youngest daughter, nicknamed Number Three. Because she was born on the seventh day of the seventh month, she was also known as Sanqiao.[4] The two older married daughters of the family were also of remarkable beauty. Within the county of Zaoyang there circulated a four-line song that voiced the admiration for the Wang girls held by all and sundry:

> Women in the world are many;
> Those with the Wangs' beauty are few.
> He who takes a Wang girl as wife
> Is better off than the emperor's son-in-law.

As the proverb says, "Failure to make a business deal is a matter of the moment; failure to marry the right wife is a woe of a lifetime." In selecting daughters-in-law, some families of distinction seek only a matching family background or rich dowry and arrange the betrothal with never a thought about other considerations. Later, when the grotesquely ugly bride is brought into the family and called upon to greet the members of the clan, imagine what poor figures the parents-in-law cut! Moreover, the discontented husband can hardly resist the temptation of illicit affairs. Yet, it so happens that ugly wives are best at bossing their husbands. If the husband reacts in the same way, he invites marital strife, but if he yields to her a couple of times out of face-saving considerations, she starts to put on airs. It was to avoid such unpleasant situations that Jiang Shize, upon learning that Mr. Wang was prone to producing beautiful daughters, had sent over betrothal gifts early on to commit Mr. Wang's youngest girl to his son, both of whom were then at a tender age. Now that Sanqiao had crossed the threshold of the Jiang house, she was perceived to be as full of grace and charm as expected. In fact, she was twice as beautiful as her two older sisters. Truly,

> Xishi of Wu[5] did not measure up to her.
> Nanwei of Chu[6] was hardly her match.
> Should she take the Bodhisattva's place,[7]
> Just as much homage would she be paid.

The handsome Jiang Xingge and his newly wedded beautiful wife were like a pair of exquisite jade statues from the hands of a master sculptor, and ten times more loving than the average married couple. After the third day, Xingge changed back into clothes of lighter colors and, declining all dealings with the outside world on the pretext of being still in mourning, stayed upstairs with his wife, enjoying every moment of the days and nights that went by. Indeed, they were never apart, whether in motion or at rest; even in their dreams they kept each other company. It has always been said that hard days pass slowly, whereas happy moments flit by all too quickly. With the passage of summers and winters, the mourning period came to an end. The spirit tablet for the deceased was removed, and the mourning clothes were taken off, but of this, we shall speak no further.

One day, it occurred to Xingge that his father's Guangdong business had been unattended to for over three years. Revenues from many accounts remained uncollected. In the evening, he said to his wife that he wished to make a trip there. At first, she agreed that he should go, but later, as she learned the distance of the journey, tears fell involuntarily from her eyes, for how could such a loving couple bear to part with each other? Nor did Xingge feel ready to leave her. After some sad laments, the matter was dropped. This happened more than once. (*Good description.*)

Time went by. Before they noticed it, another two years had elapsed. Xingge made up his mind to go. He did his packing away from home, without his wife's knowledge. It was not until five days before the auspicious day chosen for his departure that he said to her, "As the proverb says, 'He who sits idle will eat away a mountain of a fortune.' If the two of us are to start a family and build a business, we can't very well afford to give up this source of income, can we? It being now the second month of the year, with the weather neither cold nor hot, what better time than this to start on the road?"

Realizing that she would not be able to keep him home any longer, she asked only, "When are you coming back?"

Xingge replied, "I have no other choice but to take this trip, but I'll be back in one year's time no matter what. I'll just stay away longer the second time around, if that's what it takes."

Pointing at the toon tree in front of the house, she said, "Next year when this tree begins budding, I'll be expecting you back." With these words, tears fell like rain from her eyes. As he wiped away her tears with his sleeves, Xingge felt tears on his own cheeks as well. A few words hardly suffice for an adequate description of their grief at parting and their deep affection for each other.

Five days later, the night before the scheduled departure, the couple sobbingly talked the whole night through, with no wish to go to sleep. At the fifth watch, Xingge rose to get ready for the journey. He handed over to his wife all his inherited pearls and other valuables, taking along for himself only enough silver to serve as business capital, the original copies of the account books, some clothes, and bedding. Gifts to be offered to business associates had also been packed in good order. Of the two male servants, the younger one was to follow him. The older and more mature one was to stay behind to serve the mistress, run errands, and attend to the daily needs of the household, whereas two waiting women were charged with kitchen duties. There were also two maids, one called Clear Cloud, the other Warm Snow, whose job it was to serve the mistress in her private chamber, with orders not to wander too far away. Having thus assigned all the duties to the servants, Xingge turned to his wife: "Pass your time in patience. There is no lack of frivolous young men in the neighborhood. Being as pretty as you are, you'd better not look out the front door, so as not to attract undue attention." (*These words will turn out to be prophetic.*)

"Don't worry. Go quickly now and come back early."

They took a tearful leave of each other. Truly,

> *The myriad sorrows of this world*
> *All stem from parting, in life or by death.*

For whole days on the road, all of Xingge's thoughts were with his wife, to the exclusion of everything else. Some time later, he arrived in Guangdong and found lodgings in an inn. Old acquaintances came to greet him, and he, in his turn, offered them gifts and went from household to household, enjoying their hospitality in his honor. Thus, he had not a moment of rest for fifteen to twenty days in a row. He had already depleted his energy at home. The tribulations of the journey plus the now-excessive wining and dining brought on an attack of malaria, which lasted throughout the summer and turned to dysentery with the onset of autumn. With a physician checking his pulse and administering medicine every day, he finally recovered toward the end of autumn. In the meantime, his business was left unattended. It looked like he would not be able to return home in one year's time. Truly,

> For profits the size of a fly's head,
> He abandoned his love nest.

Homesick though he was, with the passage of time, he felt he might as well put aside such thoughts.

We shall leave Xingge to his travels and return to his wife, Sanqiao, who, just as her husband instructed on the day of his departure, did not look out the window or take a step down the stairs for quite a few months. Time sped by like an arrow. All too soon, the year was drawing to a close. Every household noisily lit bonfires of pine branches in the courtyard, set off firecrackers, and gathered together merrily for family feasts and games. The sight of such festivities made Sanqiao miss her husband even more. What a miserable night it was! Just as an ancient quatrain put it,

> Winter ends, but not the sorrows.
> Spring returns, but not the traveler.
> Lamenting her loneliness as the day dawns,
> She refuses to try on her New Year's clothes.

The following day was the first day of the first month of the year. In the morning, Clear Cloud and Warm Snow did all they could to urge their mistress to go to the front of the house to watch the goings-on in the street. As a matter of fact, the Jiang residence consisted of two interconnected wings that ran parallel to each other. The bedchamber was in the back wing behind the one that looked out onto the street. As a rule, Sanqiao used only the back wing. That day, unable to resist the maids' urging, she went to the front wing through a passageway. With the windows pushed open and the curtains let down, the three of them looked out from behind the curtains. That day, the street was a scene of hustle and bustle. Sanqiao remarked, "Of all these people coming and going, why isn't there a fortune-teller? If there is one, I'll be glad to have him come here so I can ask him for news about my husband."

Clear Cloud said, "New Year's Day is for everybody to relax and have fun. Who would want to be out telling fortunes?"

Warm Snow said loudly, "Ma'am, just leave it to the two of us. Within five days, we'll surely get you one."

After breakfast on the fourth day of the month, Warm Snow was downstairs relieving herself when she heard a clanging sound in the street. It came from the device called "announcer" that blind fortune-tellers use to attract attention. Before she was through with what she was doing, she hastily pulled up her pants, ran out the door, and stopped the blind man. She then turned around and ran up the stairs in one breath to report to her mistress. Sanqiao instructed her to have him sit in the reception hall downstairs and ask him to do a divination. Then she said her prayers and descended the stairs to listen to what he had to say. The blind man picked a trigram and asked what the divination was for. The two kitchen maids who came over at the commotion answered for the mistress, "It's to ask about a traveler on the road."

"Is it a wife wishing to ask about her husband?" the fortune-teller demanded to know.

"Exactly," said the maids.

And this was what the fortune-teller said: "With the green dragon in a reigning position, the wealth star is set in motion. If this is a case of a wife inquiring about her husband, the traveler is on his way home, laden with a thousand cases of treasure, and safe from the slightest hint of a storm. (*Fortune-tellers can be quite misleading.*) The green dragon being of the wood phase of the five phases and spring being the thriving season for wood, the traveler started on his way back around the time of the spring equinox and will surely be at home by the end of this month or the beginning of the next, bringing much wealth with him."

Sanqiao had the male servant give the fortune-teller three tenths of a mace of silver,[8] and, having thus sent the man on his way, she merrily went up to her room. As the proverbs go, she was "slaking thirst by looking at plums" and "allaying hunger by drawing cakes."

In most situations, if you don't get your hopes up too high, your peace of mind is not likely to be disturbed. Once you do, you indulge in wishful thinking that makes every moment of your life miserable. Believing the fortune-teller's words, Sanqiao had no other thoughts but of her husband's return. From then on, she often went to the front wing of the house and peered out onto the street from behind the curtains. The days went by, and there still was no sign of his return when the toon tree began budding at the beginning of the second month, reminding her of her husband's promise. All the more anxious, she looked out the window several times a day. Then, as if something was destined to happen, her eyes came to rest upon a handsome young man. Truly,

> *Those with predestined bonds will meet,*
> *However far apart they are.*
> *Those without will never meet,*
> *Face to face though they may be.*

Who might this handsome young man be? He was not a local resident but a native of Xin'an [New Peace] County in Huizhou. Chen Shang by name, he was also known familiarly as Daxige [Big Happy Brother], which was later changed to Dalang [Big Fellow]. At twenty-four years of age, he was a strikingly handsome young man, not any less so than Song Yu[9] or Pan An.[10] As was the case with Jiang Xingge, Dalang had also lost both parents. Having scraped together two to three thousand taels in cash as capital, he had gone into the rice and bean business, making yearly trips to Xiangyang to ply his trade. He stayed outside the city, but that day he happened to be in town to check at Squire Wang's pawnshop on Great Market Street for letters from home. The pawnshop being right opposite the Jiang residence, his steps took him past Sanqiao's window. How, you may ask, was he dressed? He was wearing, just as Jiang Xingge usually did, a Suzhou-style bell-shaped hat made of coir and a Huzhou silk robe of a fish-belly-white shade. Looking from afar, Sanqiao mistook him for her husband. She lifted the curtains and fixed her eyes upon him. When Chen Dalang raised his head and saw a beautiful young woman gazing at him from an upper window, he thought the woman had taken a fancy to him, and he also threw a significant glance at her. But in fact, it was a misunderstanding on both sides. Realizing that the man was not her husband, Sanqiao flushed crimson with embarrassment. Hastily closing the window, she ran to the back wing of the house and sank down on the edge of her bed, her heart pounding violently. (*Just like that debauched woman*[11] *when she first started out.*) In the meantime, Chen Dalang's soul had been snatched away by her gaze.

After he returned to his lodgings, his mind was still with the woman. He thought to himself, "My wife at home is not unattractive, but she's not nearly half as pretty as that woman. (*A foreshadowing.*) How I wish I could have some way to approach her! If I could just spend one night with her, I would not have lived in vain, even if it cost me all of my business capital." After a few sighs, he suddenly remembered that he had done some business with a Granny Xue, vendor of pearls, who lived on East Lane off Great Market Street. With a gift of the gab and a propensity for dropping by people's houses from street to street, she should know everyone in town and, if consulted, would surely come up with a good suggestion.

He tossed and turned all through that wakeful night to rise at the first light of dawn. Saying he had business to attend to, he asked for some cold water, washed and combed, and went to town posthaste, carrying with him a hundred taels of silver and two large ingots of gold. This is indeed a case of

> You need to work yourself to death,
> To find some enjoyment in life.

Once in town, Chen Dalang headed straight for East Lane off Great Market Street and knocked at Granny Xue's door. Her hair disheveled, Granny Xue was sorting out her pearls in the courtyard when she heard the knocking. While putting away her bags of pearls, she asked, "Who is it?" At the first few words of reply announcing that he was Mr. Chen of Huizhou, she hastened to open the door and invite him in, saying, "I haven't done my toilette yet, so I won't stand on ceremony with you. How early you are! Might I ask what brought you here?"

"I'm here specially to see you. I was afraid I might not find you at home if I came later."

"Are you here to buy jewelry from me?"

"Yes, but apart from buying pearls, I also have a big job for you."

"But I know little about things other than my own line."

"Can we talk here?" asked Chen Dalang, whereupon Granny Xue closed the door and took him into a small room.

"What can I do for you, sir?"

Seeing no one around, Dalang drew out some silver from his sleeve, untied the cloth parcel, laid the contents on the table, and said, "I'll tell you, Godmother, only if you accept them." Not knowing what he had come for, she stoutly refused to take the hundred taels of silver.

"Maybe that's not enough?" asked Dalang. He quickly added the two ingots of shining gold to the silver on the table, saying, "Please also accept these ten taels of gold. If you still refuse, I'll take that to mean you are turning me down. It is I who am asking a favor from you, and not the other way around. I have come to you because no one but you can pull off this big job. Even if it can't be done, the gold and silver will still be yours to keep. I won't ever come to claim them back. Who knows if we won't meet again later in life? I, Chen Shang, am not a petty sort!"

Dear audience, is there any procuress who does not covet money? How could the sight of so much gold and silver have failed to stir her greed? At that moment, her face breaking into a wide smile, Granny Xue said, "Please don't get me wrong. I have never, in my whole life, taken any money, not even a fraction of a penny, from any source that was not well accounted for. However, I shall respect your wish and keep the money for the time being. If I cannot be of service, I will return everything to you." So saying, she put the ingots of gold into the parcel of silver, wrapped them up together, and, exclaiming, "If I may be so bold," she excused herself and put the parcel away in her bedchamber. In a trice, she reemerged to say, "Sir, I won't presume to thank you yet, but you must tell me what this big job is that you have for me."

"I desperately need a treasure with life-saving magic powers. It's nowhere to be found except in one particular household on Great Market Street. Please, Godmother, do me the favor of going there to borrow it for me." (*A godmother doubling as a life-saving go-between.*)

The woman burst into laughter. "What a funny thing you said!" she exclaimed. "I have been living here in this alley for over twenty years without ever hearing anything about any life-saving magic thing. Tell me, which household is it?"

"The two-story house opposite my fellow townsman Squire Wang's pawnshop. Who lives there?"

After a moment of reflection, the woman said, "That's the house of Jiang

Xingge of this town. He's been traveling away from home for over a year now. There's only his wife in the house."

Dalang said, "It's precisely from her that I would like to borrow the life-saving magic thing." He pulled his chair up closer to the woman and poured out his secret to her. Barely had he finished than the woman shook her head and said, "This can hardly be done! Jiang Xingge has had this wife for less than four years, and the couple have been as inseparable as fish and water. Now that the man's had to go away, the young lady never even takes a step down the stairs—so chaste is she! Because Xingge is of a somewhat unpredictable nature and easily finds fault with people (*He is certainly not to blame for doing so*), I have never seen the inside of his house. I don't even have any idea what the young woman looks like. This job is beyond me. What you gave me is not destined for me to enjoy, after all."

At these words, Chen Dalang fell to his knees. When the woman tried to raise him, he grabbed her by her sleeves and held her so firmly on the chair that she could not budge. He said, "My life is in your hands, Godmother. To save my life, you've got to think of some ingenious way for me to get to know her. If you pull this off, I'll reward you with another hundred taels of silver. If you decline, I'll have to kill myself right now."

The woman was so alarmed that, at a loss what to do, she relented, saying, "All right! All right! Don't put me in such a spot. Please get up and listen to me."

Only then did Chen Dalang rise to his feet. With folded hands, he said, "Please tell me what good plans you have in mind."

"You'll have to give me some time," said she. "If you want it to work out, don't set a time limit. I can't possibly do it for you if you give me a deadline."

Chen Dalang said, "As long as it'll work out, I don't mind waiting a few days. But what do you propose to do?"

"Tomorrow, meet me in Squire Wang's pawnshop after breakfast, not too early or too late. Bring a lot of cash and just say that you have a business deal to make with me. That'll be part of my plan, you see. If I can manage to cross the threshold of the Jiang house (*Of first importance*), you'll be in luck. You should then quickly go back to your lodgings. Don't loiter around that house, for if your intentions are seen through, that'll be the end of it all. When I see a chance, I'll come back to let you know."

"I'll do whatever you say." With a deep bow, he happily opened the door and went on his way. Truly,

Before Xiang Yu's defeat and Liu Bang's rise,
A platform was built to honor the Marshal.[12]

Of the events of the rest of the day, there is no more to tell. On the following day, a neatly attired Chen Dalang betook himself to the Wang pawnshop on Great Market Street, followed by a page boy carrying a big leather case containing three to four hundred taels of silver. He cast a glance at the upper windows of the house opposite and took the tightly shut windows to mean that the woman was not in the front wing. Saluting the pawnshop clerk with folded hands, he asked for a wooden bench and sat down at the door, looking eastward. Before long, Granny Xue came into sight, holding a wicker box in her arms. Chen Dalang stopped her and asked, "What do you have in the box?"

"Pearls and other pieces of jewelry. Would you have any use for them, sir?"

"The very things I want to buy."

Granny Xue stepped into the pawnshop, greeted the clerk, and, with a polite word or two, opened the box. There were, in the box, about ten packets of pearls as well as a few small boxes containing fashionable ornaments in the shape of flower clusters, with kingfisher-feather inlay. The designs were most exquisite and the luster dazzled the eyes. Chen Dalang picked a few strings of extremely large white pearls and put them in a pile along with some hairpins and earrings, saying, "I'll take all of these."

Giving him a meaningful look, the old woman said, "You may use them if you want, sir, but I'm afraid you might not be ready to pay the stiff price."

Taking her hint, Chen Dalang opened his leather case, spread the silver on the table in a dazzling display (*Showing off his wealth*), and yelled at the top of his voice, "Don't tell me that with all this silver I can't afford those things of yours!"

By this time, seven or eight idle onlookers from the neighborhood had already gathered at the door. The old woman said, "I was only joking. How could I dream of taking you for less than you are? You'd better be careful with your silver. Please put it away. I'll be happy as long as we strike a fair deal."

And so the bargaining began, one asking for a high price and the other countering with a small offer, with the distance of heaven from earth between the sums. While the woman held her ground firmly, Chen Dalang picked up the pearls, and, refusing to put them down or raise his offer, he deliberately stepped out of the shop. Turning each piece over and over for a good look, he commented on which ones were genuine and which ones fake, and appraised their value while all the time letting them sparkle in the sunlight. He soon attracted a large crowd, which frequently burst into cheer.

The old woman shouted, "Buy them if you want. If not, that'll be that. Why do you have to waste my time like this!"

Chen Dalang retorted, "How do you know I'm not buying?" And the haggling started all over again. Truly,

> *The haggle over the price*
> *Caught the beauty's eye.*

Hearing the commotion opposite her house, Wang Sanqiao stepped, without realizing she was doing so, to the front wing of the house and pushed open the windows for a glimpse. There, for all to see, was the lovely sight of pearls sparkling in all their splendor. As the old woman and the customer were still locked in a haggle over price, she told her maid to have the woman come over and show her the merchandise. (*No sight, no desire. She cannot but fall into the crafty old woman's trap.*) Thus instructed, Clear Cloud walked across the street and, with a tug at Granny Xue's sleeve, said, "My mistress would like to see you."

The old woman asked deliberately, "Which family might that be?"

"The Jiang family across the street."

With one sweep of her hand, the old woman whisked away all the pearls, wrapped them up in haste, and said, "I can't afford to be held up by you like this!"

Chen Dalang insisted, "I'll add some more and we can close the deal!"

"No, I'm not selling. At your price, I could have sold them a long time ago." While saying this, she put her jewels into the box, locked it as before, and carried it away.

"Let me carry it for you," said Clear Cloud.

"No, I can manage." With never a look back, she headed straight for the house across the street. Filled with inward joy, Chen Dalang also gathered up his silver, took leave of the pawnshop clerk, and returned to his lodgings. Indeed,

> His eyes look for the victory flag;
> His ears listen for glad tidings.

Clear Cloud led Granny Xue upstairs to meet Sanqiao. At the sight of the young woman, Xue thought to herself, "What a heavenly beauty! No wonder Chen Dalang is so infatuated. If I were a man, I'd also lose my head." Aloud, she said, "I have long heard about your virtues. I regret that I haven't had a chance earlier to make your acquaintance."

"What is your honorable name, may I ask?"

"My surname is Xue. I live right near here on East Lane. In fact, I am a neighbor of yours."

"Why did you say you weren't selling these things?"

The old woman said with a laugh, "If they were not for sale, I wouldn't have taken them out. I'm just amused that the traveler, however handsome and smart he looked, knew nothing about the value of my goods." (*Clever remark.*) Having said these words, she opened the box, took out a few hairpins and earrings, and handed them to the young lady for her to look at. "Madam," she exclaimed. "You can well imagine how much it costs just to make such fine jewelry. At his ridiculous price, how am I to go back and report the loss to my employer?" She then lifted a few strings of pearls and continued, "Such top quality! He must have been dreaming!"

Sanqiao inquired about the asking price and the counter bid and remarked, "That's truly unfair to you."

"Being from a genteel family, you have seen a lot, after all. Your judgment is ten times better than a man's."

Sanqiao told her maid to serve tea, but the old woman said, "I'm not going to trouble you for tea. I need to go to West Lane for some important business. That man wasted too much of my time. This is truly a case of 'a deal that fails to go through holding up all your work.' May I leave this box here in your care, lock and all? I'll be back soon." With these words, she took her leave. Sanqiao had Clear Cloud see her down the stairs. She then went out the door and set off in a westerly direction.

Much taken with the pieces of jewelry, Sanqiao waited eagerly for the old woman to come back to talk about prices. Five days went by without the woman's making an appearance. (*The delaying tactics of a master strategist.*) In the afternoon of the sixth day, a sudden rainstorm sprang up. Before the sound of the rain had subsided, there came knocks at the door. Sanqiao had a maid open the door, and who should walk in but Granny Xue with her clothes half drenched. Carrying a broken umbrella, she chanted,

> *You don't go out when the weather is fine,*
> *But wait till raindrops pour down your head.*

She put the umbrella by the stairs and went up to the second floor. With a bow of greeting, she said, "Madam, sorry I didn't keep my word the other day."

Sanqiao hastened to return her greeting and asked, "Where have you been the last few days?"

"I went to see my daughter's new baby son and stayed there for a couple of days. I didn't get back until this morning. It started to rain when I was halfway here, so I borrowed an umbrella from a friend, but it turned out to be broken. What bad luck!"

"How many children do you have?"

"I have only one son who is already married. As to daughters, I have four. The one I went to see is the youngest. She is married as a concubine to Squire Zhu of Huizhou, who owns a salt shop outside the north city gate."

"You have too many daughters to care if they get the best deals. There's no lack of men in this area who'd take her as wife, not as concubine. How could you have married off your daughter to an outsider as a concubine?"

"You might not know that, in fact, people from other places are more gracious. My daughter may be a concubine, but the first wife only stays at home. It's my daughter who orders the maids about in the shop just as a wife would do. Every time I go there, he treats me with all the respect that an elder deserves, without the slightest neglect. Now that she's given him a son, things are even better." (*Another clever remark.*)

"You're lucky to have married off your daughter so well."

At this moment, Clear Cloud brought in tea. After the two of them drank their tea, Granny Xue said, "There being nothing to do on such a rainy day, may I make so bold as to ask for a look at your jewelry? It would be helpful if I could keep in mind some exquisite designs."

"Mine are nothing fancy. Please don't laugh." So saying, Sanqiao opened her caskets with a key and, little by little, took out quite a number of hairpins, filigrees, tassels, and the like. Granny Xue was profuse with praises. "With such a collection of treasures, I would expect you to turn up your nose at those few items of mine."

"It's kind of you to say so, but I was just going to ask you for prices."

"You are a good judge of quality," said the old woman. "Why waste my breath?"

Sanqiao put away her things and placed Granny Xue's wicker box on the table. Handing the key to Granny Xue, she said, "Please open it and see if everything is intact."

"You don't have to be so discreet." The old woman opened the box and took out the items one by one for Sanqiao's appraisal. The prices Sanqiao offered were all close to what Granny Xue would have asked. Without any objections, the old woman said cheerfully, "That'll be a fair deal. I'll be happy even if I make a few strings of cash less."

"But there's one problem. Right now, I'm not able to pay more than half of the total sum. I'll have to wait for my husband to come home to pay off the balance. He should be back in a couple of days."

"A few days won't make any difference. It's just that because I've made quite a concession on the price, I'd like to have the silver in the finest quality."

"That can be easily done." So saying, Sanqiao picked out pieces of jewelry and pearls that she liked most. She then called Clear Cloud to serve some wine for Granny Xue to stay a little longer. "How can I disturb you like this?" said the old woman.

"I have little to do most of the time," said Sanqiao. "It's so seldom that you are here to chat with me and keep me company. If you don't mind my not being a good hostess, please come visit me often."

"Thank you for such kindness, which I hardly deserve. My house is unbearably noisy, but your house is indeed too quiet."

"What line of business is your son in?"

"He does nothing more than receive jewelry dealers at home. I can't stand their daily requests for wine and other drinks. Thanks to the need to visit different households on business, I don't stay at home a lot, so it's all right. If I had to be cooped up in those six feet of space at home, I'd be annoyed to death."

"Our house being so close to yours, do come over for a chat whenever you need a break." (*Falling into the trap.*)

"But I wouldn't presume to disturb you too often."

"What kind of talk is this!" exclaimed Sanqiao.

In the meantime, the two maidservants were busily going back and forth setting the table, laying out two sets of cups and chopsticks, two bowls each of smoked chicken and meat, fresh fish, and ten dishes of vegetables and fruits, bringing the total number of dishes to sixteen. "What a fine spread!" said Granny Xue.

"These are just what we have at the moment. Please don't think ill of me for not being a good hostess." Having said this, Sanqiao poured out wine for the old woman and handed her the cup. The latter offered a toast, and the two sat down across the table from each other and fell to drinking. As it was, Sanqiao had a good capacity for wine, and Granny Xue was a veritable wine jug. As they drank, the two felt even more drawn to each other than before and wished they had gotten to know each other sooner. They drank until evening set in. As the rain had stopped, Granny Xue said her thanks and wanted to leave, but Sanqiao took out a large silver wine vessel, urged her to drink more, and, after a few more vessels, they ate dinner together. Sanqiao pleaded, "Stay around some more before I let you go with half the money I owe you."

"It's getting late," said Granny Xue. "Take your time. One night doesn't make any difference. I'll come to get it tomorrow. I'll leave the wicker box here, also, for the road will be too muddy and slippery for me to carry anything." (*Delaying tactics again.*)

"I'll be expecting you tomorrow," said Sanqiao. The old woman took her leave, went down the stairs, picked up her broken umbrella, and went out the door. Truly,

> *Goodness knows how many people*
> *Fall for a wicked crone's talk.*

In the meantime, Chen Dalang was waiting in his lodgings for news. Several days went by without any word from Granny Xue. Convinced that the old woman should be at home that rainy day, he headed into town through the rain and the mud to ask her for news, only to learn that she was not at home. He went into a wineshop, where he had three drinks and ate some refreshments before returning to Granny Xue's door, but she had not come back. As he waited, afternoon dimmed into evening, and he was on the point of turning back when Granny Xue walked into the alley with a limp, her face flushed with wine. Chen Dalang took a few steps forward, greeted her with a bow, and asked, "How is your plan coming along?"

The woman shook her hand in a gesture of negation and said, "There's still a long way to go. I've just sown the seeds. The shoots haven't come up yet. You won't get a taste until five or six years later when they blossom and bear fruit. Don't you stick your nose in here. Your old mother is not the kind that meddles in other people's affairs."

Seeing that she was addled with wine, Chen Dalang could do no more than return to his lodgings.

The following day, Granny Xue bought some fresh fruit, chicken, fish, pork, and the like, and had a cook prepare them. She then packed the food up in two boxes, and bought a jar of the best wine. With the boy from next door carrying the load, she betook herself to the Jiang residence. Sanqiao was expecting Granny Xue's visit that day. On her instruction, Clear Cloud was on the point of opening the door to take a look around for Granny Xue when whom should she see but the old woman herself. Granny Xue told the boy to put the load down by the stairs and sent him on his way. In the meantime, Clear Cloud announced the visitor to her mistress. Treating Granny Xue as an honored guest, Sanqiao went as far as the stairway to greet her and invite her up. With profuse words of thanks, the old woman bent her knees slightly in a gesture of greeting and said, "I happen to have some watery wine today and brought it along for your enjoyment."

"I shouldn't have put you to such expense," said Sanqiao. The old woman asked the two maids to bring up the food and wine, and a fine spread they made.

Sanqiao said, "You really shouldn't be so extravagant."

Granny Xue replied with a smile, "A humble household like mine has nothing fancy to offer. Just take this as a cup of tea." Clear Cloud went to fetch cups and chopsticks, while Warm Snow started lighting the portable brazier. When the wine was warm enough a moment later, Granny Xue said, "This is my treat, so would you please sit in the guest seat?"

"I am indeed much obliged," said Sanqiao, "but this being my humble house, how can I presume to accept that honor?"

After much arguing, each trying to yield the seat of honor to the other, it was Granny Xue who ended up taking the guest's seat. This being the third time they were together, they felt even more at ease in each other's company.

In the midst of their drinking, Granny Xue commented, "Your husband has been away a long time now. How can he abandon his wife like this!"

Sanqiao said, "You're right. He said he would be back in one year. I wonder what's keeping him."

The old woman pressed her point: "The way I see it, even making piles of gold and jade does not justify abandoning such a beautiful wife." She continued, "As a rule, traveling merchants take the inn as home and treat their home as an inn. Take my fourth son-in-law, Squire Zhu, for example. Ever since he's had my daughter as a concubine, he's been enjoying her from morning to night, with never a thought of the family he left behind! He goes home only once every three or four years and comes back after staying for no more than a couple of months. His first wife is virtually a widow taking care of the orphans, not knowing what he is up to behind her back." (*Convincing argument.*)

"My husband is not that kind," said Sanqiao.

Granny Xue conceded, "I was only saying that for the sake of conversation. How would I dream of comparing earth with heaven?" (*Good retreat.*) They went on to play games of riddle-guessing and dice-throwing and did not take leave of each other until they were tipsy with wine.

Two days later, the old woman came again, this time with the boy to take back her things as well as to collect payment for half of the purchase. Sanqiao kept her again for some refreshments.

Henceforth, Granny Xue frequented the Jiang residence, ostensibly to ask about Xingge, using the unpaid half of the money as a pretext. With her glib tongue and her playful ways with the maids (*Behavior befitting the character*), she won the heart of everyone in the household, high and low, so much so that Sanqiao would feel lonely if a single day went by without the old woman making an appearance. She had the old servant find out where Granny Xue lived, and, with constant invitations, visits from Granny Xue grew all the more frequent. (*Falling into the trap.*)

There are, in this world, four kinds of people with whom it would be wise not to get involved, for once you do, you'll never be able to free yourself from them. Who are these people? They are traveling monks and Taoists, beggars, vagrants, and go-betweens. The first three kinds are more tolerable than the last one, for go-betweens have access to private chambers. In moments of loneliness, nine women out of ten welcome their visits. Now, Granny Xue was not the kind-hearted sort by nature. Her sweet tongue made Sanqiao so attached to her that the latter could hardly do without her, not even for a moment. Truly,

> *You may draw the skin of a tiger, but not its bones.*
> *You may know the face of a man, but not his heart.*

More than once, Chen Dalang tried to get information out of her, but Granny Xue always put him off, saying it was not yet time. It being the middle of the fifth month, with the weather turning hot, the woman casually mentioned to Sanqiao that her home was most unfit for summer living, for it was as small as a snail's shell, with western exposure, and was far less spacious and airy than the latter's two-story house. Sanqiao said, "If you don't mind staying away from home, you may sleep here at night." (*Falling into the trap.*)

"That would be nice, but what if your husband comes back?"

"Even if he does, it won't be in the middle of the night."

"Since you don't mind my intruding—and I *am* the kind to impose myself on others, I'll bring over my bedding this very evening to keep you company. How about that?"

"I have extra bedding. You don't have to bring yours. Just tell your folks that you are staying here for the whole summer. How would you like that?"

The old woman did indeed tell her son and daughter-in-law so, and brought over nothing more than a box of toilet articles. Sanqiao said, "You didn't even have to do that! You don't really think there's a lack of combs in this house, do you?"

"My biggest fear in life is of sharing other people's combs and face-washing water. Plus, I'm afraid your combs are too nice for me. Nor would I use the maids' combs. It's better to bring my own. (*Even such trivial details are interesting.*) But, tell me, which room is for me?"

Pointing at a small rattan couch by her own bed, Sanqiao said, "I've got everything done. By staying closer, we can chat at night when sleep doesn't come to us." (*Falling into the trap.*) So saying, she took out a green gauze bed-curtain and had Granny Xue hang it up herself. The two had a drink before they retired. The two maids used to sleep at the foot of Sanqiao's bed to keep her company, but, now that Granny Xue had moved in, they were sent off to the next room.

From then on Granny Xue would return to the Jiang residence after a day of peddling her merchandise from door to door, and the Jiang residence came alive with frequent merry drinking. The bed and the couch being arranged in a "T" shape, the two women lay as close to each other as if they were side by side, though separated as they were by a curtain. At night they would chitchat, and, with one asking questions and the other answering, their gossip included all of the sordid details about happenings in the neighborhood. (*Closing in on her, step by step. A most credible detail.*) Sometimes the old woman would feign drunkenness and talk about her clandestine love affairs in her younger days, to stir up Sanqiao's amorous thoughts, and, indeed, the color came and went on the latter's fair-skinned and delicate cheeks. (*Most cunning.*) Granny Xue realized that the lewd stories were working, but found it awkward to bring up the real subject yet.

Time sped by. In no time, the seventh day of the seventh month rolled around. As it happened to be Sanqiao's birthday, Granny Xue rose bright and early and prepared two boxes of birthday presents to celebrate the occasion. Sanqiao said her thanks and asked Xue to stay for the birthday noodles. Granny Xue said, "I have a busy day ahead of me. I'll come in the evening to keep you company, and we'll watch the Herdboy and Weaving Maiden get together." (*Every word is significant.*) Having said these words, she went off.

Barely had she walked down the steps than she ran into Chen Dalang. As they could not very well talk on the street, Chen Dalang followed her into a secluded alley. Wearing a frown, he grumbled, "Mother, how you've been dragging your feet! Spring is gone, summer is behind us, and autumn is here. Day after day, you say nothing but that it's not yet time, it's not yet time, but do you know that, for me, a day is as long as a year? A few more days and her husband will be back and the whole thing will be off! Won't you be killing me? Just remember: I'll haunt you from the netherworld to make you pay me back with your life."

"Don't carry on like that. I was just on my way to invite you, and here you are. Whether the whole thing can be pulled off or not will depend on tonight. You'll have to do as I say." And she went on to instruct him to do thus and so. "Everything has to be done quietly. You must not get me into any trouble."

Chen Dalang said with a nod, "A wonderful plan! Wonderful! I'll have a handsome reward for you if it works." With that, he went merrily on his way. Truly,

The trap was laid to capture the beauty;
Brains were racked to play at clouds and rain.

To get on with our story, Granny Xue promised Chen Dalang that action was to be taken that very night. After a misty drizzle all afternoon, night fell with a darkness unrelieved by any glimmer of star or moonlight. In the inky darkness, Granny Xue took Chen Dalang to the left of the house door, where she told him to hide while she herself went to knock at the door. A paper lantern in hand, Clear Cloud opened the door. Granny Xue deliberately groped in her own sleeves and said, "I lost my Linqing[13] handkerchief. Would you be so kind as to look for it for me, dear?"

While Clear Cloud was tricked into turning her lantern toward the street, the old woman motioned Chen Dalang over, and the two slipped through the door. Having led him to hide behind the staircase (*With such meticulous planning for every move, Granny Xue could very well be a military strategist*), Granny Xue cried out, "I've found it! You don't have to look anymore."

Clear Cloud said, "My lantern happened to go out, too. Let me light up another one for you."

"I know my way about by now," said the woman. "I don't need a light." With the door closed behind them, Granny Xue and Clear Cloud groped their way up the stairs.

"What was it you dropped?" asked Sanqiao.

Pulling out a small handkerchief from her sleeve, the old woman answered, "It was this cursed thing. It's not worth much, but it's a gift from a traveler from Beijing. Isn't it true that 'the gift is trifling but it's the thought that counts'?"

Sanqiao said teasingly, "Could it be a keepsake from some old flame?"

The old woman laughed. "That wouldn't be too far from the truth." Merrily, they fell to drinking. The old woman suggested, "There being so much food and wine, why don't you offer some to the servants in the kitchen? Let them also have some fun on this night of celebration." Accordingly, Sanqiao told the maid to take four dishes and two jugs of wine downstairs. The three servants in the kitchen—two women and a man—consumed the food and wine and withdrew to their own quarters. And there we shall leave them.

In the meantime, Granny Xue asked in the midst of the drinking, "Why isn't your husband back yet?"

"It's been a year and a half now," said Sanqiao.

"Even the Herdboy and the Weaving Maiden meet once a year. And here you are, beating them by half a year. It's often said, 'In status, traveling merchants come second only to officials.' Where can't travelers find romance? It's their wives at home who suffer." (*Most cunning.*)

With a sigh, Sanqiao hung her head and fell silent. The old woman said, "Well, I shouldn't be shooting off my mouth like that. Tonight, the Herdboy meets the Weaving Maiden. It's an occasion that calls for wine and merry-making. Let me say nothing that saddens the heart." (*These are nothing less than words that sadden the heart.*) So saying, she poured Sanqiao a cup of wine.

When they were well warmed with wine, Granny Xue offered some to the two maids, saying, "This is in celebration of the tryst between the Herdboy and the Weaving Maiden. Drink your fill. I hope you will marry loving husbands who stay with you every moment of your lives."

Unable to fight her off, the two maids reluctantly drank the wine. The effect of the wine soon made them sway and tumble every which way. Sanqiao ordered them to close the staircase door and go to sleep (*Falling deeper into the trap*), whereas she and Granny Xue continued to drink at their ease.

While drinking, the old woman kept up a steady stream of chatter. "How old were you when you married?" she asked. (*There she goes.*)

"Seventeen," answered Sanqiao.

"It's not such a bad deal if you did the thing late. As for me, I lost my virginity at the age of thirteen."

"You married that early?"

"If you're talking about marriage, I married when I was eighteen. I might as well tell you, I was learning to sew in a neighbor's house when the young master seduced me. I fell for his good looks and gave in to him. At first, the pain was excruciating, but after doing it two or three times, I came to like it a lot. Was it the same case with you?"

Sanqiao giggled without answering. Granny Xue continued, "It would be better had I not experienced what it's like. Once you've had the experience, you can't get it out of your mind, and you get an itch for it from time to time. It's better during the day, but nighttime is most dreadful."

"You must have known a lot of men before marriage. How did you manage to pass yourself off as a virgin when you got married?"

"My mother was afraid of a scandal because she had some idea of what was going on. So she gave me a prescription for restoring virginity. The thing tightened up after being washed with pomegranate skin and alum. I made a great fuss about the pain and so I passed."

"But before you married, didn't you have to sleep by yourself at night?"

"I remember that before I married, I used to sleep in the same bed with my sister-in-law, head to head, foot to foot, when my brother was away. We took turns playing the man's part on each other's belly."

"What's the good of two women sleeping together?"

The old woman walked over, sat down by her side, and said, "You may not know this, but, as long as both know how to do it, it's just as much fun and provides just as much relief."

Sanqiao gave the woman a playful slap on the shoulder and said, "I don't believe this. You're lying." (*She takes the bait.*)

Seeing that Sanqiao's desires had been stirred up, the woman continued to work on her: "I am fifty-two years old, but at night, I still often have maddening fits of desire that I can hardly fight off. You are lucky to be able to stay calm, young as you are."

"You don't mean you'll have an affair with some man when your desire gets the better of you?"

"I am a withered flower, a dried-up willow tree. Who wants me anymore? I might as well tell you: I know a way to give myself pleasure, an 'emergency relief measure.'"

"You are lying. What is it?"

"I'll tell you everything about it when we get to bed in a moment," said the old woman.

At this juncture, a moth was seen fluttering over the lamp. Granny Xue swatted at it with a fan, deliberately putting the lamp out. (*The woman's craftiness is frightening.*) "Aya!" she cried. "Let me go and get another light." With that, she left to open the staircase door. In the meantime, Chen Dalang had already mounted the stairs and had been hiding by the door for some time now. This was all part of Granny Xue's scheme. "I forgot to bring a match with me," Granny Xue called out. So she retraced her steps and led Chen Dalang to lie down on her own couch, while she herself went downstairs and came up again a moment later, saying, "It's so late now that the pilot fire in the kitchen has gone out. What's to be done?"

"I'm used to sleeping with a light on," said Sanqiao. "This darkness is scary!"

"Shall I sleep in the same bed with you to keep you company?"

Wishing to ask her about the "emergency relief measure," Sanqiao said, "That'll be fine."

"You can go to bed first," said Granny Xue. "I'll join you after I close the door."

Sanqiao undressed first and got into bed, saying, "Please come quickly."

"Coming!" said Granny Xue, while dragging Chen Dalang, all naked, from the couch into Sanqiao's bed. Sanqiao touched his body and said, "For a woman of your age, what smooth skin you have!" Without a word of reply (*He can't very well talk, can he?*), the man slipped under the quilt, embraced her, and kissed her on the mouth. Still thinking it was the old woman, she put her arms around him. Suddenly, the man mounted her and started to do the real thing. Partly because she was tipsy with wine and partly because her amorous desires had been roused by the old woman, she let him have his way without bothering to find out who he was.

One was a young wife in seclusion longing for love,
The other a traveler craving romance.
She, after many agonizing nights,
Was like Wenjun when first seeing Xiangru.[14]
He, after waiting so long,
Was like Bizheng upon meeting Miaochang.[15]
A welcome rain after a long drought
Brings more joy than old friends meeting in a distant land.

Being an old hand in the world of love, Chen Dalang played the game of clouds and rain so well that the woman was brought into raptures.

After their passion had abated, Sanqiao asked, "Who are you?" Chen Dalang gave a full account of how he had seen her from the street, how he had fallen in love, and how he had pleaded hard with Granny Xue for a way to see her. "Now that I have fulfilled the dream of my life, I'll have no regrets when I die."

At this moment, Granny Xue approached the bed and said, "It's not that I was impertinent, but I thought it a shame that a young woman like you should be living all alone. I also wanted to save his life. As a matter of fact, the two of you are drawn together by a predestined bond. I had nothing to do with it."

Sanqiao said, "Now that things have come to this, what's to be done if my husband gets to hear about this?"

The old woman said, "This is a secret between us. If we bribe Clear Cloud and Warm Snow and tell them not to shoot their mouths off, who else will let on anything? Leave this to me, and I'll guarantee that you can enjoy yourselves every night without a worry. Just don't forget me in the future."

Sanqiao was in no mood at this time to concern herself with too many things, and the two resumed their amorous sport. They were still loath to part when daybreak drew near after the drum of the fifth watch. It was at Granny Xue's urging that Chen Dalang rose and went out the door in Xue's company.

Henceforth, they did not miss a single night. He came either alone or in Granny Xue's company. The latter used honeyed words and dark threats alternately on the two maids and had their mistress reward them with clothes. The man, for his part, also tipped them from time to time with a few pieces of loose silver for them to buy sweets with. The two maids were so delighted that they willingly became accomplices, greeting the visitor at night and sending him off in the morning with never an obstacle in the way. The couple came to be as inseparable as glue and lacquer, and more loving than the average lawfully wedded man and wife. With his mind set on binding the woman more securely to him, Chen Dalang showered her with nice clothes and fine jewelry and paid on her behalf all the money she owed Granny Xue. As a token of his gratitude, he gave the old woman another hundred taels of silver. In a little more than six months since he had first come to know Sanqiao, he spent nearly a thousand taels of gold. Sanqiao also gave Granny Xue gifts worth over thirty taels of silver. It was for the sake of such ill-gotten gains that the old woman agreed to be a procuress, but this is of no concern to us here.

The ancients said, "No feast does not come to an end."

> *The Lantern Festival had just gone by*
> *When the Clear and Bright Festival rolled around.*[16]

Uneasy over the thought of having neglected his business for too long, Chen Dalang now wished to return to his hometown. One night, he brought up the subject to Sanqiao, but, both being as deeply attached to each other as they were, neither could bear the thought of separation. The woman would have gladly packed up her personal belongings, eloped with the man, and lived with him ever after as his wife, but Chen Dalang objected: "This won't do. Granny Xue knows about our relationship all too well. My landlord Mr. Lü must also have his suspicions as to where I'm off to every night. What's more, there'll be a lot of travelers on the boat. Whom do you think we can fool? Nor can we bring along the two maids. When your husband comes back and finds out everything, he's not going to let the matter rest. Be patient. At this time next year, I'll come again and quietly send you a message from some secluded lodgings so that the two of us can slip away, unbeknownst to god or ghost. Wouldn't that be safer?"

"What if you don't show up by that time?" asked the woman, whereupon Chen Dalang pledged a vow. "Since you do mean it," said Sanqiao, "I will not fail you, either, whatever happens. When you get home, please send a message to Granny Xue by anyone who happens to come this way, so as to put my mind at ease."

Chen Dalang promised, "I'll surely do that. Don't worry."

A few days later, Chen Dalang hired a boat, and, after his provisions had been loaded, he went to bid Sanqiao farewell. That night they were doubly tender to each other, talking, weeping, and indulging in their desires by turns, without so much as a wink of sleep throughout the night. They rose at the fifth watch, and the woman opened a trunk, from which she took out a prized possession called the "pearl shirt." Handing it over to Chen Dalang, she said, "This shirt is a Jiang family heirloom that has a wonderful cooling effect on the body in summertime. You'll need it because the weather is getting warm. This will be a keepsake from me. To wear this shirt is to feel my body." Chen Dalang was so choked with sobs that he felt himself go limp and was unable to utter a single word. Sanqiao put the shirt on him, had a maid open the door, and saw him off as far as the door, where they took leave of each other with much emotion. As the poem says,

> *In tears, she saw off her husband years before.*
> *Today she weeps, bidding her lover farewell.*

Alas! Many a woman, fickle as water,
Attracts wild birds to replace her drake.

Our story forks at this point. After he came into possession of the pearl shirt, Chen Dalang wore it every day next to his skin. When he had to take it off before sleep every night, he put it under his quilt, and never, for a moment, did he part with the shirt. All along the journey, the boat was sailing with the wind. Within two months, he reached Maple Bridge in Suzhou Prefecture. There being in the neighborhood a trading center for brokers in rice and fuel, Chen Dalang naturally went to look for a buyer for his goods, but let us speak no more of this.

One day, at a fellow townsman's party, he met a merchant from Xiangyang, a dashing young man. This man was in fact none other than Jiang Xingge. What had happened was that after having done some trading in pearls, tortoiseshell, sappanwood, aloeswood, and the like in Guangdong, Xingge had set off together with some fellow merchants. As his fellow travelers suggested going to Suzhou to sell their goods, Xingge agreed, recalling the saying "Above, there is paradise; below, there are Suzhou and Hangzhou." A trip to such a big port would be worthwhile for some more business deals before returning home. He had arrived in Suzhou in the middle of the tenth month of the previous year. As Jiang was known in business circles as Mr. Luo, Chen Dalang had no inkling as to his true identity. At such a chance meeting, the two men, being of about the same age and similar physical appearance, came to respect and admire each other in the course of their conversation. At the dinner table, they asked for the location of each other's lodgings, and thus started a close friendship and a stream of frequent mutual visits.

After having taken care of his accounts, Xingge went to Chen Dalang's lodgings to bid the latter farewell, for he was now ready to be on his way. Dalang set out some wine, and the two fell into a most pleasant conversation. The weather being hot, for it was drawing near the end of the fifth month, they took off their outer garments as they drank. As Chen Dalang did so, the pearl shirt was exposed to full view before Xingge's eyes. However astonished he was, Xingge could not very well claim the shirt as his. Instead, he confined himself to commenting that it was a nice shirt indeed. Believing he had a friend to confide in, Dalang asked, "Do you, Brother Luo, happen to know a Jiang Xingge who lives on Great Market Street in your county?"

Being the discreet man he was, Xingge replied, "I've been away for too long. I've heard of such a man, but I don't know him personally. Why do you ask, Brother Chen?"

"To tell you the truth, my brother, I've come to be connected with him in a way." Whereupon he supplied a full account of his affair with Sanqiao. Pulling at his shirt, he said, his eyes brimming over with tears, "This shirt is a gift from her.

Now that you are leaving for home, please do me the favor of delivering a letter for me. I will send the letter to your place first thing tomorrow morning."

While he gave his promise, Xingge thought to himself, "How extraordinary! With the pearl shirt as evidence, his story must be true." Feeling as if being stabbed by needles in the stomach, on some pretext he declined more offers of wine and hastened to leave. Back in his lodgings, he sank into reflection for one moment and grew fretful the next. How he wished he could learn some magic trick to shrink the distance and be home in a trice! He packed up all of his belongings before the night was out and embarked on the boat early in the morning, ready to be on his way.

At this juncture, a man ran up to the boat, panting for breath. It was Chen Dalang. He handed over to Xingge a large package, reminding him to be sure to deliver it. Xingge's face turned ashen with rage. Speech failed him, as did his will to live or to die. It was not until Chen Dalang had left that he took a look at the envelope. It bore the line "Please be kind enough to deliver the letter to Granny Xue's house in East Lane off Great Market Street."

Angrily, Xingge ripped open the package with a single swipe of his hand, revealing a peach-pink gauze scarf more than two yards in length. There was also an oblong paper box containing a phoenix hairpin of fine white jade and a note saying, "Godmother, please do me the favor of delivering these two small gifts to my beloved Sanqiao as a token of my love. I will certainly see her next spring. Tell her to take good care of herself." In a rush of rage, Xingge tore the letter to pieces and tossed them into the river. Next, he picked up the jade hairpin and threw it onto the deck, where it broke in two. Then an idea occurred to him: "What a fool I am!" he said to himself. "Why don't I keep them as evidence?" He picked up the pieces of the hairpin, wrapped them up with the scarf, put the package away, and urged the boatman to get under way. All through the journey home he was gripped by intense anxiety.

As his house came into sight, tears fell from his eyes in spite of himself. (*Pitiable.*) "What a loving couple we used to be!" he thought. "It's my foolish pursuit of profits the size of a fly's head that made her a virtual widow in the prime of her youth and caused such a scandal. Regrets are too late now!" While on the way, he had been only too anxious to reach home, but now that he found himself approaching the house, feelings of pain and regret overcame him. His pace slackened. (*How realistic!*) As he crossed the threshold, he was obliged to curb his anger and force himself to greet his wife, though he had hardly a word to say. Sanqiao, for her part, felt so ill at ease that, with shame written all over her face, she did not presume to step forward and strike up an affectionate conversation. After he finished moving his baggage into the house, Xingge said he wanted to pay a visit to his parents-in-law, but, in fact, he spent the night on the boat.

The following morning, he went back home and said to Sanqiao, "Your parents are both gravely ill. That's why I had to stay with them for the night to take care of them. They miss you very much and wish to see you. I have hired a sedan-chair, which is waiting at the door. You may go quickly. I will follow soon."

Sanqiao had grown apprehensive about her husband's absence for the night and readily believed this story about her parents' illness. Filled with alarm, she hurriedly handed the trunk keys to her husband and mounted the sedan-chair, taking a waiting woman with her. Xingge stopped the waiting woman, gave her a letter that he took out from his sleeve, and told her to deliver it to Mr. Wang. "After giving him the letter," he continued, "you may return by the same sedan-chair."

Upon arrival, Sanqiao was surprised to find both parents in good health. Mr. Wang also gasped with astonishment at his daughter's unannounced return. As he took the letter from the waiting woman, he found, upon opening, that it was a statement of divorce that read,

> This is a statement of divorce by Jiang De, a native of Zaoyang County in the Prefecture of Xiangyang, betrothed at an early age through a matchmaker to the Wang family's daughter. Little did I expect that once married, the said woman would be guilty, as she is, of some of the seven offenses[17] that constitute grounds for divorce. Out of consideration for my sentiments for her, I cannot bring myself to reveal the details but would fain return her to her parents. She is free to remarry without any objections from me. This statement of divorce is written on this ——— day of the ——— month of the second year [1466] of the Chenghua reign period.
> (palm print)

In the envelope was also a peach-colored scarf and a broken jade phoenix hairpin. In great alarm, Mr. Wang called forth his daughter for questioning. Hearing that her husband had divorced her, Sanqiao broke down into sobs without saying a word. In a huff, Mr. Wang stormed through the streets and into his son-in-law's house. Jiang Xingge hurriedly stepped forward with a bow of greeting. Mr. Wang returned the greeting and said, "My good son-in-law, my daughter was a pure and innocent girl when she married you. What did she do wrong to make you divorce her? You owe me an explanation."

"I can't very well tell you. Ask your daughter and you'll know."

"She keeps crying without saying a word. I'm all in the dark! My daughter has always been a sensible girl, and I don't think she would be guilty of something like adultery or theft. If it's just some minor misdemeanor, please forgive her for my sake. The two of you were betrothed when you were seven or eight years old, and you have never had a harsh word for each other in your peaceful married life. You haven't even been home for more than a day since you came back from your travels. What could you have found wrong? Such heartlessness on your part will hold you up for ridicule for being a most unkind man." (*The very thing a father-in-law is likely to say under the circumstances.*)

"I will not venture to say too much to you, my father-in-law, but you may ask your daughter if she still has the pearl shirt, an heirloom of my family, that was entrusted to her care. If she still has it, well and good. If not, do not blame me for what I did."

Mr. Wang made haste to return home and asked his daughter, "Your husband is only asking you for a pearl shirt. Now tell me, whom did you give it to?" The woman flushed crimson with shame, for these words struck right on her sore point. Without knowing what to say, she burst into loud wails of grief. Mr. Wang was so disconcerted that he was at a loss what to do. In an attempt to placate her, Mrs. Wang said, "Don't keep crying like that. Tell Mom and Dad the truth, so we can help you sort things out." The daughter firmly refused to tell them anything. Instead, she kept weeping bitterly. Mr. Wang could do nothing more than hand over to his wife the divorce statement, the scarf, and the hairpin and tell her to be gentle with their daughter and gradually get the truth out of her.

The much-bewildered Mr. Wang went to a neighbor's house for some idle talk. Observing that her daughter's eyes were all red and swollen from crying, Mrs. Wang came to fear that her health would break down. After a few soothing words, she went to the kitchen to warm some wine to cheer up her daughter with.

Sitting all by herself in her room, Sanqiao began to wonder how the secret of the pearl shirt could have been divulged and where the scarf and hairpin had come from. After some moments of reflection, she said to herself, "I see. The broken hairpin means the marriage is at an end, just as a broken mirror symbolizes a broken marriage. The scarf is obviously for me to hang myself with. (*Even a guess sounds so real.*) Considering his feelings for me, he chose not to say it in so many words, so as to let me keep my good name. How sad it is that four years of a happy marriage are so suddenly brought to an end. It's all my fault, for I betrayed my husband's love. I suppose I will know no more happiness if I live on. I'd better hang myself and be done with it." At this point, she broke down in another fit of weeping. She put something under a stool to raise it, threw the scarf over a rafter, and proceeded to hang herself. However, she was not destined to die yet.

With the door left ajar, Mrs. Wang walked in with a flask of fine, heated wine. The sight of her daughter getting ready to hang herself threw her into such panic that, without stopping to put down the flask, she rushed forward to pull her daughter away. In the confusion, she kicked over the stool, and she and her daughter fell in a heap on the floor amid spilled wine. Mrs. Wang scrambled to her feet and helped her daughter up, saying, "How foolish you are! You are only in your twenties, like a flower not yet in full bloom. How could you have done such a thing! Even if your husband won't change his mind and goes through with the divorce, you, with your looks, won't have to worry about any lack of marriage proposals. You can well afford to pick a good husband and enjoy the marriage the rest of your life. Just relax and get on with your life. Forget all worries."

After he returned home and learned about his daughter's suicide attempt, Mr.

Wang also tried to comfort her with some soothing words. At the same time, he told his wife to be on alert and watch their daughter closely. A few days later, Sanqiao gave up the thought, as she saw the futility of any more such attempts. Truly,

Husband and wife are birds in the same woods,
But fly apart at the destined hour.

Let us come back to Jiang Xingge. He tied up Clear Cloud and Warm Snow with rope and beat them to make them confess. At first, they denied any knowledge of the affair, but later, unable to withstand the pain, they finally confessed all the details from beginning to end. It was thus made clear that no one else was to blame but Granny Xue, who had single-handedly pulled off the whole thing. The following morning, Xingge led a group of men to Granny Xue's house and smashed everything into pieces the size of snowflakes, falling just short of tearing the house down. Well aware that she was in the wrong, Granny Xue slipped out of the way, and no one dared to step forward to say anything. This lack of protest made Xingge feel vindicated. Upon returning home, he summoned a go-between and sold the two maids. As for the sixteen trunks of various sizes stored upstairs, he did not open any of them but wrote thirty-two sealing strips and sealed them in crisscross fashion, two to each trunk. Why did he do so? It was because, as a matter of fact, Jiang Xingge had been deeply in love with his wife. True, he had divorced her in a moment of anger, but his heart was twisted with pain. He could hardly bear the sight of anything that would remind him of her.

Let us pick up another thread of the story and tell of a man with a *jinshi* degree by the name of Wu Jie, a native of Nanjing, who was passing by Xiangyang in a boat on his way to Chaoyang County, Guangdong, to assume his newly assigned post of county magistrate. He did not bring his wife and children, and had a mind to find himself a beautiful concubine. None of the many women he saw along the way struck his fancy. Having heard that the daughter of Mr. Wang of Zaoyang County was known throughout the county for her beauty, he sought the services of a go-between and made a marriage proposal along with an offer of fifty taels of gold as a gift. Mr. Wang would have gladly accepted the proposal, but, afraid that his former son-in-law would be against the idea, he went to the Jiang household and acquainted Xingge with the fact. Xingge raised no objections.

On the eve of the wedding, Xingge hired some help and had the still-sealed and untouched sixteen trunks delivered, along with the keys, as the bride's dowry onto Magistrate Wu's boat to be handed over to Sanqiao. (*An act of kindness.*) She was overwhelmed with the sense that she did not deserve such generosity. When the story got around, some praised Xingge for his kindness, some laughed and called him a fool, and there were also those who despised him for his softness. So different indeed are human hearts.

Let us get on with our story. Chen Dalang, after having disposed of all of his merchandise in Suzhou, returned to Xin'an County, his mind still filled with thoughts about Sanqiao. The sight of the pearl shirt morning and night prompted him to sigh with emotion. Her suspicions aroused, his wife Ping-shi quietly took it away while he was asleep and hid it above the ceiling. When he rose in the morning without being able to find the shirt that he wanted to put on, he asked his wife for it, but she stoutly denied any knowledge of it. He flew into a rage and ransacked all boxes and chests. When the search proved to be futile, he let loose a torrent of angry words at his wife, who tearfully answered back, and the quarrel lasted for two to three days. Finally, in agitation, he hurriedly put together some money and, taking a page boy with him, set out on a journey back to Xiangyang.

When approaching Zaoyang, he ran into a gang of robbers, who not only made off with all of his capital, but also killed the page boy. Being keen of eye, Chen Dalang hid himself behind the rudder at the stern of the boat and was thus able to survive. Now that he could not afford the journey home, he planned to stay in the inn where he had stayed before, ask for a loan from Sanqiao, and start building his business anew. With a sigh, he stepped off the boat and went ashore.

To Mr. Lü, his landlord, who lived outside the Zaoyang city gate, he gave an account of what had happened and said that he wanted to ask Granny Xue, who was in the pearl business, to borrow some money on his behalf from some acquaintances. "You may not have heard about it," said Mr. Lü, "but that old woman caused a scandal by corrupting Jiang Xingge's wife. Last year when Xingge returned home, he asked his wife for some sort of pearl shirt, but she could not come up with an answer because she had, in fact, given it away to some lover of hers. Xingge divorced her then and there and sent her back to her parents. She has now remarried and is the second wife of *jinshi* Wu of Nanjing. As for the old woman, Jiang Xingge had her house smashed so badly that not a piece of roof tile was spared. Knowing that she would be given no peace, the old woman has moved to a neighboring county."

Chen Dalang was so shocked by these words that he felt as if a bucketful of icy water had been dumped on his head. That night, he fell ill with bouts of heat and cold. Brought on partly by depression, partly by lovesickness, and partly by the shock, the illness, with some symptoms of consumption, kept him confined to bed for over two months, with frequent improvements and relapses. With full recovery beyond sight, even the landlord's page boy attending to his needs ran out of patience. Feeling apologetic, Chen Dalang mustered enough strength to write a letter home. He then asked his landlord to find someone who happened to be available to deliver the letter and bring him back some traveling money along with a kinsman to take care of him. This was exactly what Mr. Lü wanted to hear. It so happened that there was an official courier, an acquaintance of Mr. Lü's, who was passing by Zaoyang on his way by land as well as water routes to the Huizhou and Ningzhou region to deliver official documents. To have mail delivered by him would be as quick as could be. Mr. Lü took Chen Dalang's letter and gave it to the courier, along with half a tael of silver on Dalang's behalf, asking him to deliver the letter at his convenience. Indeed, as the saying goes, "A lone traveler goes at his own pace; a courier goes with the speed of fire." In a matter of days, the courier arrived in Xin'an County and asked his way to Chen Dalang's house. After delivering the letter, he mounted his horse and galloped away. Truly,

> *A precious letter home*
> *Led to another marriage.*

When Ping-shi opened the letter, she recognized the handwriting to be her husband's. The letter said,

Greetings from Chen Shang to my good wife Ping-shi: After I left home, I ran into robbers in Xiangyang. My money was taken away and my page boy killed. The shock made me fall ill. I have been confined to bed in my old lodgings at Mr. Lü's for over two months now, without any sign of recovery. Upon receipt of this letter, please quickly send a trusted relative to see me, bringing along as much money for traveling expenses as possible. Written in haste, leaning on my pillow.

Ping-shi did not quite believe it. She thought to herself, "The last time he came back, he claimed to have lost as much capital as a thousand taels of gold. That pearl shirt must have been acquired by some improper means. And now he has come up with this story of a robbery to ask for as much travel money as possible. He must be lying." Then another thought struck her: "If he wants some trusted relative to go quickly to see him, he must be gravely ill. That part might be the truth, for all I know. Now, of whom can I ask the favor?" She kept turning the matter over and over in her mind, but, unable to put her mind at ease, she took the counsel of her father, Squire Ping. Then she put together some portable valuables, took with her the servant Chen Wang and his wife, and, in the company of her father, hired a boat and headed for Xiangyang to see her husband for herself. When they reached Jingkou,[18] Squire Ping suffered an attack of bronchitis and was escorted back home. Ping-shi and the Chen couple continued on the journey upstream.

Before many days had passed, they arrived at the city gate of Zaoyang and asked their way to Mr. Lü's house. It turned out that Chen Dalang had died ten days before. With a little of his own money, Mr. Lü had perfunctorily put the body in a coffin. Ping-shi cried until she collapsed to the ground, and remained unconscious for a considerable while. Upon coming to, she made haste to change into mourning clothes and repeatedly pleaded with Mr. Lü to open the coffin for her to see her husband once more and to transfer the body into a better coffin. Mr. Lü would not hear of it. Left with no alternative, Ping-shi could do no more than buy some boards to serve as an outer shell of the coffin. She also engaged some monks for a sutra-chanting service and burned an abundance of paper money for the benefit of the deceased. Having already obtained from her twenty taels of silver as a token of gratitude for his help, Mr. Lü said nothing to all this ado.

More than a month later, Ping-shi announced that she would like to select a propitious day and escort the coffin back home. Believing that the woman was too young, attractive, and well-provided-for to remain a widow for the rest of her life, Mr. Lü had a mind to keep her as wife for his yet-unbetrothed son Lü Er. Wouldn't that be lovely on both counts? He bought some wine, treated Chen Wang to a drink, and asked Chen Wang's wife, with promises of a handsome reward, to put the proposal tactfully to Ping-shi. Being a stupid woman, Chen Wang's wife thoughtlessly blurted out everything to her mistress. After all, what did she know about tact? Ping-shi was incensed. She gave the woman a tongue-lashing and a few slaps on the face. Even Mr. Lü was not spared a few scathing remarks from her. The humiliation reduced Mr. Lü to a resentful silence. Truly,

> *The mutton bun escaped his lips;*
> *He had but the foul smell all over his body.*

As a consequence, Mr. Lü urged Chen Wang to run away. For his part, Chen Wang also thought that to stay on would not be to his advantage any more. He took counsel with his wife. Under his instructions and with his collaboration, she stole all of Ping-shi's money and jewelry, and then the couple slipped away under cover of night. Knowing full well what had happened, Mr. Lü turned around and blamed Ping-shi for having brought along such scoundrels. "Luckily," he went on to say, "they stole only from their mistress. Wouldn't it look bad if they had stolen from someone else!" Then, complaining that the coffin was scaring his customers away, he told Ping-shi to have it removed as soon as possible. He added that, this being the wrong place for a young widow to stay, she would do well to leave. Under such pressure, Ping-shi resignedly rented a room elsewhere and hired some men to move the coffin there. Her plight hardly needs further description here.

Next door to her lived a Seventh Aunt Zhang, who was quite a sociable woman. Ping-shi's sobs frequently drew her over to offer words of comfort. She also often did Ping-shi the favor of pawning some of the latter's clothes in exchange for daily expenses, for which Ping-shi was deeply grateful. In a matter of a few months, all of her clothes had been pawned. Being good at sewing, a skill that she had acquired at an early age, Ping-shi began to consider making a living by teaching sewing skills to rich men's daughters before deciding what to do next. When she asked Seventh Aunt Zhang for advice, the latter said, "I don't know how to put this, but a rich man's house is not the best place for a young woman like you. The dead are dead and gone, which is too bad for them, but the living need to get on with their lives. You have a good part of your life ahead of you. You can't be a seamstress for some rich household until the end of your days, can you? It's such a lowly position that you'll be looked down upon. Also, what are you going to do about the coffin? That's another important thing you need to take care of. Even if you go on paying rent for it, that's no solution in the long run."

"I have also thought about all this," said Ping-shi, "but I can't come up with a better idea."

"I have an idea," said Seventh Aunt Zhang. "Don't take offense if I say so, but, for a penniless lonely widow a thousand li from home, to escort the coffin back is nothing but a lot of wishful thinking. Widowhood won't be easily maintained when daily subsistence is uncertain. But even if you do hold out for some time, what good will it do to you? As I see it, the best thing to do is to find a good match while your youth and good looks last, and give yourself up to him. Betrothal gifts can be used for their cash value to buy a piece of land to bury your husband in. Thus your future will be secure, and you'll have no regrets, dead or alive."

Convinced by her reasoning, Ping-shi reflected for some time before she answered with a sigh, "Oh well, to sell myself in order to bury my husband shouldn't be cause for ridicule."

"If you've made up your mind, I do happen to have someone for you. He's about your age. A decent man, and quite wealthy, too."

"If he's that wealthy, I'm afraid he won't take someone who's been married before."

"He's also been married before. He told me that he doesn't mind if the woman is marrying for the first time or not, as long as she is of uncommon beauty. Your looks should be attractive enough to impress him."

As a matter of fact, Jiang Xingge had indeed asked Seventh Aunt Zhang to find him a good match. As his ex-wife was a ravishing beauty, he was looking for someone as pretty. Ping-shi might not have been as beautiful as Sanqiao but was the better of the two when it came to matters of the mind and the finger.

The following day, Seventh Aunt Zhang went into town and told Jiang Xingge about the matter. Upon learning that Ping-shi was from the lower reaches of the Yangzi River, Xingge was all the more delighted. For a wedding gift Ping-shi wanted only what was necessary for the purchase of a nice plot of land for the burial of her husband. After Seventh Aunt Zhang shuttled back and forth quite a few times, both sides agreed to the deal.

To make a long story short, Ping-shi watched the lowering of the coffin into the pit, and, after the funeral, she shed bitter tears, removed Chen Dalang's spirit tablet, and took off her mourning clothes. As the wedding day drew near, Jiang Xingge sent over clothes and jewelry and redeemed all the clothes that she had pawned. On their wedding night, as was usual with wedding festivities, candles decorated with designs of dragons and phoenixes were lit in the bridal chamber amid the musical fanfare of a band. Truly,

Though the rites had been gone through before,
More loving were they than newlywed couples.

Ping-shi's gentle manners won much respect from Jiang Xingge. One day, returning home from outside, he found Ping-shi sorting out a trunk of clothes. Among the clothes, he recognized the pearl shirt. In astonishment, he asked, "Where did you get this shirt?"

"There's something strange about it." She then launched into an account of how her ex-husband had carried on about it, and how they had parted in anger after many harsh words. She continued, "When I was hard up some time ago, I thought several times of pawning it, but I was afraid of bringing it into the open, because its questionable origin might have gotten me into trouble. To this day, I have no idea where it came from."

"Was your ex-husband Chen Dalang, also called Chen Shang? Did he have a fair complexion? No beard? Long fingernails on his left hand?"

"Exactly."

Sticking out his tongue, Jiang Xingge joined his palms and looked up to the sky. "It's all too clear that heavenly principles have been at work," he exclaimed. "How fearsome!" Ping-shi asked why he said such a thing. "This pearl shirt," he explained, "was an heirloom of my family. Your husband seduced my wife and got the shirt from her as a keepsake. I didn't know anything about the affair until I saw the shirt when I met him in Suzhou. I divorced Wang-shi as soon as I returned home. Who would have foreseen that your husband would die on the road? When I remarried, I heard only that you were the ex-wife of a Mr. Chen, a merchant of Huizhou. Who would have guessed that he was none other than Chen Shang! Isn't this a heavenly retribution?"

These words made Ping-shi's hair stand on end, as a sense of awe swept over her. Henceforth, they grew even fonder of each other. This, then, is what basically constitutes our story "Jiang Xingge Reencounters His Pearl Shirt." As the poem says,

The ways of heaven are not to be slighted;
To whose advantage is the exchange of wives?
Interest must be paid on any debt incurred;
The marriage bond is but briefly suspended.

But the story continues. With a wife to take care of the household, Jiang Xingge set off a year later for Guangdong again on another business journey. This was one of those occasions when something was destined to happen. One day when he was in Hepu County[19] buying pearls, a deal had already been struck when the seller, an old man, stealthily took back a pearl of enormous size and refused to admit the theft. In anger, Xingge grabbed him by his sleeves in an attempt to search him, but the sheer force of the move brought the old man down to the ground. As the old man lay there without making a sound, Xingge hurried to help him up, only to find him dead. The old man's family and close neighbors rushed over, some weeping, some screaming, and seized Xingge. Without allowing a word of explanation, they gave him a sound beating and locked him up in an empty room. That very night, they wrote an official complaint and, after daybreak, took the defendant as well as the letter of complaint to the county magistrate's morning court session. The magistrate accepted the case, but, as there was other official business at hand, he had the accused locked up to await trial the next day.

Who, you may ask, was this county magistrate? Named Wu Jie, he was a *jinshi* of the greater Nanjing area. He was none other than Sanqiao's second husband. He originally had been assigned to a post in Chaoyang, but, as his superiors found him free from corruption, he was transferred, as a promotion, to the pearl-producing region of Hepu County. That night, Wu Jie was carefully reading by lamplight the accepted letter of complaint when Sanqiao, looking idly over his shoulders, happened to see these words: "The homicide case of Song Fu against Luo De, merchant of Zaoyang." Who could this Luo De be but Jiang Xingge? As memories of the happy marriage came flooding back to her, she appealed to her husband tearfully, her heart stricken with pain: "This Luo De is my older brother, who was brought up by my maternal uncle of the Luo family. I little expected that he would commit such a major crime while traveling on the road. For my sake, please spare his life and let him go back home."

"That'll have to depend on how the trial goes. If he is indeed guilty of murder, I can't be lenient with him."

Her eyes brimming over with tears, Sanqiao fell to her knees and pleaded piteously on behalf of the accused.

"Don't be so upset yet," said the magistrate. "I know what to do."

The following morning, as he was about to go to his court session, Sanqiao again grabbed him by his sleeve and said sobbingly, "If my brother's life is not spared, I will surely kill myself. You won't see me again."

That day when the county magistrate assumed the bench in his court, the first case he took up was the one involving Jiang Xingge. The brothers Song Fu and Song Shou tearfully pleaded that the murderer of their father should pay with his life. "Our father," they said, "was struck unconscious by the defendant in a dispute about a pearl and fell dead on the spot. Please do right by us, Your Honor." As the county magistrate took testimony from witnesses, some said the old man was knocked down and others said he fell when pushed. Jiang Xingge said in defense of himself, "Their father stole a pearl from me. I got into an argument with him in anger. Being an old man, he was not too steady of foot and fell to his own death. I had nothing to do with it."

The magistrate asked Song Fu, "How old was your father?"

"Sixty-seven."

"Elderly people faint easily without necessarily having to be hit," said the magistrate.

Song Fu and Song Shou insisted that their father was killed by the blow from Jiang Xingge.

"Whether there are injuries or not needs to be verified by a postmortem. Since you insist that he was killed, the corpse shall be sent to the county mortuary and the coroner's report will be heard during the evening session of the court."

As a matter of fact, the Songs were a prominent and respected family. The sons could hardly allow the body of their father, once a neighborhood alderman, to be exposed for autopsy in a mortuary. They pleaded while kowtowing, "There are many witnesses to our father's death. We request that the postmortem be done in our home rather than in a public place."

The magistrate said, "Without evidence of injuries to the bones, the accused will hardly admit to his crime, will he? Without duly filled-out forms of postmortem results, I can't report to my superiors, can I?" As the two brothers continued their entreaties, the county magistrate flew into a rage. "If you refuse to have a postmortem done, I can hardly try this case."

In panic, the brothers kowtowed repeatedly and said, "We will go by whatever ruling you make in your wisdom, Your Honor."

"For a sexagenarian," said the magistrate, "death is only to be expected. Suppose he did not die from a blow and an innocent man is wrongly accused. That would only serve to add to the sins of the dead. Your father lived to a venerable old age, something that you, as sons, had hoped for. Now, you wouldn't want to give him the bad reputation of having died a violent death, would you? However, though your father was not killed intentionally, he was indeed pushed. If Luo De is not severely punished, you would hardly feel avenged. Therefore, my judgment is for him to put on mourning clothes, observe the rituals in a manner befitting a son, and defray all expenses for the funeral. Will you be content with that?"

"We will not presume to be otherwise, Your Honor," said the brothers.

Xingge was overjoyed at the unexpectedly forthright verdict reached without resorting to corporal punishment. The defendant as well as the plaintiffs kowtowed in gratitude. The county magistrate went on, "Nor will I commit my judgment to paper. I will have the defendant escorted out of the court by lictors who will report back to me after what needs to be done is done. At that time, I will remove the original complaint from the file." Truly,

> Easy it is for a judge to commit karmic sin,
> Nor is it hard for him to get hidden merit.
> Observe how this Magistrate Wu of our times
> Rights the wrong and absolves guilt, to both parties' joy.

While her husband was in court, Sanqiao was as anxious as if she were on pins and needles. No sooner had she heard that the court session was over than she stepped forward to ask about what had transpired. The county magistrate said, "I made such-and-such a verdict. For your sake, I didn't put him to even one stroke of the rod."

Profuse with thanks, Sanqiao said, "After such a long separation, I am dying to see my brother to ask him how my parents are. I would be greatly obliged if you could be so kind as to arrange for us to meet."

"That can be easily done."

Dear audience, you may well ask how come Sanqiao was still so full of affection for Jiang Xingge, when she should have severed all emotional ties with the man who divorced her. The truth is that the couple had been as loving as could be. It was because of Sanqiao's misdemeanor that Xingge divorced her against his inclinations. In fact, he felt so sorry that he gave her back all the sixteen trunks intact on the night of her second wedding. Just this gesture alone was enough to melt Sanqiao's heart. Now that she was living in the midst of wealth and honor, and he was in distress, she could hardly do anything else than extend a helping hand. This is a case of returning kindness for kindness.

Now, Jiang Xingge followed the county magistrate's judgment and carefully fulfilled the ceremonial requirements asked of him, sparing no expense. The Song brothers found themselves without cause for complaint. After the funeral was over, Jiang Xingge returned under guard to the magistrate's court for a report. The county magistrate summoned him into the private quarters of his yamen, granted him a seat, and said, "My brother-in-law, I might have treated you unfairly in the lawsuit if your younger sister had not pleaded hard for you." With no inkling as to what he was talking about, Xingge was at a loss for an answer.

A moment later when they finished their tea, the county magistrate invited him into the study in the inner quarters of the yamen and called forth his concubine to greet the guest. Won't you agree that this all too unexpected reunion was as unreal as a dream? Without a salute or a word, the two of them fell into a tight embrace with loud sobs that were more heartrending than those ever heard at the funeral of a father or a mother. Overcome with pity, the county magistrate, who was standing on one side, said, "Please do not grieve so. I don't think you look like brother and sister. Tell me the truth; I'll help you out."

The two of them were so shaken by the violent shudders of weeping that neither was ready to speak. However, under the county magistrate's pressing questions, Sanqiao had no other choice but to fall on her knees to say, "I deserve to die ten thousand times for my sins, for this man is, in fact, my ex-husband."

Knowing that the truth was not to be concealed any longer, Jiang Xingge also dropped to his knees and gave a full account of their loving marriage, the divorce, and the remarrying on both sides. Having poured out the story, the two of them again fell into a tearful embrace. Even County Magistrate Wu found his own tears streaming down. "How can I bring myself to separate such a loving couple?" he said. "Luckily, no child was born during these three years. You may go together this very moment and resume your marriage." The couple took deep bows in gratitude.

With all speed, the county magistrate hired a small sedan-chair and saw Sanqiao out of the yamen. He then had some laborers carry all the sixteen trunks of dowry over to Jiang Xingge and sent a subordinate official to escort the couple out of the county. Such was the immense kindness of County Magistrate Wu. Verily,

> The Hepu pearls glowed with greater luster.[20]
> The Fengcheng swords shone in greater splendor.[21]
> Mr. Wu's kindness was admired by all.
> Wealth and beauty he coveted none.

He had never had a son, but, later, after his transfer to the Ministry of Personnel in Beijing, he took a concubine who bore him three sons in succession. All three were successful in the imperial examinations. This was believed to be a blessing for the good deeds he had done. But this happened later.

Let us return to Jiang Xingge, who took Sanqiao back home and introduced her to Ping-shi. If the first marriage were taken into consideration, Sanqiao would have taken precedence over Ping-shi. However, she had been divorced, whereas Ping-shi was married to Jiang Xingge through the mediation of a go-between, as required by proper etiquette. Moreover, Ping-shi was one year older. Therefore, Ping-shi took the position of first wife and Sanqiao became the second wife. With the two women addressing each other as "Sister," the threesome lived happily ever after, as this poem attests:

> Loving though they were for the rest of their lives,
> How shameful that she fell from wife to concubine.
> How true that vice and virtue will get their due.
> Heaven above weighs the scales; you need not seek far.

Yang Siwen Meets an Old Acquaintance in Yanshan

One night of the east wind
Swept the willow twigs clean of snow.
By the palace amid the warm mist,
Stands the colorful hill of lanterns.
The flutes and drums bring in the dusk;
The phoenix carriage returns to the palace.
A thousand doors are brightly lit;
The roads are filled with lovers.
Into the boudoirs the ladies retire
To rest after the fun and frolic.
Trying out new dresses,
They raise the bead curtains halfway.
Softly they speak, demure and shy,
Playing with silk flowers in their hands.
An occasion for reunions,
The Lantern Festival is here.

The above lyric poem to the tune of "The Jade Maiden Messenger" was written by Hu Haoran.[1] Lantern Festivals were celebrated with the most jubilation during the Xuanhe reign period [1119–25] under Emperor Huizong of the Song dynasty. Every year on the fourteenth of the first month, the eve of the Lantern Festival, the emperor would drive in his carriage between two hundred pairs of gold-trimmed red-gauze lanterns to Felicity Pool at Five Peaks Temple.[2]

By night, palm-shaped fans with long, glazed jade handles would be added on to the carriage, which was preceded by fleet-footed runners equipped with pearl-lined red-gauze lanterns. When evening set in, the emperor would return to his palace past the hill of lanterns. Members of the Office of Imperial Transportation would gather in front of the carriage and sing "Charm Follows the Poles." The carriage would turn around in a circle and then go backward all around the hill of lanterns. It was a feat, known as "Turn of the Dove" or "Stepping around Five Flowers," that invariably earned the driver a reward. The emperor himself would then ascend Extolling Virtue Tower while spectators flocked to the open-air stage shows.

On the fifteenth day of the month, the emperor would visit the Temple of Exalted Purity and remain until dusk before returning to his palace. On the day after the festival, the royal carriage would proceed again to the tower after breakfast. With the curtains drawn up, the emperor would have pedestrians summoned to his presence. Those who arrived early could thus see the Son of Heaven with their own eyes. Wearing a small cap and a red robe, the emperor would be flanked on both sides by attendants; in front of the curtains stood attendants holding golden fans. In a short while, the curtains would be let down and music struck up for all to enjoy. The resplendent light of the lanterns and candles, blended with the moonlight, shone far and wide. At the third watch of the night, a small red-gauze lamp would be lowered halfway down the tower on a rope, a signal that the imperial carriage was to return to the palace. Following is a lyric poem written by the emperor to the tune of "Jiazhong Palace: Xiaochong Hills":

> Midst the fragrance of the silks and satins,
> Gold lotuses bloom on dry land
> While my carriage goes around the city.
> In all directions stretch green wooded hills.
> The east wind, in its haste,
> Sweeps down half the stars from heaven.
>
> Ten thousand households rejoice in the peace,
> Songs fill the air on flower-strewn paths
> Where moonbeams follow at the heels.
> The royal gauze lanterns add light to the scene.
> The strains of flutes travel afar
> To the banquet in the immortal realm.

I shall now tell of a man who had always enjoyed the festivities in the Eastern Capital but, with the unexpected changing of times, came to be stranded in Yanshan Prefecture[3] and observed the Lantern Festival celebrations there. And how was the festival celebrated in Yanshan?

> Northerners though they are,
> They take joy in the festival as well.
> But instead of flutes and drums,
> Only the shrill Hun reeds are heard.
> Though every door is lit,
> No gold lotus is to be seen on the ground.
> Though nothing is left unadorned,
> No silk flowers embellish the hair.
> The Hun men wear garlic at their temples;
> The Jurchen[4] women wear chives in their hair.

The men all carry lutes;
The women beat flower drums.

Every year, the Lantern Festival in Yanshan was celebrated in imitation of the festivities in the Eastern Capital. It was not until the third year of the Jianyan period [1129] under Emperor Gaozong of the Southern Song dynasty that the festivities reached a grand scale. That year, a hill of lanterns was put up in Yanshan, an event enjoyed by officials and commoners alike.

Now, the young man of our story used to be employed in Prince Su's[5] mansion as a herald and a correspondence clerk for the imperial consort. He was named Yang Siwen but also known as Fifth Master Yang, for he was the fifth son in the family. In the Jingkang reign period,[6] he came to be stranded in Yanshan, where, luckily, he met his uncle Zhang Er, an innkeeper, who took him in as a lodger. With no other means of subsistence, Yang Siwen eked out a living by offering writing services every day in the marketplace. As the Lantern Festival rolled around, he saw that the streets were teeming with people out to view the lanterns. His uncle came to take him along to join the festivities. In a dejected mood, Siwen declined the offer. "As familiar as I am with the Lantern Festival in the Eastern Capital, how can I be expected to settle for anything less? (*How sad!*) You go ahead, Uncle. I'll catch up with you later." Consequently, Zhang Er set off alone.

By the time dusk set in, the noise on the streets had risen to such a level that, finding it hard to sit quietly, Yang Siwen could not do otherwise than go out to see the lanterns. Behold:

> *So bright were the lotus lanterns,*
> *Could they be stars blown down from heaven?*
> *Men and women thronged the streets,*
> *Like parades of celestial fairies.*
> *On the crowds the moon shed its light;*
> *Half are refugees from the old capital.*

The streets were filled with people coming and going. As he approached Blue Heaven Monastery, there came into view the golden statues of the fifty-three bodhisattvas and a hundred-foot-high bronze flagpole with an inscription in gold: "Blue Heaven Monastery of Compassion and Loyalty, constructed by imperial order." Entering the monastery, Siwen saw that both hallways were brightly lit. His leisurely steps took him to the Hall of Arhats, where he saw five hundred arhat statues in pure gold. An acolyte stood in front of the shrine asking for alms, saying, "Benefactors, please make a donation for some oil for our lamps. We shall pray for your fortune and longevity."

Detecting an Eastern Capital accent (*[Illegible] The reference to the Eastern*

Capital calls attention to the man's nostalgia for his hometown), Yang Siwen said, "May I ask the honorable monk where he is from?"

"I used to be an acolyte in River Sand Hall of Great State Councilor Monastery in the Eastern Capital. I'm now an acolyte here. Please sit down for a chat."

Seated on a stool, Siwen was watching the pedestrians passing by when a group of women keeping closely to themselves entered the Hall of Arhats. One of the women threw a glance at Siwen. As their four eyes met, Siwen noticed that the woman was dressed in the fashion of an Eastern Capital resident. She was

> *Lissome and graceful,*
> *With eyes sparkling like autumn water.*
> *She wore her jewelry like a court lady,*
> *And her headgear in the palace style.*
> *Still the fashion of the Xuanhe reign,*
> *Still the charm of the capital of old.*

The sight of someone from his native town stirred up such nostalgic emotions in Yang Siwen that he sank into dejection. As fatigue stole up on him, he drifted off to sleep. By the time he was awakened by the acolyte, the woman was nowhere to be seen. Yang Siwen sighed, "I was hoping to wait until they came out, so I could see if there might be relatives of mine among them, and now I've missed the chance."

Turning to the acolyte, he asked, "Where are the women who just came into the monastery?"

The acolyte replied, "They made a donation and left, saying that they would return tomorrow to hold a memorial service for some kinsmen. Don't feel bad, sir. You can come back to wait for them tomorrow."

Thus advised, Yang Siwen also donated some alms and took leave of the monk. After leaving the Hall of Arhats, he went around the monastery and had been looking around for some time when he suddenly noticed a lyric poem to the tune of "Ripples Sifting Sand" inscribed on the wall of the prayer hall:

> *I lean against the railings till sunset,*
> *With nothing around me but woeful sights.*
> *The frontier can be seen from up on high.*
> *In pain I hear the bugle on the tower,*
> *While the plains are under a layer of snow.*
>
> *The years speed by but my thoughts go back south,*
> *To Meridian Gate,*
> *Where the emperor rejoiced with his people.*
> *The temple keeps records from the days gone by,*
> *But the hill of lanterns is nowhere in sight.*

The poem further saddened Yang Siwen. He returned to the inn, where he spent a sleepless night. He rose upon the long-awaited first light of dawn, and the day passed without further ado.

When evening fell, he told his uncle that he was going to Blue Heaven Monastery to look for the woman he had seen the night before. Soon he found himself in the midst of the hustle and bustle of the streets. He was still walking along when he heard a peal of thunder. Afraid that it was going to rain, Siwen was about to turn back when he raised his eyes and saw

> *A bright moon shining over the Milky Way,*
> *The streets of heaven ablaze with lights.*
> *The precious candles glowing in the air,*
> *While fragrant winds caress the ground.*

Upon a closer look, he saw a large carriage approaching from the west. Several dozens of Jurchen officers followed behind as the carriage rumbled along. Behold:

> *The shouts of the guards rise to the sky,*
> *While the procession blocks the streets.*
> *In front, fifteen pairs of red-gauze lanterns,*
> *With candle flames ablaze.*
> *On both sides, twenty golden spears,*
> *Shining in dazzling splendor.*
> *The scented carriage goes by like an arrow,*
> *The attendants press ahead like a cloud.*

Behind the carriage followed several waiting women, one of whom was dressed in purple with a fish-shaped silver badge[7] at her waist, a white handkerchief in her hand, and a silk scarf around her neck. Yang Siwen took a closer look by the light of the moon and saw that she bore a striking resemblance to Lady Zheng Yiniang, wife of his sworn brother Han Sihou, protocol officer in the Diplomacy Section of the Bureau of Military Affairs.[8] She was also the adopted daughter of Imperial Consort Qiao. As her husband, Officer Han, was Siwen's fellow townsman, the two men had pledged brotherhood. Siwen used to address her as sister-in-law. Since separating, they had not heard from each other for quite some time. When their four eyes met, neither the woman in purple nor Siwen dared speak up. Instead, Siwen followed the carriage all the way to the Qin Tower in the city. The carriage drove in and the noble lady went upstairs, whereas the Jurchen officers took their seats downstairs. The Qin Tower was an impressively large restaurant, about the same size as the Baifan Tower in the Eastern Capital. There were sixty booths upstairs and between seventy and eighty tables with stools downstairs. That night, much wine was sold amid buoyant revelry.

After the noble lady entered the restaurant, Yang Siwen also went in and summoned a waiter. At the sight of Siwen, the waiter made a deep bow, but Siwen raised him up and said, "Please dispense with such ceremony." A closer look revealed him to be Chen San'er, formerly a waiter at the Baifan Tower in the Eastern Capital. Much delighted, Siwen asked him to sit, but San'er insisted that he would not presume to. Siwen said, "Both of us being from the old capital, for us to meet in a distant place is enough cause for sitting down together." The waiter sat down with an apology. Siwen handed San'er five taels of silver and told him to bring out some fine wine and dishes of meat and vegetables.

In the course of their conversation over the meal, San'er said, "When I first came here in the second year of the Jingkang reign period, I was given to a military officer as a slave. Later, when the Qin Tower opened, I thought of my days at the Baifan Tower as a waiter, and so I redeemed myself by paying the officer eighty in cash each day and came to work here. I'm so happy to see you, sir." As they conversed, a band somewhere struck up music. Siwen asked, "Where does all this music come from?"

"The music is played by the maids of the Lady of Han, who just went upstairs."

Upon Siwen's further inquiries about the lady, San'er said, "She is a most kind lady who often brings her maids and waiting women here for a cup of wine. I have often gone upstairs to serve them and she always gives nice tips."

"I ran into her entourage just now by the roadside and saw, among the maids behind the carriage, a woman who looked like my sister-in-law, Lady Zheng. I could be mistaken, though."

"I was also going to tell you that every time I went upstairs to serve them, I saw her, too, but I never dared to greet her for fear of making a mistake."

"I have a favor to ask of you. Would you go up now to serve them? Look for Lady Zheng and tell her that I am waiting for her downstairs to ask her about my brother."

Thus instructed, San'er went upstairs, while Siwen remained where he was, waiting. In a moment, San'er came down with a finger pressed against his lower lip, a gesture that Siwen knew was used by Eastern Capital residents to signal completion of a job.

"How did it go?" Siwen asked.

"I said to Lady Zheng, 'Fifth Master Yang is waiting for you to go down so that he can ask you about your husband.' The lady said tearfully, 'So my brother-in-law is here, too. Please tell him that I'll be down in a moment to speak to him.'"

Siwen thanked San'er, paid his bill, and stood waiting outside the door. Before long, he saw the attendants go in, and, a moment later, the Jurchen officers came out, escorting the carriage. After the carriage went past, Siwen saw, among the maids, his sister-in-law in a purple dress with a silver fish badge and a silk scarf around her neck. He stepped forward and asked, after some initial amenities, "Why are you not with my brother?"

Lady Zheng answered, wiping away her tears, "In the winter of the Jingkang year [1126], your brother and I went down the Huai River on a hired boat. We were at Xuyi when the boatman was hit by an arrow and the helmsman was cut down by a sword blow. I was then separated from my husband, who was captured by the barbarians. The barbarian chief, Marshal Saba, tried to take advantage of me, but I refused to submit and was brought here as a captive to Yanshan. Exasperated at my stubbornness and disgusted with my emaciated body, the marshal sold me to a family named Zu, which I later learned was in fact a brothel. Being the wife and daughter of court officials, I could not bear the humiliation of living like Su Xiaoqing.[9] I chose to die like Mengjiangnü.[10] So, when unobserved, I tried to hang myself with my girdle from a house beam, but I was found and saved from death. The Lady of Han, wife of Marshal Saba, heard about this and took pity on me. She ordered that I be taken care of and kept me as her maid. The scars on my neck have not yet healed. That's why I wear a silk scarf around it. I didn't know what had become of my husband after we parted during the confusion. Only recently did I hear that he escaped in disguise. He is now in Jinling.[11] He has taken up his old post and has been there for four years without having had the heart to remarry. I have burned incense, going as far as to burn some on the top of my head. I have also consulted fortune-tellers and prayed to the gods, hoping to escape to Jinling, but I have not yet found a way. Since I am nothing more than a slave waiting on the Lady of Han at the banquet table, I dare not talk with you for too long. Please ask every southerner you meet to send a message for me." (*This story told at the reunion could well have happened in a dream.*)

Before Yang Siwen could ask more questions, a Jurchen officer with a mace in his hand came over and yelled, "How dare you seduce one of our slaves in the middle of the night?" He raised the mace and was about to strike right at Siwen's face when Siwen ran away with all speed. The officer, being slow of foot, failed to catch up with him. Now out of the officer's reach, Siwen hastily returned in a cold sweat to his uncle's inn.

Surprised at Siwen's agitated state, Zhang Er asked, "Why do you look so flustered?" At Siwen's account of what had happened, Zhang Er heaved many a sigh. He set out some wine to drink with Siwen to cheer him up, but the latter was in no mood for wine, so disturbed was he by his thoughts of his brother Protocol Officer Han and sister-in-law Lady Zheng.

Thus it was that he spent the Lantern Festival in low spirits. When the third month came, Zhang Er said to him, "I'll be going away for a couple of days. Will you take care of the inn while I'm away?"

"Why are you going away?" asked Siwen.

"Now that the two states are at peace, I'm going to Weiyang to make some purchases. I'll be back soon."

With his uncle gone, Yang Siwen felt bored, left all alone by himself, and the long spring day made him drowsy. He went out and took a leisurely walk to the Qin Tower. After he looked around for a while, a waiter approached him and called out with a salute, "Fifth Master Yang!" It was not Chen San'er, but his face looked familiar. Who could he be?

The waiter introduced himself: "I am Little Wang. I used to work at the Yuxian Tavern in the Eastern Capital. Chen San'er was summoned by his master, the military officer, a few days ago, and he is not allowed to come out."

Now that Chen San'er was gone, Yang Siwen sank into deeper gloom. He ordered some appetizers, without really caring what they were, and asked Little Wang, "The Lady of Han who came here for a drink on the night of the Lantern Festival—do you happen to know where she lives?"

"I asked her attendants and was told that she lives behind Lord of Heaven Monastery." Before the words were quite out of Wang's mouth, Siwen raised his head and saw a poem written on the wall, its ink still wet. A closer look revealed a line of explanation that said, "This poem was written by Han Sihou of Changli when passing Lake Huangtian on a boat trip from Jinling, to mourn his deceased wife, Zheng-shi." The poem, to the tune of "Walking on Palace Steps," is as follows:

> Mix a thousand taels of powder and rouge,
> And mold a statue of Guanyin.
> The resemblance is slight, at most,
> For it lacks her wit and charm.
> I wait till dusk for dreams to begin,
> But throughout the night, I seek her in vain.
>
> Where has her sweet spirit gone?
> It may well be here on the boat.
> Without a word, I lean against the door,
> Facing the white-capped surging waves.
> Should my tears be measured as water,
> They would fill several lakes.

Yang Siwen was aghast after reading the poem. "This is my brother Han Sihou's handwriting. So he believes his wife is dead, but I saw her with my own eyes in the Qin Tower on the fifteenth of the first month. She spoke with me and said she was a maid for the Lady of Han. But he says she is dead. How strange!" In disbelief, he asked Little Wang, "Where is the man who wrote this poem? The ink is still wet."

"I have no idea. Now that the two states are at peace, envoys from the south have come here and lodged at the government inn. A group of four or five of them were here for a drink just a short while ago, and one of them must have written the poem."

Storyteller, this could not be true! How can envoys on a mission to another state go out freely to buy drinks? Well, according to *The Records of Yijian*,[12] at that time there was as yet no prohibition on official envoys' free association with local people.

To continue with our story, on that day, which was the fifteenth of the third month, Yang Siwen asked where the government inn was located. Little Wang said, "It's in the southern part of town." Thereupon, Siwen paid his bill, went downstairs, and hurriedly proceeded to the inn to look for Han Sihou. Upon arrival, he saw Su and Xu, two protocol officers, at the door, looking around idly. Being old acquaintances of Yang's, they recognized him and came over to exchange greetings.

"What brought you here, Mr. Yang?" they asked.

"I am here to look for my brother, Protocol Officer Han."

"He's inside in a discussion session. Let's go in and bring him out." So saying, they went inside and brought Han to the door.

At the sight of Protocol Officer Han, Siwen hastened to make a bow, overwhelmed by mixed feelings of joy and sadness at the reunion in Yanshan with a beloved friend far away from home.

"Is my sister-in-law well?" asked Siwen.

Tears coursed down Sihou's cheeks as he replied, "In the winter of the year of Jingkang, I hired a boat and was going down the Huai River with her when, at Xuyi, the boatman was hit by an arrow and the helmsman was cut down by a sword blow. Your sister-in-law was taken away, while I was captured and taken to an enemy camp in the wilds. At the third watch of the night, I pleaded my way out, without knowing if my wife was dead or alive. Later, while lying low in the grass, a servant of mine, Zhou Yi, saw her reject advances from the barbarian Marshal Saba and cut her own throat to end the humiliation. I made my way back to where the emperor was and regained my old post."

"Did you see what happened to her with your own eyes?"

"No. It was Zhou Yi who told me about it."

Siwen continued, "I believe she is alive. During the last Lantern Festival, I saw her with the Lady of Han on an outing to the Qin Tower. I asked Chen San'er the waiter to send a message upstairs for her to come down and see me. The first part of her account tallied with yours. She also said that you have regained your old post but have not had the heart to remarry in the last four years."

Sihou found these words hard to believe. Siwen went on, "It's easy to find out if she's dead or alive. Why don't you go with me to the residence of the Lady of Han, behind Lord of Heaven Monastery, to ask what really happened?"

Sihou agreed, "That's a good idea." He went back into the inn to notify his colleagues and then set off with Siwen, bringing a valet with him.

In a short while, they reached the area behind the monastery. It was a deserted place without a soul in sight. All that met their eyes was an abandoned house, its locked front gate covered with cobwebs, its windows laden with dust, its doorsteps overgrown with weeds, and the ground green with moss. Yang Siwen said, "This is most likely the back gate."

They walked along the wall and, dozens of steps later, came upon a house in which an old man was plaiting silk cords. They stepped forward and greeted him with a bow, saying, "Could you tell us where the entrance to the residence of the Lady of Han is?"

The old man, short in temper and rude in manners, paid them no attention. Upon further questioning, he said only that he did not know. Soon, there came along an old woman carrying a hamper and mumbling complaints against the old man. The two visitors greeted her and she returned the greeting in an Eastern Capital accent. The two men asked where the house of the Lady of Han was. The old woman was about to answer when the old man grumbled something, trying to quiet her. Ignoring him, the old woman said to the two visitors, "I am from the Eastern Capital, but this old man is from the uncivilized province of Shandong. It is my bad luck to be married to this brute who has not a grain of sense. I serve him meals and tea everyday, but he's still full of complaints. What a disgusting man! What do you have against my answering the gentlemen's questions?"

The old man started mumbling again. Paying him no attention, the old woman told the two visitors, "It is the locked empty house ahead."

Much startled, the two men asked, "But where is the lady?"

"She died the year before last. The family moved away. She was buried in the garden. If you don't believe this, would you care to go with me for a look?"

The old man objected, "Don't go! If the authorities hear about this, I'll be getting into trouble as well."

The old woman turned a deaf ear to his protests and took the visitors along. On the way, they asked, "There's a Zheng Yiniang in the lady's household. Is she still around?"

The old woman said, "Might you be Protocol Officer Han Sihou? Is the other gentleman Fifth Master Yang?"

In astonishment, the two men exclaimed, "How do you know?"

"I've heard Lady Zheng talk about you."

Sihou asked further, "How did you know her? Where is my wife now?"

The old woman replied, "Two years ago, there was a Marshal Saba who established a household here. His wife, the Lady of Han from the Cui family, was a most compassionate woman of a kind hard to come by. She often asked me into the house, and I heard her talk about a woman called Zheng Yiniang who was captured by the Marshal at Xuyi. The marshal took quite a fancy to her, but she swore never to be humiliated, and cut her own throat. Respectful of her chastity, the Lady of Han had her cremated and her ashes stored in a box. Later, after the Lady of Han died, the ash box was buried with her in this yard. Lady Zheng is dead, but she certainly looked no different than a live human being in flesh and blood. When I went into the yard, I often saw her come out. I was scared at first, but she said, 'Don't be afraid, Granny, I won't hurt you. I just want to tell you my misfortunes.'

She said she was Zheng Yiniang from the Eastern Capital. She was adopted at an early age by Imperial Consort Qiao and, later in her life, married court officer Han Sihou. She also told me that he had a sworn brother, Yang Siwen, otherwise known as Fifth Master Yang. I also learned about what happened at Xuyi. She said, 'My husband, for whom I died to preserve my chastity, is now an official in Jinling.' On rainy days, I would go into the garden to chat with her. If you want more details, you will be able to see for yourselves."

When the company of three arrived at the big locked house, the old woman climbed over the wall, followed by the two men. What came into their view was a deserted garden that had been left to run wild. They walked through the grass and the withered flowers as they searched without avail for the woman. In one of the three large rooms facing south stood a screen with a landscape by Guo Xi.[13] Sihou was looking at the painting when his eyes strayed to a few lines of writing on the wall. A closer inspection revealed a gentle and delicate penmanship that was just like that of Lady Zheng Yiniang. Overjoyed, he said, "Fifth brother, your sister-in-law is indeed here!"

"How do you know?" asked Siwen.

Sihou showed him the poem. It was a lyric poem to the tune of "Happy Events Approaching":

> With whom can I speak of the past?
> In silence, I shed tears of blood.
> When is the saddest moment of all?
> The hour when dusk sets in.
>
> I gaze from the tower and pace around.
> Who knows the pain in my heart?
> Would that I fly with the wild geese home
> While south of the Yangzi spring is in bloom!

At the end of the poem was a line that said, "Written the day after the third full moon of the year." The two men were taken aback: "So she wrote it today! Isn't this amazing!" As they moved farther along to another side, a tower came into sight. Holding on to the railings, the two men helped the old woman mount the stairs. Up there was another large screen inscribed in the same handwriting with a song titled "In Memory of My Love":

> At sunset under a lonesome spring cloud,
> I long for my love at the ends of the earth.
> Butterflies in pairs flutter in the wind,
> A sight that adds to the pain in my heart.
> All day long, I wait for him in vain;
> My youthful beauty slowly fades away.

Spring is in full splendor, mellow as wine;
Flowers fall on the steps amid birds' chirping.
By my lonely bed through the endless night,
The lamp burns out, the incense is gone.
The swings in the yard are long out of use;
The colored ropes sway for none to enjoy.
My brows always knitted,
My tears always flowing.
In silence I mount the tower
And lean against the railing.
Time flies by like a weaver's shuttle;
The waves surge forth, never to return.
My love is gone, forever;
My looks are fading, what should I do?

Having read the poem, Han Sihou said, his hand stroking the wall, "How tragic that my wife was taken captive!"

His eyes were still on the poem when he heard Yang Siwen cry out, "My sister-in-law is here!" Turning around, Sihou saw a woman with a silk scarf around her neck approaching. Upon a closer look, Siwen recognized her as the very same woman he had met at the Qin Tower. (*As in a dream.*) The old woman also cried, "The lady is here!" In amazement, the three of them rushed downstairs, only to see her turn into the left corridor at the back, heading toward a pavilion. The two men were seized with fear, but the old woman said, "Since we are already here, why don't we go into the pavilion for a look?" She led them there and found the door closed. A board on the door bore this inscription: "Memorial Hall of the Lady of Han." The old woman pushed open the latticed door and they stepped in. In the middle, set up to receive offerings, was a spirit tablet with the words "My deceased wife, the Lady of Han." To one side were a portrait of Yiniang and another spirit tablet with the inscription "Maid Zheng Yiniang." The altar in front was covered with a thick layer of dust. At the sight of the portrait, which, in clothing and appearance, differed not in the least from Siwen's description, Han Sihou broke down in passionate weeping.

The old woman said, "The box with Lady Zheng's ashes is under the table. She often spoke of it and showed it to me. It's a black lacquer box with two copper rings. Every time she mentioned the box, she would cry and say to me, 'I died with no regrets, for I died out of loyalty to my husband.'"

At these words, Sihou asked the old woman, with a promise of a handsome reward, to help him pry up the floor bricks and take out the box for a burial in Jinling. She agreed. The three of them moved aside the altar, pried up the bricks, and reached for the box. However hard they tried, the box would not budge. The harder they tried, the firmer it stuck to the ground.

"Stop! Stop!" cried Siwen. "She is showing her power, my brother. If the box is to be taken away, there must be a proper ceremony. Let's leave this place for now to prepare for a sacrificial ceremony complete with an elegy in her honor. Only then can the box be taken away."

Han Sihou agreed, "There is much sense in what you say." The three of them climbed over the wall again and went to the old woman's house, where they told the servant Zhang Jin to buy some wine, meat, incense, and candles and composed an elegy right there in the old woman's house. When daylight came, they carried the offerings with the help of the old woman and the servant, climbed over the wall, and laid everything out in the memorial hall.

By the third watch of the night, the incense and the candle had almost burned out, and the cups and plates were found to be in disarray. As the constellations crossed the Milky Way, Sihou poured out three libations and, standing by the altar table, read the elegy aloud, shedding copious tears. When the elegy was burned together with paper money, there sprang up a gust of strong wind. The candlelight flickered in a way that sent chills down their spines. As the wind blew past, a fit of weeping became audible. (*Very much like a dream.*) After the wind died down, the flicker steadied itself into a flame, bringing into view a woman with a face as fresh as a flower and with skin as smooth as jade. A silk scarf around her neck, she straightened her sleeves, moved forward in mincing steps, and greeted Yang Siwen. In astonishment, the two men returned the greeting. Han Sihou stepped forward tearfully and reached for her hand.

After much weeping, Lady Zheng said to Sihou, "By now, you should have learned what happened at Xuyi. At the Qin Tower on the night of the Lantern Festival when I met my brother-in-law, I did not have the chance to say all I wanted to say. If I had clung to life, I would have brought disgrace to my husband. Luckily, I treasured your good name like jade and treated my own life as dust. That is how we came to be parted by death, to my eternal sorrow." With these words, she broke down in another fit of weeping.

The old woman tried to comfort her, saying, "Don't cry now. Let's talk about moving your remains away from here."

Holding back her tears, Lady Zheng sat down. While the other three partook of food and wine, she did nothing more than sniff at the aroma.

"When I saw you at the Qin Tower on the night of the Lantern Festival," said Siwen, "you were waiting on the Lady of Han. Were the many attendants behind the carriage ghosts or humans?"

"In times of peace," she replied, "humans and ghosts live in separate worlds, but in these current times, humans and ghosts mix. None of those in the entourage was a living being."

Sihou said, "Since my good wife died for my sake, if only to show my gratitude, I shall never remarry. What do you say if we move your remains back to Jinling?"

The lady objected: "Please listen to me, while both Granny and Brother-in-law are here. Since you have been so kind as to take pity on my lonely soul, how would I be loath to return home with you? But you should visit me often so that our love can be kept alive across the two worlds. Should you remarry, you will certainly forget me. If it turns out that way, I would rather stay here."

No amount of persuasion from the three of them could shake her from her resolve. Turning to Siwen, she said, "My brother-in-law, how can you not know my brother! When I was alive, his weakness for women was such that it was hard to keep him in check. Now that I am dead, it is a matter of course that he will, if he is to have his way, abandon the old in favor of the new." (*Her repeated refusals are meant to strengthen her husband's resolve. But why should a ghost be jealous?*)

Siwen tried again to plead with her: "Please listen to me, my sister-in-law. My brother is now a different man. Out of gratitude for your honorable death, he will never take another woman for a wife. Now that he is here to take you back, how can you have the heart to refuse him? Please take my advice."

"I thank my brother-in-law for taking such pains to offer me words of counsel. If my husband is indeed to remain true and will take an oath now, I will gladly follow him."

At these words, Sihou poured wine on the ground and said, as an oath, "In the event that I break my promise, may I be killed by bandits when traveling on land or, if I travel on water, may my boat capsize in huge waves."

The lady protested in haste, "Stop, stop. You don't have to swear like that. Since you are determined not to remarry, my brother-in-law will be a witness." This said, a gust of fragrant wind sprang up. She disappeared as the wind blew past. Astounded, the three of them relit the candles, lifted up the brick under the altar, and took out the box without the least effort. Having gathered the things together, they climbed over the wall and went to the home of the old woman. The following evening, they thanked the old woman with three taels of silver, and Sihou presented Siwen with ten taels of gold over the latter's repeated protests. After bidding farewell to Siwen, Sihou returned to the inn, accompanied by his servant Zhang Jin, who carried the box. It was about a month later that he received his commission to return to the south. Siwen set out wine for a farewell dinner, reminding him over and over again, "Brother, don't forget my sister-in-law's words."

Carrying the box of the lady's remains, Sihou and his party left the city of Yanshan by Fengyi Gate to return south. About a month later, they reached Xuyi and found lodging in an inn. There, a man came up to Sihou with a bow of greeting. Sihou recognized him to be Zhou Yi, his former servant, who now worked at the inn. He led Sihou into a room containing a portrait of a woman on the wall and a spirit tablet, on which was written, "Lady Zheng, my master's deceased wife." To queries from a surprised Sihou, Zhou Yi answered, "Having witnessed how the lady died for you to preserve her chastity, how could I not set up a shrine in her honor?" Thereupon Sihou gave Zhou Yi a full account of everything that had happened in the house of the Lady of Han in Yanshan and showed him the box of remains. Zhou Yi kowtowed in bitter sobs. That night, Sihou and Zhou shared the same bed, head to foot and foot to head.

At the first light of dawn the following day, Zhou Yi said to Sihou, "In the old days, there were more than twenty people in your household, but now I have only my own shadow to look at. I would much rather follow you to Jinling and serve you again." Sihou agreed and brought Zhou Yi back to Jinling. Sihou returned to the tribunal and presented his superiors with the letter of reply. Zhou Yi then followed Sihou to the hills, where they selected a burial site and buried the remains with the proper rites. Beside himself with grief, Sihou went to the grave every three days with sacrificial offerings and returned only when dusk had set in. Zhou Yi was given the task of watching over the grave.

One day, Protocol Officers Su and Xu said to Sihou, "Liu Jintan, abbess of Saturn Convent here in Jinling, though a woman, is most virtuous and noble. Why don't we go to her convent for a memorial service in honor of your deceased wife?" Sihou agreed. On a selected day, he went to the convent with Su and Xu to visit Liu Jintan. You may well ask, how was she dressed?

> A sky-blue cap on her head,
> An ivory tablet in her hand.
> On her body a white silk robe,
> On her feet emerald shoes.
> Without aid of rouge or powder,
> She looked like a plum blossom in the frost.
> Elegant and pure,
> She stood like a lotus above water.
> Matchless her beauty,
> Unrivaled her grace.

The moment Han Sihou laid eyes on the abbess, his soul took flight, and he stood there stupefied, eyes unblinking and mouth agape. After the exchange of greetings, Jintan gave instructions for holding a service and invited the visitors to go inside for a look at a magic mushroom. The three of them walked past Double Purity Hall and Emerald Flower Pavilion and turned from Eight Trigram Altar into Crimson Silk Hall, where the magic mushroom was kept. While the others were gathered around the magic mushroom, Sihou slipped into the abbess's cell and looked around. His eyes swept from the bright windows and clean tables to the objects of art placed throughout the room. On the desk was an array of stationery items. From under a paperweight, he drew out a piece of paper on which was inscribed a lyric poem to the tune of "Sand of the Silk-Washing Stream" (*Very much like Chen Miaochang.*[14] *This must be the way with all nuns and monks*):

My beauty is untouched by worldly dust,
In my star cap, cloud cape, and purple skirt.
With the door shutting out the slanting sun,
I strum idly my zither of jade.

Flowers in this lonesome convent pain my heart.
The moon by the window fills me with longing.
To return to the secular world,
What a blessing that would be!

Han Sihou's desires had already been stirred up at the first sight of Jintan's beauty. These words plunged him deeper into yearning. He wrote a lyric poem to the tune of "The Moon over the West River":

Such beauty needs no rouge and powder.
Such a plum is no common flower.
All day long, she ponders the Daoist truth,
To the neglect of the world of romance.

On her cap are the stars of the Big Dipper,
From her staff hangs the Daoist canon.
When shall I enter this fairyland
And ride the colored phoenix with her?

Clapping his hands, he chanted the poem at the top of his voice. Jintan's expression hardened. In rage, she lashed out, "What is the meaning of this? How dare you take advantage of my helplessness to sully the name of my convent! Get me my sedan-chair! I'm going to the authorities. They will know what to do with you."

However hard Su and Xu tried to stop her, she turned a deaf ear. Han Sihou took out from his bosom the poem she had written and showed it to them, saying, "Don't be so upset, my good abbess. Who is the author of these lines?"

Jintan was so consternated that she wished she could hide herself. Her scowl softened to a radiant smile. She laid out a banquet in honor of the guests. Amid the drinking and the carousing, everything about the memorial service was forgotten. Both being amorously disposed toward each other, they did not part company until well intoxicated with wine.

Now this Liu Jintan was a native of the Eastern Capital. Her husband, Feng the Sixth, had been the recipient of edicts in the Bureau of Military Affairs. During the Jingkang reign period, the couple had fled to Jinling on a hired boat. When on the Huai River, Feng the Sixth was shot by an arrow and fell into the water to his death. His wife, Liu-shi, vowed to enter the Daoist order in Saturn Convent in honor of her late husband's memory. Her fame having thus spread to the court and through the public, she was appointed to be its abbess. After this visit, Han Sihou began to frequent the convent.

One day, Su and Xu pooled their money, prepared some gifts, and treated Liu Jintan and Han Sihou to dinner at the convent. After several rounds of wine, Su and Xu held up their cups and made this suggestion to Sihou and Jintan: "Your love for each other is due to a predestined marriage bond. With all the rumors floating around, you can't very well go on like this. Why don't you, Jintan, return to secular life and marry our brother with proper ceremonies, complete with wedding gifts and a matchmaker? Wouldn't that be nice!"

Sihou and Jintan accepted their counsel. Jintan paid a fee for permission to return to secular life. Sihou selected a day, and the wedding ceremony duly took place. She ceased to mourn her deceased husband, nor did he continue to visit his wife's grave. Hand in hand, they leaned against the window and exchanged tender words of love.

Some days after the wedding, Zhou Yi, whose job it was to watch the grave, went to the Han residence to find out why Mr. Han had stopped visiting the grave. He asked the gatekeeper, "Why has the master not been seen at the grave for some days?"

The gatekeeper replied, "Mr. Han is newly married to Liu Jintan of Saturn Convent and has no time to go to the grave anymore."

Being a tactless northerner, Zhou Yi smoldered with indignation at these words. As coincidence would have it, he ran straight into Sihou, who was on his way out. After the greeting, Zhou Yi exploded, "Master, what a heartless man you are! Lady Zheng died for your sake. How could you have taken another wife?" While lashing out at him, Zhou Yi also wept for Lady Zheng.

Afraid that the commotion would not reflect well on his newly wedded status, Han Sihou sharply ordered the gatekeeper to drive Zhou Yi out. A dispirited Zhou Yi returned to his hut by the grave. That day being the Clear and Bright Festival,[15] Zhou Yi tearfully complained to the grave about what had happened. At the third watch of the night, Lady Zheng called out to Zhou Yi, "Where does your master live now?"

Zhou Yi told her all he knew about how Sihou had broken faith and remarried. "He now lives on Sanshiliuzhang Street. Why don't you go and settle things with him?"

The lady answered, "That's exactly what I'm going to do."

Zhou Yi woke up with a start from the dream. A cold sweat broke out all over his body.

In the meantime, the newly wedded happy couple were enjoying the moonlight at a table laid out with wine. In the midst of the drinking, Liu-shi suddenly grabbed Sihou and, with her willowlike eyebrows knit in an angry frown and her starry eyes wide open, she cried, "You owe me too much! Pay me back with your life!" The voice was that of Lady Zheng.

Seized with fear and at a loss what to do, Sihou pleaded, "My good wife, please forgive me." But the grip remained firm. While he was struggling, Su and Xu, out on a walk in the moonlight to visit Sihou, appeared on the scene. At the sight of Liu-shi keeping a tight grip on Sihou, the two men came forward and released him. Sihou scurried away and, after taking counsel with Su and Xu, decided to have Priest Zhu of Iron Chain Temple of Bamboo Bridge perform an exorcism. Zhang Jin the servant was sent immediately to bring the priest over.

When he saw Liu-shi, Priest Zhu said, "The injustice done to her was so great that this case is beyond me. The only thing left for me to do is to offer her some soothing words."

Slapping her own face and mouth, Liu-shi gave the priest a tearful account of what had happened in Yanshan, adding, "Please be compassionate in your judgment, Your Honor."

The priest tried to placate her by saying repeatedly, "There will surely be a memorial service for you to redeem your soul. If you refuse to stop this behavior, you will be violating the laws of heaven."

At these words, Liu-shi thanked the priest with a sob and said, "I will go now."

It was some moments before Liu-shi regained consciousness. The priest drew a magic charm for her to eat[16] and posted some ghost-expelling signs on the door before he left. That night passed without further ado.

The following day, Sihou brought some incense and paper to Bamboo Bridge to thank the priest. Barely had he sat down when a servant of his came to report that his wife was possessed again. To Sihou's pleas to go to his house for another exorcism, the priest replied, "If this thing is to be put to an end once and for all, you will need to dig up the grave and dump the box of remains into the Yangzi River. Only then will you never be bothered again." Sihou had no better choice than to do as the priest said. He hired laborers, went with them to the grave, dug it open, took out the box, and threw it into the Yangzi River. From then on, Liu-shi was herself again. How preposterous that such ingrates were not met with retribution from heaven!

So Sihou betrayed Zheng Yiniang and Liu Jintan betrayed Feng the Sixth. In the eleventh year of the Shaoxing reign period [1141], the emperor moved to Qiantang,[17] followed by officials and civilians. Sihou also left Jinling and took his family farther south. When they reached Zhenjiang, Sihou wished to revisit the scenic Jin Mountain. He hired a boat and went on board with his wife, Liu-shi. When they were in midstream, the boatman burst into a song to the tune of "Happy Events Approaching":

> With whom can I speak of the past?
> In silence, I shed tears of blood.
> When is the saddest moment of all?
> The hour when dusk sets in.

> *I gaze from the tower and pace around.*
> *Who knows the pain in my heart?*
> *Would that I fly with the wild geese home*
> *While south of the Yangzi spring is in bloom!*

Sihou was appalled, for it was the very poem that was written on the screen by Zheng Yiniang, maid of the Lady of Han in Yanshan. "Where did you learn this poem?"

The boatman answered, "Recently, an envoy went up north to Yanshan and heard this song all over the city. The lyrics were originally on a screen in the house of the Lady of Han and were recorded by an old woman who plaits cords for a living. (*Picking up an earlier thread.*) The story is that there was a Zheng Yiniang, wife of an official south of the Yangzi, who died to preserve her chastity. Later, her husband took her remains back to the south, and the poem came to be spread throughout the empire and beyond."

These words were like ten thousand knives stabbing at Sihou's heart. Tears coursed down his face. In a trice, a storm sprang up. Waves surged furiously, sending up sheets of spray and mist. Strange-looking fish appeared and vanished, and river monsters threw the waves higher. There emerged from the waves a man wearing a square cap, who grabbed Liu-shi by her hair and threw her into the river. "Madam fell into the water!" The maid shouted at the top of her voice and called Sihou for help, but Liu-shi was already far beyond any hope of rescue. The next moment, a woman appeared. A silk-scarf around her neck, her eyes blazing with anger, she seized Sihou and dragged him into the depths of the waters, and there he drowned. There was nothing the boatman could do, much as he wished to help. In low spirits, he went back home. Alas! Such has been the fate of all heartless ingrates of times old and new, and therefore I pass this story on. As the poem says,

> *She betrayed her husband and drowned to death,*
> *He wronged his wife and perished in the waves,*
> *Dying as did Cao E,[18] the filial daughter,*
> *If not like Qu Yuan the loyal minister.[19]*

Yu Boya Smashes His Zither
in Gratitude to an Appreciative Friend

What a lie that Bao Shu was cheated out of his silver!
Who recognized Boya's talent in playing the zither?
An evil lot are those claiming friendship nowadays,
Unworthy of loving thoughts over seas and lakes.

When it comes to friendship, none since ancient times has measured up to that between Guan Yiwu [d. 645 B.C.E.] and Bao Shuya [also known as Bao Shu].[1] When both were engaged in business dealings, they divided their profits between them. Though Guan Yiwu took the larger share of the profits, Bao did not think Guan was a greedy man, for he knew Guan to be poor. Later, when Guan Yiwu became a prisoner, it was Bao who came to his rescue and recommended that he be made prime minister of the state of Qi [during the Spring and Autumn period]. Such is the stuff of which true friendships are made.

Now there are different kinds of friends. Those who are bound together by deeds of kindness are friends who truly know each other; those who show utter devotion to each other are friends of the heart; those who find much in common with each other are friends truly appreciative of each other. They all fall into the general category of friendship.

I now propose to tell a story about a certain Yu Boya. Dear audience, those of you who would like to hear it, please lend me your ears. Those who do not want to hear it are free to do whatever you wish. Truly,

What is meant for an appreciative ear
Is not to be wasted on just anyone.

As the story goes, during the Spring and Autumn and the Warring States period, there lived a man named Yu Rui, courtesy name Boya, in Yingdu, capital of the state of Chu, in what is now Jingzhou Prefecture in Huguang.[2]

Though a native of the state of Chu, Yu Boya was destined for a career as an official in the state of Jin, where he rose to be a senior grand master. By order of the king of Jin, he went on an official visit to Chu. It was actually a mission that he had solicited. He did so partly because, with his superior abilities, he was sure that he would acquit himself well as the king's emissary and partly because he could take the opportunity to visit his hometown, thus accomplishing two purposes at the same time. So he traveled by land to Yingdu, where he had an audience with the king of Chu and transmitted to him the message from the king of Jin, whereupon the king of Chu laid out a feast in his honor, treating him with great courtesy.

Yingdu being his hometown, Boya naturally went to visit the family graves and meet with relatives and friends. However, now that he was serving another state and was bearing orders from his king, he refrained from staying longer. As soon as his official business was over, he bade a respectful adieu to the king of Chu, who gave him gifts of gold, colored silk, and a canopied four-horse carriage.

Now, because he had been away from Chu for twelve years and missed the scenic rivers and mountains of his home state, Boya wished to make a big detour by water on his return journey so as to see the sights to his heart's content. He therefore said to the king of Chu, not in all honesty, "I have an unfortunate affliction that makes the rapid speed of carriages too much for me to bear. I humbly request permission to go by boat instead, which would make it easier for me to undergo treatment." The king of Chu approved Boya's request and ordered the navy to provide him with two big boats, one for his exclusive use as the emissary from the state of Jin and the other, of a lower ranking, for his servants and the luggage. Magnificent boats they were, with brocade canopies, tall masts, and decorated oars made of fragrant wood. The ministers of the court escorted Boya and his entourage all the way to the riverbank before they bade him farewell.

> To satisfy his wish to see the sights,
> He thought nothing of the distance.

Romantic scholar that he was, Boya found the sights to be all that he had hoped to enjoy. With sails unfurled, the boats rode on the undulating green waves, the distant wooded mountains and clear waters within full view. Before many days had passed, he found himself and his entourage at the mouth of Hanyang River. It was the fifteenth night of the eighth lunar month, the night of the Mid-autumn Festival. Suddenly, a storm sprang up. With waves leaping high and rain pouring down in sheets, the boats had to be moored at the foot of a hill. A while later, the wind died down, the waves subsided, the rain stopped, and the clouds cleared, revealing a bright, rain-washed moon that shone with double its usual brightness.

Sitting alone in the cabin and feeling bored, Yu Boya told his page boy, "Put some incense in that incense burner. I'm going to play my zither to express my feelings." Thereupon, the page boy lit the incense and put the zither case on the table. Boya opened the case, took out the zither, tuned it, and began to play. Before he had finished a piece, a string broke with a sharp twang. Startled, Boya told the page boy to ask the head boatman what kind of place this was. The head boatman replied, "This is just the foot of a hill where the storm took us. There are some grass and trees around, but no houses." (*True enough.*)

Much taken by surprise, Boya thought to himself, "So, this is a deserted hill. If it were a town or a village where some intelligent person eager to learn listened secretly to my music, that would explain why the music suddenly changed in tone and why the string snapped. But in this deserted place at the foot of a hill, how can there be anyone listening to my music? Ah yes, I know. It must be an assassin sent by some enemy of mine, or it could be some robbers waiting here for the night to deepen before coming onto the boat to get my possessions." So thinking, he said to the attendants by his side, "Go ashore and look around for me. If there's no one in the depths of the willow grove, then search in the reeds."

Thus instructed, the men called out to other servants, and they all assembled, ready to use the gangplank to get to the rocky shore. At this moment, a man's voice was heard from the shore, saying, "The gentleman in the boat need not be suspicious. I am not a robber but a woodcutter. I had finished cutting firewood for the day and was on my way home after dark when I was caught in a bad storm. My rain gear not being enough to protect me from the rain, I found shelter by a rock. Then I heard the gentleman play the zither and stayed to listen."

Boya burst into laughter. "Imagine a woodcutter in the hills having the audacity to say he listens to music! Well, I won't even bother to find out whether that claim is true or not. Now, my men, tell him to leave."

Instead of leaving, the man on the rocky shore said loudly, "Sir, you've got it all wrong! Haven't you heard the sayings 'In a neighborhood of ten households, there are bound to be loyal and trustworthy people' and 'If there is a gentleman in the room, another gentleman will come to the door'? You, sir, in your contempt for these backwoods, think that no one around here would listen to music. Well, if so, there shouldn't be a zither player at the foot of a deserted hill, either."

Impressed by the man's refined speech, Boya began to think that this woodcutter might truly have been listening to his music. He told his men to quiet down and went to the cabin door. His displeasure having given way to delight, he asked, "Since the gentleman on the rocky shore has been standing and listening to my playing for quite some time, does he, by any chance, know what I was playing?"

"If I didn't know," said the man, "I wouldn't have stayed and listened. What you have been playing, sir, is a melody set to what Confucius wrote in memory of [his student] Yan Hui. The lines go like this, 'How tragic that Yan Hui died so early; / Memories of him have whitened my hair. / By living happily in poverty,'— and at this point, a string on your zither snapped before the fourth line could be played. But I remember the fourth line. It says, 'A good name he left for posterity.'"

Overjoyed upon hearing this, Boya said, "You are indeed a gentleman of culture. But it is difficult to talk with you across such a distance." Turning to his men, he said, "Put out the gangplank and the handrail and invite the gentleman to come aboard for a chat."

The servants put out the gangplank, and the man boarded the boat. He was indeed a woodcutter, with a broad-brimmed bamboo hat, a straw cape, a carrying pole with its load, an ax tied to his waist, and straw sandals on his feet. The servants, who had little appreciation for refined speech, assumed a contemptuous look at the sight of a mere woodcutter. (*Those who worship money and bully the poor and the humble don't know the good from the bad and, as such, will never rise above the servant class.*) "Hey, woodcutter!" they called out. "When you go into the cabin, be sure to kowtow to our master, and be respectful when you answer his questions. He's a highly placed official, you know."

The woodcutter was by no means of the common run. "You don't have to be so rude," he said. "Now, let me get myself ready before I go in." So saying, he took off his bamboo hat, under which was a blue cloth cap. Then he took off his straw cape, revealing a blue cloth shirt, a long bag worn around his waist, and a pair of cloth pants. All calm and collected, he put his cape and hat, his load and its carrying pole, and his ax outside the cabin door. (*What great composure! He has lost his respect for Boya by now.*) He removed his sandals, shook off the muddy water, put them on his feet again, and walked into the cabin, which was brightly lit by the candles on the emissary's writing desk.

The woodcutter bowed deeply with one hand cupped in the other before his chest but did not drop to his knees. "Greetings, sir," said he.

Being a minister in the court of Jin, Yu Boya, as a rule, would not deign to glance at a common laborer who was not wearing a robe. Now, he was afraid that to leave his seat and return the greeting would be beneath his dignity as an official, and yet, since he had already invited the man onto the boat, he could not very well drive him out. Left with no alternative, Boya lifted a hand slightly and said, "You, my good man, need not stand on ceremony." He then told his page boy to bring a seat. The page boy put a small stool in a spot usually assigned to lower-ranking people. Disregarding the usual decorum due to a guest, Boya said to the woodcutter, pushing out his lips, "You may sit." By addressing the man simply as "you," he made no secret of his unwillingness to play the good host.

Without any of the usual obligatory words of demurral, the woodcutter sat down in a dignified manner.

Slightly annoyed that the man had sat down without saying any polite words, Boya refrained from asking the man's name, nor did he instruct the servants to serve tea. After sitting silently for quite some time, he spoke up out of curiosity, "So, you are the one who was listening to my music?"

"Yes, sir."

"Let me ask you something. Since you were listening to my playing, you must know something about the history of the zither. Who invented the zither? What good does the zither do?"

Before he had finished with his questions, the head boatman came in to report that, the wind being favorable and the moonlight as bright as day, they were ready to be on their way. But Boya said, "Wait a moment."

The woodcutter said, "I thank you, sir, for being so kind as to ask me a few questions, but if I ramble on too long, I'm afraid I will prevent you from taking advantage of the favorable wind."

Boya said with a smile, "I'm just not sure if you know anything about the zither. If what you say makes sense, I won't mind even losing my official title, let alone being delayed on my journey."

"In that case," said the woodcutter, "I will make bold to speak out of turn. The first zither was made by Fuxi.[3] He saw the essence of the five planets fly through the air and fall on a *wutong* tree.[4] Then a phoenix descended onto the same tree. The phoenix, the king of all birds, eats only bamboo seeds, perches only on *wutong* trees, and drinks only from sweet springs. Knowing that *wutong* provides good timber, Fuxi thought that a musical instrument made of wood containing cosmic essences would produce the most elegant music. And so he ordered that the tree be cut down.

"The thirty-three-foot-tall tree, in harmony with the thirty-three layers of heaven, was cut into three segments, representing heaven, earth, and people respectively.[5] Fuxi tapped the upper segment, but finding the sound too delicate and soft, he put it aside. He then took up the bottom segment, tapped it, and, finding the sound too coarse and thick, put it aside as well. When he tapped the middle segment, he discovered that the sound was neither too delicate and soft nor too coarse and thick. The timber was put into an ever-running stream to soak for seventy-two days, in harmony with the seventy-two divisions of the year.[6] When the time was up, it was taken out of the water, dried in the shade, and, on a chosen auspicious hour of an auspicious day, was made by Liu Ziqi, the master craftsman, into a musical instrument.

"Because it produced the kind of music heard only in the Jasper Pool, it was named the jasper zither.[7] It is three feet six and one-tenth inches long, in harmony with the three hundred and sixty-one degrees of the cosmic circumference; eight inches wide in front, in harmony with the eight solar terms of the year;[8] four inches wide at the back, in harmony with the four seasons; and two inches thick, in harmony with the two elements of heaven and earth. It has a Golden Boy head, a Jade Maiden waist,[9] a fairy's back, a dragon's pond, a phoenix's pool,[10] jade tuning pegs, and gold frets. The frets are twelve in number, in harmony with the twelve months. There is also another fret in the middle, which stands for the leap month. There were originally five strings, which, on a cosmic scale, stood for the five phases of metal, wood, water, fire, and earth, but on the zither itself they also represent the five musical notes.

"During the time of Yao and Shun, the five-string zither was played to accompany the singing of the poem 'The South Wind,' and peace reigned throughout the land.[11] Later, when King Wen of the Zhou dynasty was incarcerated in Youli Prison, he added a string to his zither so as to enhance the dolefulness of the tone and express mourning for his son Boyikao. That added string came to be called King Wen's [lit. trans. of *wen* is "civilian"] string. Thereafter, King Wu of Zhou, while surrounded by singers and dancers between campaigns against King Zhou of the Shang dynasty, added another string to the zither to enhance the forcefulness of the tone. That string came to be called King Wu's [lit. trans. of *wu* is "military"] string. The zither with the original five strings plus the two added strings then became known as the Wen and Wu seven-stringed zither.

"As for the zither: there are six things to be avoided, seven situations in which it should not be played, and eight superior qualities that it alone possesses.

"What are the six things to be avoided? They are severe cold, scorching heat, strong winds, torrential rain, sudden peals of thunder, and heavy snow.

"What are the seven situations in which the zither should not be played? When there is a death, when other musical instruments are being played, when one is busy with miscellaneous things, when one has not washed oneself clean, when one is not properly attired, when no incense is being burned, and when no appreciative listener is present.

"What are its eight superior qualities? Well, in short, they are its delicacy, uniqueness, serenity, elegance, dolefulness, grandeur, sweetness, and lingering vibrations.

"When the zither is played to perfection, a roaring tiger that hears it will quiet down and a screaming monkey that hears it will stop its cries. This is what refined music can do."

Boya was impressed by the man's eloquence but thought he might have been merely reciting what he had learned by rote. But then another thought struck him, "Even if he memorized all this by rote, it's a very creditable effort. Let me test him further."

This time not addressing the man simply as "you" (*Now, watch how Boya gradually changes his tone.*), he asked again, "Since you, my friend, know so much about music, let me ask you another question. Once, when Confucius was playing the zither in a room, Yan Hui entered from outside. Puzzled when he detected a trace of a thought about killing in the rumbling notes, Yan Hui questioned Confucius about it. Confucius replied, 'A moment ago, when I was playing, I saw a cat chasing a rat. I hoped that the cat would get the rat and was afraid that it would miss its prey. And this thought about killing came through in the music.' This shows what a profound master of music the sage's student was. If I play the zither while thinking about something, would you, my friend, be able to guess what it is?"

The woodcutter replied, "I will 'try to surmise what is in another man's thoughts,' as is said in *The Book of Songs*. Please play something, sir, and I will try my best to guess. If I fail to guess right, please do not take offense."

Boya replaced the broken string and thought for a while before playing a few strains, thinking of high mountains. The woodcutter said in praise, "How beautiful! How majestic! You, sir, were thinking of high mountains."

Boya did not reply. After another few moments of concentration, he started playing again, this time thinking of flowing water. The woodcutter again broke into praises. "How beautiful! What a magnificent torrent! You, sir, were thinking of flowing water."

Astounded that the man had guessed right both times, Boya pushed the zither aside, stood up, and exchanged formal greetings as a host with his guest, Ziqi the woodcutter. (*According to* The Atlas, *there is a Boya Terrace in Haiyan County, Jiaxing Prefecture, Zhejiang. To one side of the terrace is the Listening to Zither Bridge. This could very well be the place where Zhong Ziqi listened to Boya play the zither. Generally speaking, stories are not accurate records of facts. Neither is this one. It proposes only to make the point that an appreciative friend is hard to come by.*)

"How discourteous of me!" Boya exclaimed over and over again. "Buried in the rock is a piece of fine jade. If people are judged only by their appearance, wouldn't many talents of the land go unrecognized? What, may I ask, is your honorable name?"

The woodcutter raised himself slightly from his seat and replied, "My surname is Zhong, my given name Hui, and my humble courtesy name Ziqi."

With hands respectfully folded before his chest, Boya said, "Please accept my greetings, Mr. Zhong Ziqi."

"May I ask your name, sir?" said Ziqi in his turn. "And where do you serve, sir?"

"My humble name is Yu Rui. I serve as an official in the court of the state of Jin. I am here in this country as an emissary."

"So, you are none other than His Honor Yu Boya himself."

Boya moved Ziqi to a seat reserved for a guest of honor, and he himself sat as the host at the head of the table. He then bade the page boy serve tea and, after tea, some wine.

"I may be a poor host, but let's have a chat over a cup of wine."

"What an honor for me," said Ziqi.

The page boy took away the zither, and the two men sat down for wine. Boya asked again, "Judging from your accent, I believe Mr. Zhong is a native of Chu, but where is your honorable residence?"

"Not far from here, in the Ma'an Mountains, there's a place called Village of Worthy Men. That's where my humble home is."

Boya nodded. "Truly a village where worthy men gather," he commented. "What is your occupation?"

"Nothing more than cutting firewood for a living."

Boya said with a smile, "Well, Ziqi my friend, this humble official shouldn't be speaking out of turn either, but with your ability, why not seek fame and glory and find a position in a royal court and a place in the annals of history? My humble opinion is that you should not waste your talents among woods and rivers in the company of woodcutters and herdsmen and end up rotting with the grass and the trees."

"To be honest," said Ziqi, "I have my aged parents to take care of, and I have no siblings to help me do it. So I will continue to cut firewood for a living until my parents live out the rest of their days. I cannot bring myself to exchange even one day of taking care of my parents with the highest official title in the land."

"Such great filial piety is quite exceptional," said Boya.

They drank a while longer, toasting each other by turns.

Ziqi never lost his composure, not when he was being insulted earlier, nor when he was treated with much respect (*Well-made comment.*), which gained him even more respect and affection from Boya.

"May I ask your age?" said Boya.

"I have frittered away twenty-seven years."

"This humble official is older by ten years. If Ziqi is not disdainful, I would like us to pledge brotherhood, to do justice to our appreciation of each other and our friendship." (*Who else would be willing to do this?*)

"You are quite mistaken, sir. You are a famous official in your country, whereas I, Zhong Hui, am but a lowly woodcutter in a poor village. How would I dare aspire to claim connections with you and make demands on your kind attention?"

"I may have acquaintances all over the land, but how many among them understand my heart? In my busy, mundane life as an official, I consider it my greatest fortune to get to know such a worthy man as you. If you think I judge people by wealth and status, you are not doing me justice!" Thereupon he bade the page boy build up the flame in the incense burner, light some joss sticks of superior quality, and, in that very cabin, the two men performed the eight-bow ritual of pledged brotherhood, Boya as the older brother and Ziqi the younger. They pledged to address each other henceforth as brothers and never to betray each other in life or in death.

The ceremony over, more wine was heated and served. Ziqi insisted that Boya take the seat of honor, a courtesy Boya did not decline. Cups and chopsticks changed places, and Ziqi left the guest's seat. Addressing each other as brothers, they went on talking. (*From discourtesy to suspicion, to trust, to affection, and eventually to inseparable devotion, the friendship of the ancients is truly unmatchable.*) Indeed,

> You never tire of a guest who shares your mind,
> Nor of one with an appreciative ear.

In the course of their animated conversation, the moon paled, the stars dimmed, and the first faint glow of dawn lit the eastern sky. All the boatmen rose, readied the ropes and the sails, and prepared to set sail. Ziqi stood up to bid Boya farewell.

Offering a cup of wine to Ziqi, Boya held the latter's hand and said with a sigh, "My good brother, I met you too late in my life, and now we have to part in such haste!"

When Ziqi heard this, tears fell from his eyes into the cup in spite of himself. He finished the wine in one gulp, filled another cup with wine, and offered it to Boya in return. Neither of them could bear the thought of parting.

"I'm not ready to part with you yet, my brother," said Boya. "I would like to invite you to leave with me and then stay with me for a few days. Would that be agreeable to you?"

"It's not that I don't want to go, my brother," said Ziqi, "but I have my parents to look after. [As Confucius says,] 'While your parents are alive, do not travel far.'"[12]

"But you can go home, tell them about it, and come to visit me in Jinyang.[13] By telling them about it, you will be 'making your whereabouts known to them.'"[14]

"I don't want to promise lightly because I do not want to go back on my words later. If I give you my promise, I will certainly fulfill it. (*Words of* [illegible].) Should my parents not approve my request, I would only be giving you false hopes while you wait for me thousands of li away, and I would be committing an even greater wrong."

"What a true gentleman my good brother is! All right, then, I'll come to see you next year."

"When will you be arriving next year, my good brother?" asked Ziqi. "Tell me, so that I know when to wait for you."

Counting on his fingers, Boya said, "Yesterday was the Mid-autumn Festival. With daybreak, it's now the sixteenth day of the eighth month. My good brother, I will be coming to visit you on the fifteenth or sixteenth day of the second month of next autumn. If I fail to arrive by the twenty-first day of that month or by the last month of autumn, I'll be breaking my promise, and I'll be no gentleman." He then turned to his page boy and said, "Tell the scribe to write down in the engagement book my good brother Zhong's address and the date of my visit next year."

Ziqi said, "In that case, I will stand by the river to wait for you on the fifteenth and sixteenth days of the second month of next autumn. I will do so without fail. Now, it's already light. I should be going."

"Not so fast, my good brother," said Boya.

He bade the page boy bring over two ingots of gold, and without wrapping them, he held them in his hands and said, "My good brother, this is a small gift from me, to be used toward supporting your parents. Please don't think that this is inadequate for a scholar's parents." Ziqi did not think it appropriate to decline the offer, so he accepted the gift.

After another bow of farewell, he left the cabin with tears in his eyes. He picked up his carrying pole, put his cape and hat in the load, attached the ax to his waistband, walked up the gangplank, holding onto the handrail, and went ashore. Boya saw him off at the bow of the boat, and they bade each other a tearful farewell.

We shall say no more of Ziqi's return home for the moment but will continue our story with Boya, who sounded the drum for the boats to set sail. However beautiful the scenery along the river, Boya had lost all interest in sightseeing. All his thoughts were with the one who understood his music. Several days later, he left the boat and continued the rest of the journey on land. Wherever he stopped, he was provided with horse carriages for transportation, for local officials knew him to be a senior grand master in the state of Jin, not someone to be slighted. So he traveled in this manner all the way back to Jinyang, where he reported to the king about the mission, but of this, no more.

Time flew. Quite unnoticeably, autumn, winter, and spring went by, and summer rolled around. Ziqi was never absent from Boya's thoughts, even for one day. With the Mid-autumn Festival drawing near, he asked the king of Jin for leave to return to his hometown, and the king approved the request. Boya gathered his things together and went, as before, by river in a big detour. Once on board, he told the boatmen to tell him the name of every place where the boat was to moor. As coincidence would have it, exactly on the fifteenth night of the eighth month, the boatmen came to report, "We are near the Ma'an Mountains."

Vaguely recalling the place where the boat had moored last year when he met Ziqi, Boya told the boatmen to stop there, cast the anchor to the bottom of the river and drive in a wooden stake next to the shore so they could tie the boat to it. It was a clear night, and a moonbeam shone through the portiere of the cabin door. Boya had a page boy roll up the portiere and walked out to stand at the bow, where he gazed up at the handle of the Big Dipper. The vast expanse of the water, lit as bright as day, joined the sky at the horizon. His thoughts went back to this time last year when, with the rain just over and the moon shining brightly, he had met his true friend, and this happened to be a glorious night as well. His friend had promised to wait for him at the riverside, but why was there no trace of him? Could he have broken his promise?

After waiting for a while longer, he thought, "Ah, I know. There are so many boats coming and going, and I'm not in the one I had last year. How can I expect my brother to see me right away? Last year, my zither playing caught his attention. Tonight, let me play my zither again. When my brother hears it, he'll surely come to greet me." So thinking, he bade the page boy bring a table to the bow of the boat and put the zither on the table.

With incense burning and his seat in place, Boya opened the zither case, tuned the strings, and started playing, but the notes sounded mournful. He stopped. "Ah," he said to himself, "the notes are so mournful. This must mean that one of my brother's parents has passed away. Last year, he did say that his parents were quite advanced in years. Either his father or his mother must have died. Being the filial son that he is, he has his priorities and would rather break a promise to me than be remiss in his duties toward his parents. That's why he chose not to come. After daybreak tomorrow, I'll go up on the rocky shore and visit him at home."

He had the page boy take away the zither table and retired to his cabin for the night. But he was awake the whole night through, waiting for a daybreak that just would not come. As soon as the moon's shadow on the portiere vanished and the sun appeared at the top of the hills, Boya rose, straightened his clothes, told his page boy to follow him, and took out two hundred taels of gold. "My brother will need this for the funeral if he's in mourning," he said to himself.

In one jump, he landed on the rocks and began walking along a woodcutters' path, which took him to the mouth of a valley more than ten li away. He stopped and stood still.

"Why have you stopped, Master?" asked the page boy.

"There is one mountain to the south and another one to the north, and there is one road leading to the east and another one leading to the west. From the mouth of the valley, I can take either of these two thoroughfares, but I wonder which one leads to the Village of Worthy Men. Let's wait for someone who knows the area well and ask him for directions before continuing on our way."

Boya sat down on a rock to rest a little, and the page boy stood behind him. Soon, an old man came into view, walking slowly down the road on Boya's left-hand side. His beard flowing like threads of jade, his silvery hair tied up in a knot, he wore a bamboo hat and farmers' clothes. In his left hand he carried a rattan walking stick, and in his right hand, a bamboo basket. The old man advanced slowly in Boya's direction. Boya rose, adjusted his clothes, and stepped forward with a bow.

Unhurriedly, the old man put down the basket and returned the greeting. He raised his walking stick with both hands, saying, "What can I do for you, sir?"

"Could you tell me which of these two roads leads to the Village of Worthy Men?"

"Well, the two roads lead to two different villages, both called Village of Worthy Men. The one to the left is the Upper Village of Worthy Men, and the one to the right is the Lower Village of Worthy Men. They are separated by a thirty-li thoroughfare. You, sir, having just come out of the mouth of the valley, are at the very midpoint of the road, which stretches fifteen li to the east and fifteen li to the west. Now, which village do you have in mind?"

Boya was at a loss for words. He thought to himself, "My brother is an intelligent man, but how could he have been so careless? That night when we met, he should have told me clearly that there are two Villages of Worthy Men, one upper and one lower."

While Boya was in the midst of these reflections, the old man said, "You look thoughtful, sir. Whoever gave you directions must have spoken only about the Village of Worthy Men, without specifying whether it's the upper one or the lower one. That's why you, sir, are at a loss."

"Exactly," said Boya.

"There are about ten to twenty families in these two villages. They are mostly people who chose to live here in seclusion. I have been living in these mountains longer than others. As the saying goes, 'After thirty years of life in the same neighborhood, you form ties everywhere.' My neighbors are either my relatives or my friends. You, sir, must be visiting a friend. If you could tell me your friend's name, I'll tell you where he lives."

"I'm looking for the Zhong family."

At the mention of the Zhong family, tears fell from the old man's age-dimmed eyes. "Please visit any other household but the Zhongs."

"Why?" asked Boya, startled.

"Which member of the Zhong family do you want to see, sir?"

"Ziqi."

The old man burst into loud sobs. "Ziqi, Zhong Hui, was my son. On his way home, late on the fifteenth night of the eighth month last year, he met Mr. Yu Boya, senior grand master of the state of Jin. They chatted and found that they had much in common. Before he left, he was given two ingots of gold as a gift. My son then bought books and applied himself to his studies. I am such an old and stupid man that I did not stop him. By day, he chopped firewood and carried heavy loads; by night, he labored at his studies, exhausting himself both mentally and physically until he contracted consumption and died after a few months."

At these words, Boya felt as if his insides had split open. His tears flowing like a gushing spring, he let out a loud cry, fell to the ground by the cliff, and fainted.

Mr. Zhong Senior put his hands around Boya and, turning to the page boy, asked, "Who might this gentleman be?"

The page boy whispered into the old man's ear, "He is none other than Master Yu Boya."

"So, he is my son's good friend." So saying, Mr. Zhong Senior raised Boya up. Upon coming to, Boya sat on the ground, foaming at the mouth, beating his chest with both hands, and crying bitterly. "My good brother," he wailed, "last night when my boat cast anchor, I blamed you for having broken your promise. Little did I know that you had already become a ghost in the Nine Springs.[15] What a short life for a man of such talent!"

Mr. Zhong Senior wiped away his tears and said some comforting words.

When he finished weeping, Boya rose and saluted Mr. Zhong Senior anew, not as just any elderly man, but as an uncle, as if the two clans had been friends for generations.

"Uncle," said Boya, "is your son's coffin still at home or is it already buried in an open space?"

"It's a long story. My wife and I sat by his bedside before he died, and these were his last words: 'How long one gets to live is a matter dictated by divine will. While living, your son has failed to provide good support for you. After I die, please bury me by the river at the foot of the Ma'an Mountains because I wish to keep the promise I made to Yu Boya, grand master of Jin.' I have fulfilled my son's last wish. To the right of the path that you, sir, just traveled along is a mound of newly dug earth, and that is my son Zhong Hui's grave. Today being the one hundredth day after his death, here I am, carrying a string of paper coins to be burned at his grave. I certainly did not expect to run into you here, sir!"

"In that case," said Boya, "I'll go with you, Uncle, so that I can bow to the grave." So saying, he instructed the page boy: "Carry the bamboo basket for Grandpa."

Supporting himself on his walking stick, Mr. Zhong Senior led the way, followed by Boya, with the page boy bringing up the rear. Upon reentering the mouth of the valley, Boya saw that there was indeed a mound of newly dug earth to the left of the path.

Boya adjusted his clothes and bowed deeply. "My good brother," said he, "in life you were an intelligent man. After death, you will be a deity responsive to prayers. Accept this bow from me, your unworthy brother, as my final farewell!" After bowing, he burst into loud wails again, wails that caught the attention of people all around this hilly region. Passersby as well as local residents, hearing that a court minister was here to mourn Zhong Ziqi, flocked to the grave and vied with one another for a better view. (*How vulgar, these rubberneckers!*)

Since he had not brought any sacrificial items, Boya found that he lacked the means to express his condolences. He told the page boy to take the zither from its case and put it on the stone altar. He then sat cross-legged in front of the grave and tearfully began to play. Hearing the clear, ringing notes of the zither, the onlookers clapped their hands and, laughing, went their separate ways.

"Uncle," said Boya, "I am overcome by grief when I play the zither to mourn my brother, your son. Why did these people laugh?"

Mr. Zhong Senior replied, "These are rustic people with no understanding of music. They laughed because they thought music is for entertainment."

"I see. Do you, Uncle, know what I've been playing?"

"I was quite studious when I was young, but now that I'm old and all my five senses are working only half as well as they used to, I have long since lost my ability to appreciate music."

"In that case, let me recite to you the short lyrics that I improvised to express my condolences for your son."

"I would be pleased to hear them," said the old man.

So Boya began to recite:

"I met you last spring at the riverside; [16]
I am here again, but where might my true friend be?
The sight of your grave gives me pangs of grief,
Pangs of grief that bring tears to my eyes.
Happily I came, sadly I go;
Gloomy clouds gather on the riverbanks.

"Ziqi! Ziqi! My good brother!
Our bond was worth a thousand pieces of gold;
We had more to talk about than the world could hold.
After this song of mine comes to an end,
I shall never play the zither again;
For you dies this three-foot jasper zither!"

Boya drew a small knife from inside his robe, cut the strings of the zither, raised it with both hands, and smashed it with all his might against the stone altar. The zither broke into pieces, and the jade tuning pegs and gold frets scattered everywhere.

Aghast, Mr. Zhong Senior asked, "Why did you smash your zither?"

And this was Boya's reply:

"The zither smashed, the phoenix's tail grew cold. [17]
Now that Ziqi's gone, for whom can I play?
All call themselves friends and give you a smile,
But to find a true friend is all too hard."

Mr. Zhong Senior said, "I see. How sad! How sad!"

"Do you, Uncle, live in the Upper Village or the Lower Village?"

"My humble home is the eighth house down the road in the Upper Village. Why do you still want to know?"

"I am too grief-stricken to follow you home, Uncle, but I have here forty [sic] taels of gold, half of which I wish to give to you on behalf of your son, for your daily subsistence. The other half is for you to buy a few *mu* of land with which to earn enough income to pay for the annual sacrificial rites at your son's grave. After I return to my court, I will submit a memorial to ask for retirement. After I retire, I will come to the Upper Village of Worthy Men to escort you and my aunt to my humble home, where you will live for the rest of your lives. I am Ziqi, and Ziqi is me. (*Such is the friendship between the ancients. The rich, frivolous men of today should be ashamed to death.*) Uncle, please don't reject me as an outsider." So saying, he had his page boy bring out the gold, and he himself handed it to Mr. Zhong Senior. Weeping bitterly, he prostrated himself on the ground. Mr. Zhong Senior returned the courtesy with a salute. Boya lingered for a while longer before they bade farewell to each other.

This story is titled "Yu Boya Smashes His Zither in Gratitude to an Appreciative Friend." A poet of later times had this to say in praise:

Snobs mingle with snobs,
Nor do scholars value true friends.
Boya's loyalty after Ziqi's death
Lives on in the story of the smashed zither.

Judge Bao Solves a Case through a Ghost That Appeared Thrice

Gan Luo achieved fame young, and Ziya late; [1]
Peng Zu lived long, and Yan Hui died early; [2]
Fan Dan was penniless, and Shi Chong rich; [3]
It is all a matter of time and fate.

The story goes that during the reign period of Yuanyou [1086–93] in the Song dynasty, there was, in the imperial court, a chamberlain for ceremonies by the name of Chen Ya. After a failed attempt to impeach Zhang Zihou,[4] Chen Ya was demoted to pacification commissioner of the Jiangdong Circuit and concurrently magistrate of Jiankang [present-day Nanjing].

One day, he was feasting with his assembly of officials in the Riverside Pavilion when he heard someone cry outside, "I can tell your fortune even without knowing the five phases and the eight characters in your horoscope!"[5]

"Who has the temerity to make such a claim?" said the magistrate.

Those officials who had seen the man before replied, "This is Bian'gu, fortune-teller from Jinling."

"Bring him over to me."

And so the man was brought to the pavilion. There, for all to see, was

A man in rags with a brimless and tattered hat,
A frosty beard, sightless eyes, and stooping shoulders.

Carrying his walking cane, Bian'gu entered the pavilion and, with a deep bow, groped for a place to sit before he sank down on a step. The magistrate said in anger, "Being a blind man unable to read the classics, how can you think so highly of yourself that you speak so lightly of the five phases?"

Bian'gu replied, "I can foresee changes by listening to the clicking of bamboo tablets and predict life or death by listening to the sound of footsteps."

"How accurate are you?" Even as the magistrate spoke, a painted boat was seen coming downstream, its oars creaking. The magistrate asked Bian'gu what he could make of it. Bian'gu rejoined, "The creaking of the oars sounds sad. That boat must be carrying some high official's coffin."

The magistrate sent someone to make an inquiry. Sure enough, the boat was carrying a coffin in which lay the body of Director Li of Linjiang District [in present-day Jiangxi Province], who had died at his post, on its way to Director Li's hometown. Agape with astonishment, the magistrate exclaimed, "Even if Dongfang Shuo[6] were reborn, he couldn't be as good as you are." He gave the fortune-teller ten jars of wine and ten taels of silver before sending him away.

This is a man able to tell things by the sound of oars. Now, let me tell of another fortune-teller, Li Jie by name, who was a native of Kaifeng, the Eastern Capital. He traveled to Fengfu County, Yanzhou Prefecture, and opened a fortune-telling shop in front of the county yamen. Under a Tai'e sword[7] covered with gilded paper, he hung up a sign that said "Death to all those with little learning but too much readiness to echo the views of others." And he was indeed most accurate in his applications of the yin and yang theories in his divinations.

> *Well-versed in the* Book of Changes *of Zhou,*
> *Knowing all methods of divinations,*
> *He read signs in all patterns in heaven,*
> *And was a master of feng shui on earth.*
> *Knowing all there was to know about the stars,*
> *He told fortunes with divine accuracy.*
> *Conversant with every law of destiny,*
> *He never missed the mark in his prophecies.*

He had just hung up the signboard when a man walked into the shop. How did he look? He had

> *A bag on his back, a cap on his head,*
> *A black double-collar shirt with a silk waistband,*
> *A clean pair of shoes and socks on his feet,*
> *And a scroll of writings in his sleeve.*

After exchanging a greeting with the fortune-teller, the man gave the date and the hour of his birth, and the astrological chart was drawn. But, quickly, the fortune-teller announced, "No, I can't do this for you."

The man, Sun Wen by name, was chief clerk at the Fengfu County yamen. He asked, "Why won't you tell my fortune?"

"Your Honor, this is too difficult a job for me."

"What do you mean?"

"Stay away from wine, and stop covering up for anyone."

"I haven't been drinking, nor am I covering up for anyone."

"Give me the date and the hour of your birth again, in case there was a mistake."

The chief clerk repeated the information. The fortune-teller set to work again and then said, "Sir, you'd better give up."

"I don't mind hearing whatever you've come up with."

"It doesn't look good." So saying, the fortune-teller wrote a quatrain that said,

> This is the day the white tiger arrives,[8]
> Bringing with it sorrow and misery.
> At midnight, before dawn,
> All your kith and kin will be in mourning.

The chief clerk read it and asked, "What does all this mean?"

"I won't keep anything from you, sir, but you are going to die."

"In what year am I going to die?"

"This very year."

"Which month?"

"This very month."

"On which day?"

"This very day."

"At what hour?"

"Around midnight tonight, at the third quarter of the third watch."

"If I do indeed die tonight, you'll be off the hook, but if I don't, I'll settle the score with you tomorrow at the county court."

"If you don't die tonight, sir, come again tomorrow and cut off my head with this sword, which is meant for all those who have little learning but are much too ready to echo others' views."

At these words, the chief clerk fumed with rage. With one swipe, he grabbed the fortune-teller and threw him out of the shop. How did this end for the fortune-teller?

> For all his knowledge of human affairs,
> He brought upon himself sorrows galore.

From the county yamen emerged several officers, who blocked Chief Clerk Sun's way and asked what the commotion was all about. Sun complained, "What an unreasonable man! I asked him to tell my fortune. I did this just for fun, but he said that I was going to die at the third quarter of the third watch tonight. I am a perfectly healthy man. How am I going to drop dead this very night just like that? I'm taking him to the county yamen to have the court settle the matter."

Someone in the crowd said, "If you believe in fortune-telling, you'll end up selling your house. If you make a living telling fortunes, you do nothing but make up stories." The crowd pacified Sun and sent him on his way.

Turning back, they scolded the fortune-teller, saying, "Mr. Li, now that you've offended this well-known chief clerk, you won't be able to keep your business here. It's always easier to tell if someone is going to be poor and lowly than to say how long someone is going to live. You are not King Yama's father or a brother of the Judge of the Dead. How can you be so sure about the exact hour of someone's death? You'd better use some ambiguous words."

"If I say only things that please people, I'll be sacrificing accuracy. And yet, when I speak the truth, I give offense. Oh well, as the saying goes, 'If this place doesn't tolerate me, there will be places that do!'" (*Cynical words.*) With a sigh, he picked up his things and moved his business elsewhere.

Now, even though Sun had been calmed by the crowd, he still felt uneasy. After disposing of his official business for the day, he returned home in dejection. Noticing his knitted brows and worried look, his wife asked, "Is there anything troubling you? Is some work at the yamen baffling you?"

"No. Don't ask."

"Were you punished in any way by the magistrate today?" she pressed.

"No."

"Did you fight with someone then?"

"No. It's just that I went to a fortune-teller in front of the county yamen, and he said that I would die around midnight tonight at the third quarter of the third watch."

His wife bristled at these words. Her willow-leaf-shaped eyebrows raised high, her starry eyes opened wide, she said, "For a perfectly healthy man to die this very night! How preposterous! Why didn't you take him to the county court?"

"I did try, but the onlookers stopped me."

"Husband, you just stay at home. Am I not usually the one who goes forward and pleads to the magistrate on your behalf when the need arises? (*Women who seek publicity are to be feared.*) Now this time, let me go find that fortune-teller and say to him, 'My husband doesn't owe the government or anyone any money, nor is he driven to desperation by some lawsuit. How can you say he's going to drop dead tonight?'"

"Don't go. After I live through tonight, I'll deal with him tomorrow myself. That'll be better than having a woman take care of this."

Evening fell. The chief clerk said, "Give me a few cups of wine. I want to stay awake the whole night through." Several cups later, he got quite drunk before he knew it, and, his eyes glazed with wine, he dozed off on his folding chair.

His wife said, "Husband, how can you go to sleep?" She called out for Ying'er the maid. "Come here," said she, "and shake Father to wake him up."

Ying'er came over, shook him, and called his name but to no avail. "Ying'er," said the wife, "let's carry him to the bedroom." If this storyteller had been born in the same year as the chief clerk and grown up with him shoulder to shoulder, I would have put my arms around his waist and dragged him back to where he had been. He should have stayed awake throughout the night, sipping his wine. The last thing he should have done was go to bed to sleep. But as it was, he died that very night, a death more tragic than that of Li Cunxiao [d. 894], as described in *The History of the Five Dynasties,* and of Peng Yue [d. 196], as described in *The History of the Han.* Indeed,

> *The cicada feels first the autumn winds,*
> *And he had a foreboding of his death.*

With the husband already in bed, the wife told Ying'er to put out the kitchen fire, adding, "Did you hear Father say that a fortune-teller told him today that he was going to die at midnight tonight?"

"Yes, Mother, I did indeed. What nonsense!"

"Ying'er, let's do some sewing and stay awake tonight to see if that's really going to happen. If not, we'll deal with that fortune-teller tomorrow. Don't go to sleep!"

"I wouldn't dare!" said Ying'er. But before the words were quite out of her mouth, she started drifting off to sleep.

"Ying'er! I told you not to sleep, but you are already dozing off!"

"I am not!" But even as she spoke, she fell asleep again.

Her mistress woke her up and asked, "What time is it now?"

At this moment, Ying'er heard the county yamen's night-watch drum striking the third quarter of the third watch.

"Ying'er!" exclaimed Mrs. Sun. "Don't sleep! This is the moment!"

But Ying'er fell asleep again, this time giving no response. All of a sudden, Mrs. Sun heard her husband jump out of bed, and then, the middle door of the house made a noise. Hurriedly, she woke up Ying'er, and by the time a lamp had been lit, they heard the outer gate opening. Carrying the lamp, the two gave chase, and what did they see but a man in white walking out with a hand over his face and throwing himself with a splash into the Fengfu County river. Indeed,

> *When life comes to be filled with pain,*
> *To the east wind one gives oneself away.*

The river was a tributary of the Yellow River, and it was quite impossible to retrieve the body in the rapid currents. Mrs. Sun and the maid stood by the river and burst out crying, "Chief Clerk! Why did you have to throw yourself into the river? Who is going to support the two of us now?"

They started shouting for the neighbors to come out. Mrs. Diao from up the street, Mrs. Mao from down the street, Mrs. Gao and Bao from across the street, all rushed over.

After hearing Mrs. Sun's story of what had happened, Mrs. Diao said, "How very strange!"

Mrs. Mao said, "I saw him return home in his black shirt, carrying documents. I even exchanged greetings with him." Mrs. Gao said, "That's right, so did I!" Mrs. Bao had this to say, "My husband went to the county yamen on some business in the morning and saw the chief clerk grabbing the fortune-teller. He told me about it when he came home. Who would have thought that he would really die!"

And then Mrs. Diao put in, "Oh, Mr. Sun, how could you have died without even a word to us neighbors!" With these words, tears dropped from her eyes. Mrs. Mao commented again, "How sad! Especially when you think of all the kindnesses he did!" She also burst into tears. (*Nice description of a bunch of garrulous old women.*) Mrs. Bao wailed, "Mr. Sun, when shall we ever get to see you again?"

Losing no time, the local headman reported the matter to the authorities, and, as would be expected in such a case, Mrs. Sun had some sutras chanted in memory of the deceased.

With the snap of a finger, three months sped by. One day, Mrs. Sun and Ying'er were sitting at home when two women, flushed red with wine, came in the door, one carrying a bottle of wine and the other holding two rice-plant blossoms. Raising the cotton portiere, they stepped in, saying, "Yes, this is the place."

Mrs. Sun looked up and saw that they were matchmakers with surnames that could not have been any other than the common Zhang and Li. Mrs. Sun said, "Long time no see, grannies!"

The matchmakers said, "Sorry to disturb you, ma'am! We didn't hear about it earlier, so please forgive us for not sending any incense or paper money. How long has it been since your husband died?"

"I just observed the hundredth day of his death the day before yesterday."

"How time flies! So it's been more than one hundred days. What a nice man he was. Whenever I greeted him, he always greeted me back. Since he's been gone for so long, you must be very lonely. Why don't we make a match for you?"

The widow rejoined, "Where can I ever find a man as good as he was?" (*Good men often don't know what happens right under their noses, and the chief clerk was one of them.*)

The matchmakers said, "But that's not all that difficult! We do have a good candidate for you."

"Stop it! How can there possibly be anyone like my deceased husband?"

The two matchmakers had some tea and left, but a few days later, they came back for a second attempt. The widow said, "Don't come again with any of your marriage proposals unless you can meet all three of my conditions. Otherwise, don't bring up this subject ever again. I'd rather live out my days as a widow." So she listed her three conditions, and as a consequence, the two lovers, whose love bond dated back five hundred years, came to be punished according to the law of the land. Truly,

> *The case of the deer baffled the Qin prime minister;* [9]
> *The dream about butterflies confused Zhuangzi.* [10]

"What three conditions?"

"First, my deceased husband's surname was Sun, and Sun must also be the surname of whomever you propose. Second, my deceased husband was the number one chief clerk in Fengfu County. Your man must have the same post. Third, I'm not leaving this house. He has to move in." (*Clever words.*)

At these demands, the two matchmakers said, "Hooray! So you want to marry a man with the surname of Sun, with the same job as your deceased husband, and who will move into your house. Well, other conditions might be harder to meet, but these three things are no problem! Let me tell you, ma'am, your deceased husband, being the number one chief clerk of Fengfu County, was called Big Chief Clerk Sun. The man we have in mind for you used to be the number two chief clerk of the county. Now that Big Sun is dead, number two has become number one. He is known as Young Chief Clerk Sun. And he's willing to move in. Now what do you say?"

"This is too much of a coincidence to be true!" exclaimed the woman. (*Clever words!*)

Matchmaker Zhang said, "I am seventy-two years old. If I fabricated anything, may I change into seventy-two dogs to eat shit at your house!"

"If it's indeed as you say," said the woman, "please go ahead and make the proposal to him. I wonder if there's a predestined marriage bond between him and me."

"Today being an auspicious day," said Matchmaker Zhang, "write us a note on some lucky red paper."

"I don't have such stationery at home," said the widow.

"I've got some with me," said Matchmaker Li. So saying, she produced from her apron a sheet of floral-patterned paper. Truly,

> *Egrets are not seen till the snow melts away;*
> *Parrots in willows are not noticed till they talk.*

Then and there, the widow had Ying'er bring over a brush-pen and an ink slab. The note thus drawn up was taken away by the matchmakers. As was expected, betrothal gifts were offered, and messages traveled back and forth. Before two months were out, Young Chief Clerk Sun had moved in, and a nice, loving couple the two turned out to be.

The days went by. One evening, the couple, in an inebriated state, told Ying'er to make some soup to sober them up. While she was trying to make the kitchen fire, Ying'er said aloud resentfully, "If the old chief clerk were alive, I'd have gone to bed by now. But these two make me work!" Noticing that one end of the fire tube was blocked and would not burn, she bent down to knock it against the foot of the stove. She had knocked just a few times when the stove gradually rose until it was more than a foot up in the air. A man appeared, pushing up the stove with his head, his neck framed by the railings of a well, his long hair coming loose, his tongue hanging low, his eyes dripping blood. (*First apparition.*) He cried, "Ying'er! Help your father!'

Ying'er was so frightened that with a loud scream, she collapsed on the ground, her face sallow, her eyes glazed over, her lips purple, her fingernails turning blue. We do not know what was happening to her internal organs, but her limbs had all gone limp. Truly,

> *Weak as the waning moon at the fifth watch,*
> *Feeble as the spent oil lamp before dawn.*

The couple rushed over to bring Ying'er back to consciousness. After feeding her with some "soul-pacifying" liquid, they asked, "What did you see that made you faint?"

Ying'er said to the woman, "I was making a fire when the stove gradually went up in air, and I saw the deceased chief clerk, his neck framed by the railings of a well, his eyes dripping blood, his hair hanging loose. He called my name, and I was so scared I fell to the ground."

At this account, the woman slapped Ying'er on the face and said, "A fine maid you are! You could have just said that you're too lazy to make the soup. You didn't have to come up with such tricks, faking death and all! Well, no more work for you now. Put out the fire and go to sleep." And Ying'er did as she was told.

Back in their own room, the woman whispered to her husband, "Second Brother, that girl saw something. We can't keep her any longer. Let's send her away."

"But where?"

"I have an idea."

After breakfast the next morning, Young Sun went off to the yamen for work. The woman called Ying'er over and said to her, "Ying'er, you've been with me for seven or eight years now, and I like you a lot. But you're not working as hard as when the other chief clerk was alive. Is it because you are thinking of marriage? If so, let me make a match for you."

"How could I dream of marrying? But who are you marrying me off to?"

The man Mrs. Sun had in mind was to be the cause of vindication for the deceased Big Sun. Truly,

> *Cicadas in the trees aren't heard till the wind dies;*
> *The moon outside isn't seen till the lamp goes out.*

To pick up our story, Ying'er was married off, without having any say in the matter, to a fellow called Wang Xing, nicknamed Wang the Wino, a drinker and a gambler. Less than three months into the marriage, he had used up all of Ying'er's dowry.

One day, in a drunken state, the man came home and yelled at Ying'er, "You cheap slut! How can you watch me live in such misery without going to your master and mistress to borrow a few hundred in cash?"

Unable to bear such abuse, Ying'er put on a skirt, tied it up around her waist, and walked all the way to Young Sun's house. At the sight of Ying'er, the woman said, "Ying'er, you are a married woman now. What could you have to say to me?"

"To be honest with you, this is a bad marriage for me. My husband drinks and gambles, and in less than three months, he has spent all my dowry. There's nothing for it now but to ask you for a loan of a few hundred cash to tide us over."

"Ying'er," said the woman, "being married to the wrong man is your problem. Now, here's one tael of silver for you, but don't come here again." Ying'er accepted the silver and thankfully took her leave.

But the money was gone in a matter of four or five days.

One evening, an inebriated Wang Xing walked up to Ying'er and said, "You worthless slut! Why don't you go again and get something from your mistress when you see me in such misery?"

"The last time I went, I was given a good talking-to for that one tael of silver. How can you tell me to go again?"

"You cheap slut! If you don't go, I'll break your leg!"

Unable to fend off the stream of curses, Ying'er could not do otherwise than go to Sun's house before the night was out, but upon reaching the house, she found the gate closed. She thought of knocking but checked herself for fear of being scolded. In a quandary, she saw nothing for it but to turn back. After passing two or three houses, she heard a man say, "Ying'er, I have something for you." Now, this man makes me fear for Mrs. Sun and Young Sun! Truly,

> *A turtle in water—black amid blue;*
> *A crane on a pine branch—white amid green.*[11]

Ying'er turned around to look at the man, and there he stood, under the eaves of a house, wearing a cap, a red robe, and a waistband with a horn clasp and carrying a scroll of documents in his arms. In a subdued voice, he continued, "Ying'er, I'm the dead chief clerk. I can't tell you where I live now, but hold out your hand, I've got something for you."

Ying'er held out her hand. The moment something was placed in it, the man disappeared. Ying'er saw that in her hand was a package of loose silver. She returned home, and at her knock, Wang Xing said from within, "Sister, what took you so long at your mistress's house?"

"Let me tell you what happened. I went there to borrow some rice, but their gate was closed. I didn't dare to knock for fear that she might get angry. When I turned back, I saw the deceased chief clerk standing under the eaves of a house, wearing a cap, a red robe, and a horn waistband, and he gave me a package of silver. Here it is."

"You slut! What nonsense is this! You have some more explaining to do about that package of silver, but get inside first."

Ying'er went in. "Sister," said Wang Xing, "I remember what you said before about seeing the dead man by the stove. There must be something fishy about all this. I said those things a moment ago because I was afraid that the neighbors might hear you. Put the silver away for now. Let's wait until tomorrow morning to go to the county yamen to press charges against them." Truly,

> Flowers wither when given too much care;
> Willows flourish when left unattended.

The next morning, Wang Xing thought to himself, "Hold it! I can't press charges for two reasons. First, he is the number one chief clerk in the county. How could I ever dare make an enemy of him? Second, there's no hard evidence. Even these loose pieces of silver would be confiscated, and it would be a lawsuit without a suspect. I'd better redeem a few pieces of clothing from the pawnshop, buy a couple of boxes of sweets for Mr. Sun with the money, and pay him a visit." His mind thus made up, he went out and bought two boxes of sweets.

After dressing up neatly, the couple went to Sun's house. At the sight of the neatly dressed couple bearing boxes of gifts, Mrs. Sun asked, "Where did you get the money?"

Wang Xing replied, "I earned two taels of silver drawing up a paper for the chief clerk. So I'm bringing some gifts for you. I've given up drinking and gambling."

"Wang Xing," said Mrs. Sun, "you may go home now, but I'd like to keep your wife here for a couple of days."

After Wang Xing was gone, the woman said to Ying'er, "I need to travel to Eastern Peak Temple to offer some incense. Go with me tomorrow."

Nothing of note occurred that night. The next morning, after washing up, the chief clerk went to the yamen, whereas his wife, after locking up the gate, set out with Ying'er on their journey. After burning some incense in the main hall of Eastern Peak Temple, they went to offer more incense in the corridor. When they were passing the Shrine of Retribution, Ying'er's skirt belt came loose. While Ying'er was busy tying up her belt, Mrs. Sun went ahead on her own. Suddenly, a statue of a judge wearing a cap, a red robe, and a horn waistband called out from inside the shrine, "Ying'er, I am the deceased chief clerk! (*Third apparition*.) Redress the wrong done to me! I've got something here for you."

Ying'er took the object and said, looking at it, "How very strange for a clay statue to talk! Why did he give me this?" Truly, this is something

> Unheard of since the beginning of the universe
> And hardly ever seen from time immemorial.

Hastily Ying'er hid the object in her bosom and did not dare to reveal anything about this to Mrs. Sun. After offering incense, they went their separate ways.

Upon hearing Ying'er's account of what had happened, Wang Xing asked to see the object and found it to be a scroll of paper bearing the following inscription:

The big daughter's child, the small daughter's child,
The former sowed for the latter to reap.
To know what happened at the third watch of the night,
Remove the fire and drain the water underneath.
In the second or third month of next year,
Ju Si will come to solve this riddle.

Unable to make head or tail of it, Wang Xing told Ying'er, "Don't let anyone else know about this. It looks like something's going to happen in the second or third month of next year."

In the time it took to snap a finger, the second month of the new year rolled around. A new county magistrate came to replace the old one. A native of the town of Jindou in Luzhou, he was called Bao Zheng [999–1062], the very Judge Bao who came to be so celebrated in stories of our day. Later known as Academician Bao after he rose to that post in the Longtu Pavilion Imperial Academy, he was, at the time this story took place, a county magistrate serving in his first official post. From an early age, he had been known for his intelligence and integrity. While serving as a county magistrate, he manifested a deep understanding of hidden human feelings and solved cases that would have baffled others.

On the third night after taking up office, before he began to attend to official business, he had a dream in which he was seated in a hall with a couplet posted on the wall:

To know what happened at the third watch of the night,
Remove the fire and drain the water underneath.

The next morning, Magistrate Bao called a court session and asked all the clerks on duty to explain these two lines, but no one was able to come up with an answer. He then asked for a blank placard and had none other than Young Sun copy the couplet onto it in the regular style of calligraphy. The magistrate then added with his vermilion brush-pen: "A reward of ten taels of silver will be offered to anyone able to solve this riddle." The placard was hung on the gate of the county yamen, and soon a large crowd of county employees and commoners had gathered, all attracted by the reward offer and jostling one another for a better view.

Wang Xing was buying some date cakes near the county yamen when he heard that the magistrate had hung out a placard bearing a couplet that no one could interpret. He went to take a look. When he saw two lines that he had seen on the scroll from the judge at the Shrine of Retribution, he was quite shocked. "If I go and tell the truth," he thought, "that new county magistrate is so unpredictable that I'm afraid I might give him offense. But if I don't say anything, no one else will ever know what is behind these two lines."

After returning home with the date cakes, he told his wife about this. Ying'er said, "The dead chief clerk has appeared three times, telling me to redress the wrong done to him. We also got a package of silver from him without having done anything to earn it. If we don't go to the authorities, I'm afraid the ghosts and gods will be after us."

Wang Xing remained undecided. Once again, he headed for the county yamen and there ran into a neighbor, a county clerk named Pei. Knowing Clerk Pei to be a wise man, Wang Xing pulled him into a secluded alley and consulted him. "Should I or should I not come forward?"

"Where's that scroll from the Shrine of Retribution?" asked Pei.

"It's hidden in my wife's clothes trunk."

"First, let me go to the yamen to report the matter on your behalf. In the meantime, go back to get that scroll and bring it to the yamen. When the magistrate calls you, you can present it as evidence."

So Wang Xing went back home. Clerk Pei went into the yamen and waited until Magistrate Bao dismissed the court session. Observing that Young Sun was not around, Pei approached the magistrate and, falling to his knees, said, "Your Honor, my neighbor Wang Xing is the only one who knows the story behind the couplet on the placard. He says that he received at the Shrine of Retribution in Eastern Peak Temple a scroll of paper on which were written these two lines and a lot more."

"Where is this man Wang Xing?" asked the magistrate.

"He has gone back home to get the scroll."

Magistrate Bao sent an officer to bring Wang Xing to court posthaste.

Meanwhile, Wang Xing, back at home, opened his wife's trunk and took out the scroll. As soon as he spread it out for a look, he let out a cry of dismay. It was now a blank piece of paper without the slightest trace of a character. Losing all courage to go to the county yamen, he stayed indoors in trepidation. But the officer dispatched by the county magistrate arrived. How could Wang Xing resist the fiery zeal of a county administration in its first term of office? Resignedly, he took the blank paper and followed the officer to the yamen and straight into the inner hall.

Magistrate Bao dismissed his attendants, keeping only Clerk Pei by his side, and asked Wang Xing, "Mr. Pei said that you received a scroll of paper from Eastern Peak Temple. Show it to me."

With one kowtow after another, Wang Xing said, "My wife made an incense-offering trip to Eastern Peak Temple last year. While she was passing the Shrine of Retribution, a god gave her a scroll of paper. It contained, among other lines, the very couplet inscribed on Your Honor's placard. I put the scroll in a trunk, but when I went just some moments ago to take it out, I found it to be blank. It is here now. Everything I said is true."

Magistrate Bao took the scroll. After one look, he asked, "Do you remember what was written on it?"

"Yes, I do." Right away, Wang Xing started reciting the lines.

After taking down every word on a piece of paper, Magistrate Bao perused the lines for a while before he said, "Wang Xing, let me ask you, what did that deity say to your wife when he gave her the scroll?"

"He told her to redress the wrong done to him."

The magistrate flew into a rage. "You are lying! How can a deity have grievances that need to be redressed by humans? And he begs your wife, of all people, to help him? (*Exactly so.*) Whom are you trying to fool with such nonsense?"

Wang Xing hastened to reply with another kowtow, "Your Honor, there is an explanation for this."

"Then tell me! And be specific! I'll have a reward for you if what you say makes sense. If not, you'll be the first one to be put under the rod!"

"My wife Ying'er used to be a maid serving Big Chief Clerk Sun of this county. A fortune-teller predicted that he was going to die at the third quarter of the third watch that very night, and so he did. His widow married Young Chief Clerk Sun, her current husband, and married Ying'er off to me. The first time the deceased chief clerk appeared to my wife was in the kitchen of the Sun house. With the railings of a well around his neck, his hair coming down loose, his tongue hanging out, and his eyes dripping blood, he cried, 'Ying'er, help your father!' The second time was at the gate of the Sun house one night. This time he wore a cap, a red robe, and a horn waistband. He gave my wife a package of loose silver. The third time was in Eastern Peak Temple, where he appeared as a judge of the Shrine of Retribution and gave my wife this scroll, telling her to redress the wrong done to him. The judge looked exactly like Big Sun, my wife's deceased master." (*Clear exposition.*)

At this account, Magistrate Bao burst into a peal of laughter. "So that's what happened!" By his order, his men apprehended the Sun couple and brought them to court.

"A fine thing the two of you did!" he said to the couple.

Young Sun retorted, "I didn't do anything wrong!"

Magistrate Bao launched into an explication of the inscription given by the judge at the Shrine of Retribution. "As for the first line, 'The big daughter's child, the small daughter's child,' well, 'a daughter's child' is a 'grandchild,' which is the character *sun,* a surname that is obviously shared by the two chief clerks, the big one and the small one. As for the line 'The former sowed for the latter to reap,' 'to reap' means to have something to live on, a reference to the fact that you, at no expense to yourself, took his wife and enjoy his family property. As for the third and fourth lines 'To know what happened at the third watch of the night / Remove the fire and drain the water underneath,' Big Sun died at midnight, and to find out the cause of his death, one would have to drain the water under the fire. Ying'er saw her master by the kitchen stove, his hair coming down loose, his tongue hanging out, his eyes dripping blood. These are signs of death by strangulation. There were the railings of a well around his neck. A well is the source of water. The kitchen stove is the source of fire. As for 'the water underneath,' there must be a well under your kitchen stove, and the dead body must be inside the well. 'The second or third month of next year' is now. As for the line 'Ju Si will come to solve this riddle,' well, the characters *ju* [sentence] and *si* [the sixth of the twelve Earthly Branches], when put together, make the character *bao,* which means that I, Bao Zheng, would be here to serve as the judge and solve the riddle to redress the wrong done to him." (*Well explained.*)

He then ordered his men and Wang Xing to take Young Sun under guard to his own kitchen and, whatever the circumstances, bring back the dead body. Somewhat skeptical, the men went to Sun's house. When they removed the stove, a stone slab underneath came into view. When the slab was pried open, they saw that there was indeed a well. They hired some laborers to drain the well. A man and a bamboo basket were let down into the well, and sure enough, the man came up with a dead body. The men gathered around for a look and found that the face appeared as if still alive. Some of the men recognized it as the face of Big Sun. Around his neck there was indeed a piece of silk with which he had been strangled. Young Sun was so frightened that he was struck dumb, his face turning the color of mud. The others were also appalled.

What had happened was that the younger Sun had once almost frozen to death in the snow. Big Sun saw him and, taking pity on the fine-looking young man, brought him back to life and later taught him to read and write. Little did he expect that his wife would carry on an affair with the young man. On the day that the older Sun came home after having his fortune told, the younger Sun happened to have sneaked into his house. Hearing that the older Sun was to die at around midnight, the younger man took the opportunity to get him drunk and then strangled him and threw him into the well. The younger Sun then walked toward the river, covering his face with his hand, and threw a rock into the water, making a loud splash, to make people believe that the older Sun had thrown himself into the river. The kitchen stove was then moved to cover the well. Later, the couple got married through the services of the matchmakers.

The officers reported the matter to Magistrate Bao. The Sun couple confessed without being put under the rod and were sentenced to death as repayment for Big Sun's life. Keeping his promise to an insignificant villager, Magistrate Bao gave Wang Xing the reward of ten taels of silver. Wang Xing, in his turn, gave Clerk Pei three taels as a token of his gratitude, but that need not be gone into here.

Having solved the case in the first few days of his term of office, Magistrate Bao became a well-known figure, and his name spread throughout the land. Even today, stories about how he solved his cases among mortal beings in daytime and among ghosts at night still circulate far and wide, as testified by the following poem:

> *The lines contained a most baffling riddle;*
> *Judge Bao's verdict amazed ghosts and deities.*
> *Let it be known to those guilty of crimes:*
> *Never assume that heaven does not know.*

Madam White Is Kept Forever
under Thunder Peak Tower

Hill beyond green hill, tower beyond tower,
When will songs and dances by West Lake ever cease?
Enchanted by the warm breezes,
The sightseers take Hangzhou for Bianzhou.[1]

Our story takes place by beautiful West Lake amid green hills and clear waters. In the Xianhe reign period [326–34] during the Jin dynasty, when a raging mountain flood swept past West Gate, an ox was suddenly seen in the water, glittering all over with the color of gold. The ox then followed the receding flood all the way to North Hill, where it became lost to view, destination unknown. The event caused quite a stir throughout the city of Hangzhou, for the residents believed that the ox was an apparition of some deity. Thus, a temple was built and named Jinniu [Golden Ox] Temple. At West Gate, now called Yongjin [Golden Flood] Gate, a temple dedicated to General Jinhua [Golden Splendor] still stands.

At the time, a foreign monk with the Buddhist name Hunshouluo commented when viewing the hills of Wulin County on one of his wandering journeys: "A little peak in front of Spirit Vulture Hill [Grdhrakuta] has suddenly disappeared. So, here's where it has flown to." Reacting to the disbelief these words generated among his audience, he continued, "As far as I remember, that little peak is called Spirit Vulture Peak. It has a cave in which lives a white ape. Let me try to call the ape out by way of proof." And indeed, a white ape emerged in response to his calls.

At the foot of the hill was a pavilion, now called Cold Fountain Pavilion. In the middle of West Lake stands a solitary hill. When the poet Lin Hejing[2] was living as a hermit on that hill, he had stones and earth carried over and a walkway built between Broken Bridge to the east and Sunset Peak to the west. The walkway thus came to be called Solitary Hill Road. During the Tang dynasty, Prefect Bai Juyi[3] also had a causeway built, reaching from Green Screen Hills to the south and Sunset Peak to the north, and it came to be called the Bai Causeway. The two roads were often damaged by mountain floods, and money had to be withdrawn from government coffers each time to pay for repairs. Then, during the Song dynasty,

Su Dongpo,[4] who was prefect of Hangzhou, bought timber and stones, hired laborers, and had the two water-damaged roads repaired and reinforced. Railings on the six bridges were painted vermilion, and peach and willow trees were planted all along the causeway. In the balmy days of spring, the scenery is most picturesque. Later, it came to be known as the Su Causeway. Two stone bridges were built by Solitary Hill Road to part the flow of the water. The one to the east is called Broken Bridge and the one to the west Xiling Bridge. Truly,

> *Three hundred temples half hidden in the hills;*
> *Two tall peaks locked in faint, fluffy clouds.*

But, storyteller, you may well object, why talk only about the scenery of West Lake, men of immortal fame, and sites of historic interest? Well, let me now launch into the story proper and tell of a dashing young man who, because of his encounter with two women while touring West Lake, caused quite a sensation throughout the romance-filled streets of the region's cities and towns, providing material for a love story from the writer's pen. Now what was the young man's name? What manner of women did he encounter? What did he do to cause a sensation? There is a poem in testimony:

> *In the dismal rain of the Qingming season,*[5]
> *The wayfarer on the road is stricken with grief.*
> *"Where, pray, might I find a wineshop?"*
> *The herdboy points to Apricot Village afar.*

The story goes that in the Shaoxing reign period [1132–62], after Emperor Gaozong of Song moved to the south, there lived, in Black Pearl Lane by the Reward the Troops Bridge in Lin'an Prefecture, Hangzhou, a certain Li Ren. He served as a petty official in the treasury of the Southern Song court while doubling as bursar for a Marshal Shao. His wife had a younger brother, Xu Xuan, who was the oldest son of the family. Xu's father used to own an herbal medicine store, but both parents had died when Xu Xuan was still a boy. Now twenty-two years old, Xu Xuan worked as an assistant in an herb store owned by a distant uncle, Squire Li. The store was situated at the corner of Officials Street.

One day, Xu Xuan was attending to his business in the store when a monk appeared at the door and said after a greeting, "This poor monk is from Baoshu Pagoda Monastery. I sent some steamed buns and twisted rolls to your house the other day. Now that the Clear and Bright Festival is drawing near, I hope that you, Master Xiaoyi [Oldest Son], will come to our monastery to offer incense in memory of your ancestors. Please do remember to come."

"I'll surely be there," promised Xu Xuan. The monk took his leave.

In the evening, Xu Xuan returned to his brother-in-law's house. Being a bachelor, he lived with his older sister's family. That evening, he told his sister, "A monk from Baoshu Monastery came today and asked me to go and burn sacrificial straw baskets.[6] So I'll make the trip tomorrow to honor our ancestors."

He rose bright and early the next morning and bought some paper horses, candles, sutra streamers, and strings of paper coins. Afterwards he ate breakfast, changed into new clothes, socks, and shoes, wrapped the baskets and offerings in a piece of cloth, and went to Squire Li's house on Officials Street. When Squire Li asked where he was off to, Xu Xuan replied, "I'm going to Baoshu Pagoda to offer incense in memory of my ancestors. Please give me a day's leave, Uncle."

"All right, but come back as soon as possible."

Xu Xuan left the store. He took Peaceful Longevity Lane and Flower Market Street, crossed Well Pavilion Bridge, went through Qiantang Gate behind Clear River Street, crossed Stone Box Bridge, and passed the Monument to the Release of Captured Living Creatures.

Once he arrived at the monastery, he sought out the monk who had brought him steamed buns and made his confession. He then burned the baskets containing the paper offerings and went up to the main hall to watch the monks recite the scriptures. After a vegetarian meal, he bade the monk good-bye and left to take a leisurely walk around.

He crossed West Peace Bridge and Solitary Hill Road and went to the Temple of the Four Sages, meaning to continue on to Lin Hejing's grave and Six Ones Spring. But all of a sudden, clouds gathered in the northwestern sky, and a fog closed in from the southeast. The drizzle that followed soon grew into a steady rain. As it happened to be around the Clear and Bright Festival, the Lord of Heaven, in observance of the laws of nature, lent a determined insistence to the rain so as to speed the growth of flowers. Seeing that the ground outside was wet, Xu Xuan took off his new socks and shoes and stepped out of the temple to look for a boat. There being none in sight, he wasn't sure what to do, when suddenly, he was over-joyed to see an old man rowing a boat in his direction. A closer look revealed the boatman to be Grandpa Zhang. "Grandpa Zhang," cried Xu Xuan, "please take me on board!"

At the cry, the old man looked around and saw that it was Master Xiaoyi. Rowing his boat toward the shore, he said, "Master Xiaoyi, so you're caught in the rain! How far do you want me to take you?"

"I'll get off at Golden Flood Gate."

The old man helped him into the boat and rowed away from the bank toward Harvest Joy Tower. Before they had gone more than a hundred feet, they heard a cry from the shore, "Grandpa, would you give us a ride, please?"

Xu Xuan turned to look and saw a woman wearing a white silk blouse, a fine flaxen skirt, and white hairpins in her jet-black hair, which was arranged in a chi-gnon covered in mourning white. By her side stood her maid, dressed all in green. Her hair was fastened in two knots, each tied with a bright red string and adorned with a piece of jewelry. She was carrying a package in her hand. Both appeared eager to get on the boat.

Old Man Zhang remarked to Xu Xuan, "As the saying goes, 'When there's a wind blowing, you need do nothing to keep the fire going.' Since we don't have to do anything extra, why don't we take them on board?"

"Have them come down, then," said Xu Xuan. (*The beginning of all the troubles to come.*)

So the old man drew the boat up to the shore, and the woman and her maid stepped on board. At the sight of Xu Xuan, the woman flashed a smile, revealing dainty white teeth between red lips, and dropped a curtsy. Xu Xuan rose with alacrity and returned the greeting. After the woman and the maid were seated in the cabin, the woman kept casting significant glances at Xu Xuan, who found his desires stirring, despite his prudishness, at the sight of such an enchanting beauty accompanied by a flower of a maid. (*It so happens that prudish ones tend to be the easiest to catch.*)

"May I ask your name, sir?" said the woman.

"I am Xu Xuan, the oldest son in the family."

"Where do you live?"

"I live in Black Pearl Lane by Reward the Troops Bridge and work in an herbal medicine store."

Now that the woman had asked her questions, Xu Xuan thought it was his turn. Rising from his seat, he inquired, "May I ask your name, madam? And where do you live?"

"I am the younger sister of Officer White [Bai] of the imperial guards. My husband, Zhang, has unfortunately passed away and is buried here on Thunder Peak. The Clear and Bright Festival being near, I took my maid to sweep his grave and make some offerings today. We were on our way back when we got caught in the rain. If you hadn't taken us in, we would have been in quite a sorry state."

After they had chatted for a while, the boat approached the shore. The woman said, "I left home in such haste that I didn't bring enough travel money. Could you please lend me some money so that I may pay the boatman? I'll surely pay you back." (*An excuse for continuing the association.*)

"As you wish, madam, but don't worry about such a trivial amount," Xu Xuan assured her.

After the boatman was paid, the rain came down even harder. As Xu Xuan helped her go ashore, the woman said, "My house is at the entrance to Double Tea Lane by Arrow Bridge. If it's not beneath you, please follow me to my humble home for tea, so that I can repay the money."

"Oh, don't worry about such a trifle. It's getting late now. I'll come for a visit another time," said Xu Xuan. And so, the woman and her maid took leave of him.

Xu Xuan then went through Golden Flood Gate and wended his way under the eaves of the houses to Three Bridges Street, where Squire Li's brother's herb store was located. Xu Xuan walked up and saw the younger Squire Li at the door.

"Brother Xiaoyi," said Li, "where are you going at this late hour?"

"I went to Baoshu Pagoda on an incense-offering trip and got caught in the rain. Could you lend me an umbrella?

"Old Chen!" cried out Li. "Get Master Xiaoyi an umbrella!"

Soon, Old Chen emerged with an umbrella. Opening it, he said, "Master Xiaoyi, this umbrella is the work of Honest Shu by Character Eight Bridge on Clear Lake, and a fine umbrella it is, with its eighty-four ribs and purple bamboo handle. It's not torn anywhere, either. So don't ruin it! Be sure to take good care of it!" (*Remarks quite unexpected. A comic touch.*)

"Of course, don't worry," said Xu Xuan as he took the umbrella. After some words of thanks to Squire Li, he left, heading in the direction of Sheep Dike. As he approached Rear Market Street, he heard someone call, "Master Xiaoyi!" Turning to look, he saw a woman standing under the eaves of the small teahouse at the entrance to Shen's Well Street, the very Madam White who had been his companion on the boat.

"Why are you here, madam?"

"With the rain pouring like that, my shoes became wet, so I had Little Green go home to fetch an umbrella and my galoshes. Now that it's getting dark, may I share your umbrella for part of the way?"

So they walked as far as the dike, sharing one umbrella. "Now where do you want to go, madam?"

"To Arrow Bridge after crossing that bridge."

"Well, I'm heading for Reward the Troops Bridge, which is quite close by. You might just as well take the umbrella. I'll come to get it tomorrow." (*Volunteering to continue the relationship and inviting trouble. There's no one more tender, affectionate, and [illegible] than Madam White.*)

"You're too kind. Thank you so much," said Madam White.

Keeping under the eaves, Xu Xuan walked on in the rain. Upon arriving, he ran into Wang An, his brother-in-law's servant, who had just returned after looking vainly for him to deliver his galoshes and umbrella.

Xu Xuan ate supper at home and spent a wakeful night, tossing and turning, thinking about the woman. When he finally fell asleep, the events of the day reappeared in a dream, stirring up amorous passion. At the roosters' crow, he woke up and realized that it had all been but a dream. Truly,

> His heart as wild as a fast-running ape or horse,
> His amorous desires kept him awake till dawn.

When it grew light at last, he rose, washed, did his hair, ate breakfast, and went to the store. With his mind in a fluster, he could hardly concentrate on his job. In the early afternoon, he thought to himself, "How am I going to get the umbrella back and return it without having to tell a lie?" Addressing the older Squire Li, who was sitting by the counter, he said, "My brother-in-law wants me to go home earlier than usual today to deliver a present for him. May I take the rest of the afternoon off?"

"All right, go ahead. Come in earlier tomorrow!"

After chanting his good-bye, Xu Xuan headed straight for Double Tea Lane by Arrow Bridge and asked for directions to Madam White's house, but no one knew where it was. He was wondering what to do when Little Green, Madam White's maid, appeared, coming from an easterly direction.

"Sister!" exclaimed Xu Xuan. "Where exactly do you live? I've come to get my umbrella."

"Follow me, sir."

And so he did. A few moments later, she announced, "Here we are!"

He saw that the house was two-storied with a double door flanked by four long, latticed windows, two to each side. A finely woven vermilion curtain hung in the middle of the door. The main hall was lined with twelve black lacquer arm-chairs and decorated with four landscape paintings by famous artists of olden times. Opposite the house stood the mansion of Prince Xiu, father of Emperor Xiaozong of Song.

Disappearing behind the curtain, the maid said, "Please come in and take a seat, sir!"

Xu Xuan followed her to the inner section of the house. Little Green then whispered, "Ma'am, Master Xiaoyi is here!"

"Invite him in for tea," said Madam White from inside.

Xu Xuan had not made up his mind what to do, but Little Green kept urging him to go in, and so he did. There came into view four veiled latticed windows. When the blue cotton portiere was raised, he saw a small parlor with a table on which stood a pot of bearded calamus. Two paintings of beautiful women hung on either side, and on the central wall was a picture of a deity. On another table was a bronze vase in the shape of an incense burner.

Madam White stepped forward and said with a deep bow, "I'm much indebted to you, Master Xiaoyi, for having taken such good care of us upon our first encounter yesterday. How can I ever thank you enough?"

"Oh, it's hardly worth mentioning."

"Please sit and have some tea," said Madam White. After they finished the tea, she continued, "Let me serve you some wine as a token of my gratitude."

Before Xu Xuan could decline the offer, Little Green had laid out a fine spread of vegetables and fruits.

"I thank you, madam, for your hospitality, but I really shouldn't be imposing on you like this." After drinking a few cups of wine, he rose and said, "It's getting late. As I have quite a long way to go, I beg to take leave of you now."

"A relative of mine borrowed your umbrella from me last night," said Madam White. "Please have a few more cups while I try to have it sent back."

"It's getting late. I really must be going."

"Just one more cup!"

"But I've had enough. I'm much obliged!"

"If you insist on leaving now, please be good enough to come back tomorrow for the umbrella." (*Trying again to continue the relationship. Another twist in the plot.*) There was nothing Xu Xuan could do but take leave of her and return home.

The next day, after working in the store for a little while, he got away again on some excuse and went to Madam White's house to reclaim his umbrella. Again, she kept him for wine.

"Please give me back my umbrella," said Xu Xuan. "I don't want to impose on you like this."

"But since the wine is ready, please take just one little cup," the woman insisted. Xu Xuan felt he had no choice but to sit down. Madam White filled a cup, handed it to Xu Xuan, and said, her cherry-red lips moving, her pearly teeth glistening, her voice sweet and coquettish, her face radiant with joy, "My respects to you, sir. As they say, 'To an honest person, be honest.' The fact is, my husband has died. Judging from your kindness to me the first time we met, I believe that I must have a pre-destined marriage bond with you and that the feeling is mutual. Wouldn't it be nice if you could find a matchmaker and we two who are made for each other can join in blissful marriage?"

These words set Xu Xuan to thinking. "That would indeed be a good match. To have such a wife wouldn't be a bad deal at all. I am more than willing, but there's one matter to consider. Working during the day for Squire Li and lodging at night at my brother-in-law's house, I have saved a little money, but it's just enough for my own clothes. How can I afford to have a family?"

As he sat there, pensively silent, Madam White asked, "Why don't you answer me?"

"I'm very honored, but the fact of the matter is, I don't have the means to comply with your wish."

"That problem is easily solved," replied Madam White. "I have money to spare. You needn't worry on that score." To Little Green, she said, "Go up and get an ingot of silver for me."

Holding on to the railing, Little Green went up and down the stairs and handed a package to Madam White. "Master Xiaoyi," said the woman, "Take this. When in need, come here again for more." So saying, she gave the package to Xu Xuan with her own hands. Xu Xuan opened the package and saw inside fifty taels of snow-white silver. He put it in his sleeve and rose to go. Little Green returned his umbrella to him. Umbrella in hand, Xu Xuan took his leave, went straight home, and hid the silver. The night passed without further ado.

In the morning, he rose and went to Officials Street to return the umbrella to Squire Li. With some loose pieces of silver, he bought a fat and juicy roast goose, fresh fish, lean meat, a young chicken, fruit, and a jar of wine and carried them home. He gave everything to the housekeeper and the maids for them to take care of.

His brother-in-law, Officer Li, happened to be at home that day, and Xu Xuan invited him and his sister to sit down around the dinner table with the fine spread on it. Much taken aback at the invitation, Officer Li said to himself, "Why is he going to so much expense today? I've never seen him with a wine cup. Something's wrong here!"

The three sat down in order of seniority. After a few rounds of wine, Officer Li said, "My honored brother-in-law, why are you going to so much expense when there's nothing special happening?"

"I'm much obliged to you, Brother-in-law, but please don't make fun of me. This is really not worth mentioning. I am very grateful to you and Sister for taking care of me all these years. But, as they say, one guest should not impose himself on two hosts. I'm a grown man now and should make sure I'll have support in my old age. I've had a marriage offer. Could you, my brother-in-law and sister, please make the necessary arrangements on my behalf so that I can settle down once and for all?"

At these words, his brother-in-law and sister thought to themselves, "This is a man who hardly ever parts with a penny. And now, with what little he has spent, he expects us to get a wife for him?" Exchanging glances, the husband and wife refrained from answering. After the meal was over, Xu Xuan went back to work.

A couple of days later, Xu Xuan wondered, "Why does Sister still keep silent about the matter?" He asked his sister, "Have you consulted Brother-in-law about what I said the other day?"

"No."

"Why not?"

"Well, unlike other things, this isn't something that should be done in a rush. Also, your brother-in-law's been looking worried the last couple of days, so I haven't dared ask him, so as to avoid adding another burden to his mind."

"Sister, why are you dragging your feet? What's so difficult about it? You're ignoring me only because you're afraid I'll be making a demand on my brother-in-law's pocket!" With that, he rose, went to his bedroom, opened his trunk, and took out Madam White's silver. Handing the ingot to his sister, he said, "Now, no more excuses. I need Brother-in-law to make the arrangements for me."

"So, you've saved up quite a tidy sum all these years while working for Uncle! No wonder you are talking about getting married! You go along now and leave the money here with me."

When Officer Li returned, Xu Xuan's sister told him, "Husband, you know why my brother is talking about marrying? The fact is, he has saved up quite a tidy sum for himself and has offered some to me. It looks like we'll have to take care of this matchmaking business."

"So that's what it is!" exclaimed Officer Li. "Well, it's a good thing he has some private savings. Show me the money." Promptly, his wife handed the silver to him. He turned the ingot over and over in his hand, examining the characters engraved on it. "We're in trouble!" he burst out in alarm. "This means death for the whole family!"

Seized with fear, his wife asked, "What can be so terrible?"

"A few days ago, fifty large ingots of silver disappeared from Marshal Shao's treasury. The seal and lock on the door are intact, and there is no underground tunnel that leads to it. And now, Lin'an Prefecture has been given the urgent task of hunting down the thief, but there's no clue whatsoever. Goodness knows how many people have been implicated! Bulletins have been posted, complete with the serial numbers of the missing ingots. The bulletin says, 'Whoever captures the thief and finds the silver shall receive a reward of fifty taels. Anyone who withholds information or gives shelter to the thief shall be duly punished, and all members of his family shall be banished to remote regions.' Now, the serial number on this ingot is exactly the same as the one in the bulletin, which means that the silver comes from Marshal Shao's treasury, and there's a big hue and cry after it! Indeed, 'In a spreading fire, you can't afford to take care of all your relatives.' If this theft is discovered, I won't be able to talk my way out of trouble. I don't care whether he stole it or borrowed it, but it's far better to have him punished than to be implicated myself. I'll have to take the silver to the authorities, so as to protect our family." His wife was so stunned at these words that her jaw dropped and she stared at him, her eyes unblinking.

And so, off he went to the prefectural yamen to surrender the ingot of silver. His report deprived the prefect of a whole night's sleep.

The next day, He Li, the arrest officer, was summoned posthaste. Taking a few assistants and a team of lictors keen of eye and swift of movement, Officer He Li went straight to Squire Li's store on Officials Street to apprehend the thief Xu Xuan. At the store counter, the men gave a shout and bound Xu Xuan with rope. Beating a drum and a gong along the way, they took him to the yamen of Lin'an Prefecture, where Prefect Han happened to be holding court. Xu Xuan was taken to the middle of the hall and made to kneel down.

"Beat him!" roared the prefect.

"Hold the torture for now, Your Honor," protested Xu Xuan. "First, let me know the charge against me."

Furiously the magistrate thundered, "What does a thief have to say for himself when the evidence is there? How dare you try to claim innocence! Fifty of the largest ingots of silver have disappeared from Marshal Shao's treasury, with the seal and lock intact. Officer Li has brought in one of the ingots, and the other forty-nine ingots must be in your possession. If you are able to steal without touching the seal, you must be a sorcerer as well as a thief! All right, hold the beating for now, but bring me some animal blood!"[7]

Now realizing what this was all about, Xu Xuan shouted at the top of his voice, "I'm not a sorcerer! Let me explain!"

"All right, go ahead and tell me where you got the silver."

Thereupon, Xu Xuan gave a detailed account of how he had lent his umbrella and had gotten it back.

"What manner of woman is Madam White?" the prefect demanded. "And where does she live?"

"She says she's the younger sister of Officer White of the imperial guards. She lives in the black house on the slope opposite Prince Xiu's mansion at the entrance to Double Tea Lane by Arrow Bridge."

Right away, the prefect ordered Arrest Officer He Li to escort Xu Xuan to Double Tea Lane to apprehend the woman and bring her to court.

Thus ordered, He Li and his men hurried to the black house opposite Prince Xiu's mansion on Double Tea Lane. When they got there, all they saw were four windows looking out onto the street, a big double door, a heap of garbage on the steps leading up to the door, and a bamboo pole across the door. The men stood astounded. Then they set out to a search for some neighbors and came back from one end of the street with a Mr. Qiu Da, a maker of artificial flowers, and from the other end of the street a Mr. Sun, a cobbler. The latter was so overwhelmed by the shock that he had a rupture and collapsed to the ground. Other neighbors came over and told the officers, "There isn't any Madam White around here. About five or six years ago, an Inspector Mao who used to live there died in an epidemic, as did all other members of his family. Since then, because ghosts have often been seen coming out of the house in broad daylight to buy things, no one has dared to live in it. A few days ago, a madman was seen standing in front of the door chanting greetings."

By He Li's order, the bamboo pole barring the door was removed. As the door opened, a gust of foul-smelling wind sprang up from the deserted interior of the house. Astounded, the men staggered back, while Xu Xuan stood speechless.

Among the officers was a stout-hearted Mr. Wang, the second son in his family, better known as Wino Wang the Second because of his weakness for wine. "Follow me!" shouted Wino Wang the Second as he led the men in.

The walls, the parlor, and the table and chairs were all there as Xu Xuan had described them. When they came to the staircase, Wino Wang was made to go up first, and the rest of the men followed. They found the upper floor covered with a layer of dust three inches thick. Continuing on to a bedchamber, they pushed open the door and saw that, on a canopied bed surrounded by trunks and cases, sat a woman in white, as pretty as a flower and as fair as jade. Lacking the courage to step forward, the men said, "Are you, madam, a goddess or a ghost? We are ordered by the prefect of Lin'an to summon you to court to bear out Xu Xuan's testimony." The woman did not move.

"It won't do if none of us dares to go forward!" exclaimed Wino Wang. "Bring me a jar of wine. She can't hurt me after I drink, and I'll be able to take her to the prefect."

Two or three men promptly hurried downstairs and came back with a jar of wine. Wang the Second broke the seal over the mouth of the jar and drank up the wine. "She can't hurt me now!" With that, he hurled the empty jar at the bed curtains. It would have been a different story had he not done so, but as he did, they heard an earsplitting crack, like a bolt out of the blue. Everyone collapsed to the floor in shock. By the time they scrambled to their feet to look around, the woman had vanished. All they saw was a heap of glittering silver. Moving closer for a better view, they exclaimed, "Good!" They counted forty-nine ingots in all.

"Oh well, at least we can take the silver to the prefect," they said, and they returned to the Lin'an prefectural yamen carrying the silver.

After hearing He Li's report, the prefect concluded, "This must have been the work of a demon spirit. Very well, then, the neighbors are innocent and can go home." He then dispatched a messenger to take the fifty ingots of silver to Marshal Shao along with a report containing detailed explanations. Xu Xuan was charged with "having committed an improper act" and was given a few thrashings of the rod. Though spared the disgrace of a facial tattoo, he was sentenced to hard labor in a Suzhou Prefecture prison camp until his term expired.

Feeling guilty for having informed on Xu Xuan, Officer Li gave Marshal Shao's fifty-taels reward to Xu Xuan for use on his journey. The squire wrote two letters on behalf of Xu Xuan, one addressed to Warden Fan and the other to Mr. Wang, the owner of an inn by Lucky Bridge. After a violent fit of sobbing, Xu Xuan bade farewell to his brother-in-law and his sister and was put into a cangue. Escorted by two guards, he left Hangzhou and embarked on a boat at East New Bridge.

In a matter of days, the party arrived in Suzhou. The first thing Xu Xuan did upon arrival was to present the letters to Warden Fan and Mr. Wang. On his behalf, Mr. Wang bribed high and low throughout the yamen. The two guards were then sent on to the Suzhou prefectural yamen to deliver the official documents as well as the convicted man. Once they got a return message, they went back. Warden Fan and Mr. Wang managed to get Xu Xuan released on bail. After settling down in a room on the upper floor of Mr. Wang's inn, Xu Xuan gloomily wrote a poem on the wall:

> Alone in a tower, I look toward home;
> Sadly, I watch the setting sun by the window.
> A man of honesty throughout my life,
> I was doomed when I met the bewitching one.

Where could the one in white have gone?
And where could the one in green be now?
Here, in Suzhou, away from kith and kin,
I'm overwhelmed with nostalgia for home.

Only when there is a lot to say will the story be a long one, but at this point in our narration, there being little to tell, let us skip over the more than six months that flitted by like an arrow amid the busy risings and settings of the sun and the moon. During all this time, Xu Xuan continued to stay with Mr. Wang. Now, toward the end of the ninth month, Mr. Wang was standing idly at the door of his inn, watching the goings-on in the street, when he saw, coming from afar, a sedan-chair with a maidservant walking by its side.

"Might this be Mr. Wang's inn?" asked the maid upon drawing near.

Mr. Wang hastened to reply with a bow. "Yes. Are you looking for someone?"

"We're looking for Mr. Xu Xiaoyi from Lin'an."

"Just a moment. Let me have him come out."

The sedan-chair parked in front of the door, while Mr. Wang went inside and cried out, "Brother Xiaoyi! You have visitors!"

Xu Xuan hurried out to the door with the innkeeper. Who should be there but Madam White in the sedan-chair, attended by Little Green!

"Oh, you'll be the death of me yet!" burst out Xu Xuan. "You stole silver from an official's treasury and got me into goodness knows how much trouble, and there's no one who can right the wrong done to me. Now that I've come to such a pass, why do you have to run after me like this? I'm ashamed to death!"

"Don't blame me, Master Xiaoyi," pleaded Madam White. "I'm here today to explain. Let me go in first." So saying, she had Little Green take the luggage and got down from the sedan-chair.

"Since you're an evil spirit, you cannot come in," announced Xu Xuan. With that, he blocked the door and refused to let her enter.

With a deep curtsy to the innkeeper, Madam White said, "I'm not trying to hide anything. You, sir, can see that I am not an evil spirit. Look at the seams in my clothes and the shadow I cast in the sun. Unfortunately for me, my husband died and left me a victim of such abuses! Whatever was done was my husband's doing. I had nothing to do with it. I came all this way just to explain to you because I was afraid you might bear a grudge against me. After I've said what I came to say, I'll happily take my leave."

"Please go in and be seated while you talk," said Mr. Wang.

"Yes, let's go inside and speak to the mistress of the house," said Madam White, whereupon the onlookers who had gathered at the door went their separate ways.

Once inside, Xu Xuan addressed the innkeeper and his wife. "I've been punished by the law because of her theft. I wonder what she has to say for herself, rushing all the way here like this."

"It was out of the best intentions that I gave you the silver my deceased husband left behind," explained Madam White. "I had no idea how he had come by it."

"But when the officers went to arrest you, why was there so much garbage at the door? And why is it that we heard one loud bang behind the bed curtain and then you disappeared?"

"When I heard that you had been arrested because of the silver, I was afraid you might name me. How embarrassing it would be if I were brought to the authorities and had to show my face in public! So I saw nothing for it but to seek refuge in my aunt's house by Splendid Treasure Temple. Then I arranged to have garbage piled up at the door and silver placed on the bed. I also asked the neighbors to lie on my behalf."

"So you got away free and left me behind to be caught up by the law!"

"I put the silver on the bed because I thought that would close the case. How was I to know that so many things would happen? After learning your whereabouts, I brought some money and came all this way by boat to look you up. And now that everything has been explained, I'm leaving. You and I are not predestined to be husband and wife after all!"

"Madam," put in Mr. Wang, "you can't leave like this after such a long journey. Stay here for a few days before you decide what to do next."

Little Green urged, "Since the host is offering to keep you, why don't you stay here for a couple of days, madam? You did once promise to marry Master Xiaoyi."

Without missing a beat, Madam White said, "How humiliating! I can't be as unwanted and eager to be married off as that! I came only to set the record straight." (*Calculatedly going the other way, to throw off suspicions.*)

"Since you promised to marry him," said Mr. Wang, "why do you have to go? Stay!" And he dismissed the sedan-chair carrier, but of this, no more.

Several days later, Madam White having done her best to win Mrs. Wang's heart, the old lady persuaded Mr. Wang to use his powers of persuasion on Xu Xuan and make the match. The eleventh day of the eleventh month was then chosen for the wedding ceremony, to mark the beginning of a long and blissful marriage.

In the twinkling of an eye, the auspicious day rolled around. Madam White took out some silver and asked Mr. Wang to prepare the wedding feast. After the bride and the groom made their wedding bows in the main hall and partook of the wedding feast, they retired to the curtained bed in their bedchamber. Madam White used such charms on Xu Xuan that he was thrown into as much ecstasy as if he had met a divine being. How he wished he could have known her earlier! They were still sporting joyfully when the roosters crowed three times and the eastern sky began to brighten. Truly,

In joy, the night goes by all too quickly;
In loneliness, the hours drag on, and dawn never comes.

Henceforth, the two spent all their time in delirious pleasure at Mr. Wang's inn, as inseparable as fish and water. The days grew to months. Soon, six months had slipped by, bringing in the balmy days and blooming flowers of spring. Noticing the hustle and bustle in the streets, Xu Xuan asked his host, "Why is everybody out on the street? What's all this excitement about?"

"Today being the fifteenth day of the second month, men and women are going out to see the image of the Reclining Buddha," explained Mr. Wang. "Why don't you also go to Chengtian Monastery for some fun?"

"Right! I'll go, but let me tell my wife about it first." So Xu Xuan went upstairs and said to his wife, "Since today is the fifteenth day of the second month, there are lots of men and women out to see the Reclining Buddha. I want to go and take a look, too, but I'll be back soon enough. If anyone asks for me, just say I'm not at home. Don't go out to be seen in public."

"But what's there to see? What's so bad about just staying at home?" protested Madam White. "Why do you have to go?"

"I'll just go and have a little fun. I'll be back soon. No harm can come of it."

So saying, Xu Xuan left the inn. In the company of a few acquaintances, he went to the monastery to see the Reclining Buddha. After touring all the halls along the corridors, he was on his way out when he saw a priest wearing a Daoist robe, a casual head wrap, a yellow silk waistband, and a pair of hemp shoes sitting in front of the monastery gate, selling medicine and distributing charms and holy water. Xu Xuan stopped to watch.

"This poor priest is from the Zhongnan Mountains," announced the priest. "I dispense charms and holy water everywhere I go in my travels, to cure diseases and dispel disasters. Those afflicted with ailments, please come forward." Espying a column of black vapor over Xu Xuan's head, the priest immediately concluded that this man was being haunted by an evil spirit. "You there!" he called out. "An evil spirit has been haunting you for some time now, and it's doing you no little harm! Let me give you two charms to save your life. One is for you to burn at the third watch of the night, and the other is to put in your hair."

Xu Xuan took the charms with a deep bow, thinking to himself, "I do have the feeling that she's most probably an evil spirit. So it's true." Thankfully, he took leave of the priest and returned to the inn.

At night, while Madam White and Little Green were asleep, Xu Xuan rose and said to himself, "It should be the third watch of the night by now."

With that, he put one of the two charms in his hair and was about to burn the other when Madam White spoke up with a sigh, "Brother Xiaoyi, we've been husband and wife for quite some time now, and yet, instead of showing me affection, you believed some stranger and try to burn a charm in the middle of the night to exorcise me! Well, go ahead and burn it!" So saying, she grabbed the charm and burned it up. Nothing happened.

"Are you convinced now?" asked Madam White. "Imagine accusing me of being an evil spirit!"

"It wasn't my idea," protested Xu Xuan. "A mendicant priest in front of Reclining Buddha Monastery said that you are."

"All right, let me go with you tomorrow and see what manner of priest he is."

The next morning, Madam White rose bright and early. After she had completed her toilette, put on her jewelry and her white outfit, and instructed Little Green to take care of things in their rooms on the second floor of the inn, husband and wife made their way to Reclining Buddha Monastery. There, they saw a crowd gathered around the priest, who was distributing charms and holy water. Her bewitching eyes wide open, Madam White walked up to the priest and shouted at the top of her voice, "How dare you, a priest, tell my husband that I am an evil spirit and write up a charm to subdue me!"

The priest shot back, "With my Five Thunders heaven-centered orthodox method, I can make any demon reveal its true shape as soon as it swallows my charm."

"In the presence of everyone here, why don't you make me eat one of those charms of yours?" challenged Madam White. Accordingly, the priest drew a charm and gave it to Madam White, who took it and swallowed it up. The onlookers watched intently, but nothing happened.

They commented, "How can you accuse such a nice lady of being an evil spirit?" And they went on berating the priest while he stood there stupefied, fear written all over his face.

Madam White addressed the crowd, "You all witnessed how he failed to trap me. Now, let me try something on him that I learned as a child. Watch!" As she murmured something quite incomprehensible, the priest huddled up and rose in the air as if clutched by an invisible hand. The onlookers stood aghast. Xu Xuan was dumbfounded.

"If it were not for my respect for all of you," said Madam White, "I would keep him up there in the air for a year." She blew a puff of air, and the priest came down to the ground. How he wished his parents had given him two wings at birth! As he raced off, the crowd dispersed.

Needless to say, the husband and wife went back home together. With Madam White paying for the daily expenses, theirs was truly a harmonious conjugal life in which:

> *The husband sings, the wife follows;*
> *The mornings delightful, the nights joyous.*

Time flew by like a darting arrow. Again, the eighth day of the fourth month, Sakyamuni's birthday, rolled around. On the streets, people were seen taking donations from door to door and carrying cypress shrines to the monasteries where statues of Buddha would be washed. To Mr. Wang, Xu Xuan commented, "The customs here are the same as in Hangzhou."

At this point, a young neighbor called Iron Head remarked, "Brother Xiaoyi, there's a Buddhist gathering at Chengtian Monastery today. Why don't you go and take a look?"

Xu Xuan went inside and told Madam White about it. "What's there to see?" said she. "Don't go!"

"It'll just be a harmless little trip to kill some time," insisted Xu Xuan.

"If you're determined to go, let me dress you up. Your clothes are too old and ugly." So saying, she had Little Green bring over a few fashionable pieces of clothing, which turned out to fit him so well that they seemed to have been tailor-made for him. They included a black hat with a pair of white jade rings dangling at the back, a blue silk robe, and a pair of black boots. Carrying in his hand an exquisite folding silk fan bearing gold-traced portraits of women and adorned with a coral pendant, Xu Xuan looked the very picture of elegance from head to foot. In a voice as sweet as that of an oriole, the woman admonished him, "Come back early, husband! Don't make me worry about you!"

Accompanied by Iron Head, Xu Xuan went to Chengtian Monastery to watch the Buddhist gathering. Everyone who saw him gave a cheer, for he was a marvel to the eye. A man was heard saying, "Last night, some jewelry and other valuables worth four to five thousand strings of cash disappeared from Squire Zhou's pawnshop. They reported the case to the authorities, along with a list of the missing items. The search is on, but the thief hasn't been found yet."

Xu Xuan heard these words, but not seeing their significance, he continued to tour the monastery with Iron Head amid the jostling crowds of men and women who had come to offer incense. Then he told himself, "She wants me to be home early, so I'd better go." But, when he turned around, he didn't see Iron Head anywhere. As he went out the gate alone, he ran into a group of five or six men who looked like yamen lictors, with identification badges hanging at their waists. Upon taking one look at Xu Xuan, one of the men commented to the others, "What this man wears and holds in his hand look like you know what."

Another lictor, who happened to know Xu Xuan, accosted him, saying, "Master Xiaoyi, would you please show me your fan?"

An unsuspecting Xu Xuan handed the fan to him.

"Look!" the man exclaimed, "the pendant of this fan exactly fits the descriptions on the list!"

All shouting "Get him!" the men threw a rope over Xu Xuan and tied him up, much like

Black vultures chasing a baby swallow;
Hungry tigers devouring a lamb.

"This is a mistake," protested Xu Xuan. "I'm innocent!"

"Whether you are or not, we shall see when we get to Squire Zhou's house in front of the prefect's tribunal! They lost jewelry and other valuables worth five thousand strings of cash, a pair of white jade rings, and an exquisite folding fan with a coral pendant. How can you protest your innocence, with the actual stolen objects right here on you? And a reckless fellow you are, too, coming out into the open and showing them off from head to foot! What do you take us for?"

Xu Xuan was petrified. It was quite a while before he was able to speak. "So that's what happened," he said. "Yes, yes, there is indeed a thief."

"You can tell that to the Suzhou prefectural yamen," said the men.

The next day, the prefect called the court to order, and Xu Xuan was led into his presence. "Where are the valuables that you stole from Squire Zhou's treasury?" the prefect began. "Out with the truth, or you'll be put under the rod!"

"Your Honor, please do right by me! These clothes and everything else I'm wearing were given to me by my wife, Madam White. I have no idea where they're from, and that is the truth, as Your Honor will surely see in your wisdom!"

"Where is your wife?" thundered the prefect.

"She's on the upper floor of Mr. Wang's inn by Lucky Bridge."

Right away, the prefect ordered Arrest Officer Yuan Ziming to escort Xu Xuan there and bring the woman to court posthaste.

Stunned by the sight of Arrest Officer Yuan Ziming, the innkeeper, Mr. Wang, asked, "What is this all about?"

"Is Madam White upstairs?" asked Xu Xuan.

"Soon after you and Iron Head left for Chengtian Monastery, she said to me, 'My husband is off to the monastery for some fun. He told Little Green and me to take care of things upstairs, but he's been gone for so long that we're going to the monastery to look for him. Could you please keep an eye on our rooms?' And so they left. They did not return that night, and they haven't shown up so far. I thought you had all three gone to visit some relatives."

By order of the officers, Mr. Wang searched for Madam White throughout the house, back and front, but without success, whereupon Yuan Ziming brought Mr. Wang to see the prefect.

"Where is Madam White?" asked the prefect.

Mr. Wang gave a detailed account of what he knew and added, "Madam White must be an evil spirit."

After further questioning, the prefect announced, "Put Xu Xuan in jail for now!"

Through bribery, Mr. Wang managed to have himself released on bail to wait for a settlement of the case.

Now, Squire Zhou was sitting idly in the teahouse opposite his house when a servant came to report, "The jewelry and the valuables have all been found! They're right there in the treasury, in a trunk that used to be empty."

Upon hearing this, Squire Zhou rushed home and saw that the items were indeed there, with only the cap, the jade rings, the fan, and the pendant still missing. "All too clearly, they've wronged Xu Xuan, an innocent man," said he to himself, "and that's not right." Secretly, he approached the officials in charge of the case and pleaded with them to charge Xu Xuan for a minor offense only.

Now, Officer Li, who had been sent on a mission by Marshal Shao, went to Suzhou and took up lodging at Mr. Wang's inn. Upon hearing Mr. Wang's account of how Xu Xuan had first come to him and then been charged with a crime, Officer Li thought to himself, "Now I can't very well stand by and do nothing. He's a member of the family, after all." So he felt obliged to seek help from acquaintances and pay bribes high and low. (*Good for him, Officer Li!*) Finally, the prefect settled Xu Xuan's case after a thorough interrogation, attributing the offense squarely to Madam White and convicting Xu Xuan only on the charge of "failure to report the presence of an evil spirit to the authorities." He was given a hundred lashings and sentenced to a labor camp in Zhenjiang Prefecture, three hundred and sixty li away.

"Going to Zhenjiang is not bad," remarked Officer Li. "I have a sworn uncle, Li Keyong, who owns a medicinal herb store there by Needle Bridge. I'll write a letter for you to present to him." Left with no other choice, Xu Xuan borrowed travel money from his brother-in-law, took grateful leave of Mr. Wang and his brother-in-law, bought wine and a meal for the two yamen guards, and packed his belongings for the journey. Mr. Wang and his brother-in-law accompanied Xu Xuan for some distance before they returned home separately.

On the road, Xu Xuan and the guards ate and drank when necessary, traveling by day and resting at night. In a matter of days, they arrived in Zhenjiang. Xu Xuan's first priority was to seek out Li Keyong, so he found his way to the herb store by Needle Bridge, where he saw an assistant at the door, tending to his business. As Squire Li emerged from inside, the two guards and Xu Xuan hastened to chant their greetings. "I am a relative of Officer Li of Hangzhou," said Xu Xuan. "I have a letter from him."

The assistant took the letter and handed it to Squire Li, who opened and read it. "So, you are Xu Xuan, I presume?" asked the old gentleman.

"Yes, I am."

Li Keyong ordered that a meal be served to the three men. He then had a clerk take them to the prefectural yamen, where they delivered the official documents and paid to have Xu Xuan released on bail. The guards returned to Suzhou with the yamen's letter of reply, while Xu Xuan followed the clerk back to Squire Li's house, where Xu Xuan thanked Li Keyong and paid his respects to Mrs. Li. Li

Keyong said to her, having read Officer Li's letter, "Xu Xuan used to work in a medicinal herb store." Thereupon, he hired him to work in his store. At night, Xu Xuan slept on the upper floor of Mr. Wang's tofu store on Fifth Lane. Li Keyong came to be impressed by Xu Xuan's meticulous work.

The store already had two managers, a Manager Zhang and a Manager Zhao. The latter was by nature an honest and law-abiding man, whereas the former was a crafty and treacherous one who took advantage of his seniority to bully younger men. Displeased by the arrival of a newcomer because he feared his services might no longer be needed, he thought up an evil plan to give vent to his jealousy.

One day, Li Keyong paid a visit to the store and asked, "How's the newcomer doing?"

Manager Zhang thought to himself, "Here he falls into my trap!" Aloud, he said, "He's all right, except for one thing."

"What one thing?"

"He's interested only in the bigger transactions and turns away clients who don't bring much profit. That's why he's not popular among our clients. I've tried several times to talk some sense into him, but he just won't listen."

"I can easily take care of that," said old Squire Li. "Let me talk to him. He'll surely listen to me." (*The whole story is a fabrication.*)

Having overheard the conversation, Manager Zhao said privately to Manager Zhang, "We should all be nice to one another. Since Xu Xuan is a newcomer, you and I should by rights be taking good care of him. If he does anything wrong, we should tell him face-to-face rather than criticize him behind his back. If he hears about this, he'll say we're jealous." (*Manager Zhang* [illegible].)

"What does a young man like you know?" snapped Manager Zhang.

The hour being late, they went back to their respective lodgings.

Later, Manager Zhao went to Xu Xuan's place and offered him this advice, "Manager Zhang spoke ill of you to the squire out of jealousy, so you should be more careful. In future, just remember to treat clients alike, regardless of the volume of the sales."

"It's so kind of you to give me this advice," said Xu Xuan gratefully. "Let's go for a drink!"

The two men went to a wineshop and took their seats. After the waiter set out the dishes they had ordered, they drank a few cups of wine.

"The old squire is a straightforward man who can't stand being contradicted, so you'd do well to humor him and be patient in your work," admonished Zhao.

"Many thanks for your kindness! How can I ever thank you enough?" exclaimed Xu Xuan.

After another couple of drinks, Zhao said, noticing that it was quite dark, "It's late. We'd better go before the roads are too dark for walking. We'll meet again some other time."

Xu Xuan paid the bill, and they went their separate ways. Feeling the influence of the wine, Xu Xuan was afraid that he might inadvertently bump into people and chose to make his way home under the eaves of the houses along the street. As he was walking, a window above him opened, and down onto his head came a stream of ashes from charcoal used to heat irons. He stopped in his tracks and cursed, "What swine did that? Don't you have eyes? What a thing to do!"

A woman hurried downstairs and apologized, "Please don't get angry, sir! It was my fault for being so careless. Please don't take it amiss!"

In his half-drunken state, Xu Xuan raised his eyes and saw that the woman was none other than Madam White. Rage seized him. With the flames of fury leaping three thousand feet high, he burst out, "You foul evil spirit! A fine mess you got me into! I've been punished twice by the law because of you!" As the saying goes, he who harbors no indignation is no gentleman; he who is free of venom is not destined for greatness. Truly,

> *Iron boots are worn out in the hunt for her;*
> *But here she is; you need not have searched.*

"Why do you always appear wherever I am? If you are not an evil spirit, I don't know what is!" So saying, Xu Xuan lunged forward and held Madam White in a firm grip. "Do you want to settle this in or out of court?"

"Husband," Madam White said with a placating smile, "as they say, husband and wife for one night, tender lovers for a hundred nights. I have a long story to tell you. Listen to me. The clothes were left behind by my deceased husband. It was out of my deep love for you that I asked you to put them on. How could you repay my kindness with such hostility and turn me into an enemy?"

"But why did you disappear when I came back that day to look for you? Mr. Wang said that you and Little Green went to the monastery to look for me. And how is it you manage to be here now?"

"I did go to the monastery, where I heard that you had been captured and taken away. I had Little Green make inquiries, but she wasn't able to find out anything more. We thought that you must have escaped. I was afraid they would be after me next, so I had Little Green hire a boat and we hurried to my uncle's home in Jiankang Prefecture. I arrived here only yesterday. I know that I got you in trouble with the law twice, and I wondered how I would ever have the nerve to face you! Scolding me won't serve any purpose now. But since we were a loving wedded couple, we can't very well end the relationship just like that, can we? After all, you and I had vowed to live the rest of our lives together in a love as eternal as Mount Tai and the East Sea. For the sake of old times, could you take me to your lodging? Wouldn't it be nice if you and I could grow old together until the end of our days?"

Upon hearing these honeyed words, Xu Xuan felt his anger turn to joy. He lapsed into silence, but lust took possession of him, and thoughts of being with her began to stir in him. Instead of returning to his lodging, he spent the night with Madam White at her place upstairs.

The next day, upon returning to Mr. Wang's inn on Fifth Lane, he announced to Mr. Wang, "My wife and maid have come from Suzhou." After explaining further, he added, "I'd like to have them move in here and join me."

"How nice! You needn't have asked!" exclaimed Mr. Wang.

That very day, Madam White and Little Green moved into Mr. Wang's inn and took up lodging on the upper floor. The following day, they held a tea party for the neighbors, and the day after that, the neighbors reciprocated in Xu Xuan's honor. The feast over, the neighbors dispersed and went their separate ways, but of this, no more need be said.

On the fourth day, Xu Xuan rose early and, after combing his hair and washing, said to Madam White, "I'm going to see the neighbors and thank them and then go to work. You and Little Green just stay where you are and keep an eye on the place. Don't, on any account, go out the door!" After this admonition, he went to the store to tend to the business, and henceforth, he left early for work and came home late in the evening.

Time flashed by, and the sun and moon shot back and forth like a busy shuttle on a loom. Another month went by.

One day, Xu Xuan asked Madam White if she could visit his employer Squire Li and the Squire's wife and family. Madam White said, "Since you're working for him, it's only right that I go to see him, so that there will be more mutual visits in the future."

The next day, a hired sedan-chair was brought to the house for Madam White. With Mr. Wang carrying gift boxes on a pole over his shoulder and Little Green bringing up the rear, they went to Squire Li's house. Madam White got out of the sedan-chair, went into the house, and asked to see the squire. Li Keyong emerged with alacrity from the interior of the house to greet her. Madam White curtsied deeply and bowed twice to Mr. Li and then twice to Mrs. Li before presenting herself to the other women of the family.

Now, this Li Keyong, albeit advanced in years, was a lustful man. At the sight of Madam White's ravishing beauty, truly,

> His three souls took leave of his body;
> His seven spirits gave him the slip.

The squire gazed raptly at Madam White. As dinner was served in honor of the guests, Mrs. Li commented to her husband, "What a nice young woman! She's not only beautiful but also gentle, courteous, meek, and well behaved."

"Hangzhou women are indeed pretty," the squire remarked. After the meal, Madam White thanked the hosts and returned home.

Li Keyong thought to himself, "What must I do to spend a night with that woman?" As he knitted his brows, he hit on a plan. "My birthday is coming up on the thirteenth day of the sixth month. I can take my own sweet time and make her fall into my trap that day!"

Time flew by. Soon after the Dragon Boat Festival was over, the sixth month began. The squire said to his wife, "Mother, the thirteenth being my birthday, let's set out a feast and invite relatives and friends for an entire day of fun. It will be a joyous day to remember for the rest of my life."

That very day, invitations were sent to relatives, neighbors, friends, and assistants of Squire Li's store. The next day, all the invited guests came to offer gifts of candles, noodles, and handkerchiefs. On the thirteenth, the [male] guests attended the feast, which was an all day affair. On the following day, the women came to offer their congratulations. About twenty women arrived, including Madam White, who was extravagantly arrayed in a blue blouse woven with golden thread, and a scarlet gauze skirt and her hair glittered with hairpins of silver, gold, pearl, and jade. Taking Little Green with her, she went inside to offer birthday wishes to Squire Li and pay her respects to the hostess.

A feast was laid out in the east hall. In point of fact, Li Keyong was a miser who, if he were to eat a flea, would save a hind leg for later. It was out of his lust for Madam White's beauty and for the purpose of trapping her that he set this grand feast. (*Feminine beauty can change a miser's ways.* [Illegible].) The wine cups were passed around the feast table, and in the midst of the drinking, Madam White rose to go to the lavatory. Squire Li had already instructed his most trusted maidservant to lead Madam White to a secluded room behind the house should she need to relieve herself. Having thus drawn up his plans, he hid himself there in anticipation. Truly,

> *He need not scale walls or crawl into holes*
> *But steals the fragrant jade, risk-free.*

So when Madam White rose to relieve herself, the maidservant led her to the secluded room behind the house, as instructed. After the maidservant left, the squire, finding it hard to suppress his lustful longings and yet afraid to go straight in, peeked through a chink in the door. Everything would have been all right had he not taken that peek, but he did, and the sight that met his eyes gave him such a shock that he turned on his heels and ran. As soon as he gained the rear section of the house, he collapsed on his back.

> *Dead or alive, no one could be sure,*
> *But his limbs were not moving at all.*

What the squire had seen was no pretty woman but a coiled-up white snake, its body as thick as a water bucket and its eyes as large as lanterns, emitting a myriad of golden rays. (*The evil spirit is showing its true shape at last, but by choosing this*

*moment to do so, it scares off Squire Li. How remarkable that an evil spirit should
also know the importance of chastity!*)

Scared half to death, he turned on his heels and ran, but stumbled and fell.
When the maidservants helped him up, they saw that his face was green and his
lips were white. Terrified, a store assistant fed him pills to pacify his spirits. When
he came to, his wife and the guests who had joined the crowd around him asked,
"What happened to frighten you like that?"

Instead of telling the truth, Squire Li replied, "I got up too early this morning,
and I've been working too hard these last few days. All this brought on a headache
so bad that I passed out." After he was taken to his own room to lie down in bed,
the guests resumed their seats at the table and drank a few more cups of wine before
thankfully taking their leave when the feast came to an end.

Back at home, Madam White gave herself up to thinking, for she was afraid
that Squire Li would tell Xu Xuan her true form the next day when they met in the
store. An idea came to her. While she was taking off her clothes, she heaved a sigh.

"Why are you sighing? Didn't you have fun at the feast?"

"Husband, you won't believe this! Squire Li was in fact using the birthday
celebrations to cover up his evil designs. When I went to the lavatory, I had no idea
that he was already hiding there. He tried to force himself on me, tugging at my
skirt and pants. I almost screamed but was afraid to alarm all the people there. So
I knocked him down. He was too ashamed to admit the truth and told them that
he had fainted. Curse my luck! If only I could get back at him!"

"Since he didn't have his way with you in the end, we'll just have to put up with
it because he's my employer. We have no other choice. Just don't accept his next invitation, and that will be it."

"What? How are you going to face the world if you don't take my side and do
something about it?"

"Well, my brother-in-law wrote to him on my behalf asking for his help, and
he was kind enough to take me on as a manager of his store. What do you want me
to do now?"

"What kind of man are you? He took liberties with me, and you'll continue
working for him?"

"But where do you want me to go? How am I going to make a living?"

"A store manager is a lowly position. It would be better if we could have an
herb store of our own."

"It's all very well for you to say, but where's the money?"

"You needn't worry. That can be easily taken care of. I'll give you some silver
tomorrow so you can rent a house first, and we'll go from there."

As the saying goes, "What's true today was true in olden times, and what was
true in olden times is true today." Everywhere, there are, and have always been,
people who go out of their way to help others. Living next door to them was a man

called Jiang He, who, throughout his life, was given to altruistic deeds. The next day, equipped with Madam White's silver, Xu Xuan asked Jiang He to rent a house by the Zhenjiang ferry pier and buy a set of drawered cabinets in which he could gradually lay up a stock of medicinal herbs. By the tenth month of the year, with all the necessary preparations completed, a day was chosen for the opening of the store, and Xu Xuan quit his job. Troubled by an uneasy conscience, Squire Li knew better than to call him back.

After he opened the store, Xu Xuan found to his surprise that his business prospered day by day and was yielding substantial profits. He was selling medicinal herbs at the door one day when a monk approached with a register of alms, saying, "I'm a monk from Golden Hill Monastery. The seventh day of the seventh month is the birthday of Yinglie the Dragon King. I humbly ask you to offer incense and make donations at the monastery for the occasion."

"You don't have to record my name in your book, but I have here a piece of fine fragrant wood[8] that you can burn as incense." So saying, Xu Xuan opened a cabinet, took out the wood, and handed it to the monk. The monk accepted the piece of wood, saying, "Please be at the monastery on that day!" With a bow, he left.

Having witnessed the scene, Madam White remarked, "How foolish of you to give that lousy bald one such a good piece of wood. He's only going to buy wine and meat with it!"

"I gave it to him in good faith. If he squanders it, that's his problem." (*Both are right.*)

All too quickly, it was again the seventh day of the seventh month. Xu Xuan opened up the shop and saw that the street was a scene of bustling traffic. Jiang He, who was helping out, suggested, "Master Xiaoyi, since you made a donation the other day, why don't you take a trip to the monastery today just for fun?"

"Let me get my things in order and then we can go together. Wait for me a little while."

"All right, I'll go with you."

Xu Xuan hastily put things in order and went to the interior of the house, where he said to Madam White, "I'm going to Golden Hill Monastery to burn some incense. You take care of the house."

Madam White replied, "As the saying goes, 'One never goes to the temple without a reason.' Now, what's your reason for going?"

"First, I've never been there, so I want to see it. Second, having given a donation the other day, I'd like to offer some incense."

"If you're so determined to go, I can't stop you, but you have to promise me three things."

"What three things?"

"First, don't go into the abbot's cell. Second, don't talk with the monks. Third, come back as soon as possible. If you don't, I'll have to come and get you."

"Fair enough. I'll do as you say." He changed into clean clothes, shoes, and stockings and slipped his incense box into his sleeve. Then, together with Jiang He, he walked to the riverside, got on a boat, and went to Golden Hill Monastery.

They started their tour from Dragon King Hall, where they burned incense. Afterward, they took a leisurely walk around the monastery. Xu Xuan followed the crowd and was approaching the door of the abbot's cell when he suddenly recalled his wife's admonition. "My wife warned me not to enter the abbot's cell," he said. He stopped in his tracks and stayed outside.

"It's all right," said Jiang He. "She's at home, so she won't know. Just tell her you didn't go in." (*What a liar!*) With that, they went in, took a look around, and came out.

Sitting in the center seat in the cell was a monk of great moral integrity. With finely marked eyebrows, bright eyes, a round head, and a monk's robe, he did indeed possess the looks of a truly great master. At the sight of Xu Xuan passing by, he called out to his attendant, "Bring me that young man, quick!"

The attendant looked around, but unable to recall the young man's features as he stared at the masses of people before him, he said to the abbot, "I have no idea where he's gone."

At these words, the abbot picked up his cane and left the cell to search on his own. He didn't see Xu Xuan anywhere and went outside, where a crowd was waiting for the stormy waves to subside before embarking on the boats. But the tempest rose higher. Amid laments of "This is no time to go," there, for all to see, came a boat speeding toward them as if on wings.

Xu Xuan commented to Jiang He, "This big storm has stranded all of us here. How can that boat go so fast?" Even as he spoke, the boat drew near. Two women, one in white and one in green, were seen coming to shore. What was Xu Xuan's astonishment when, upon a closer look, he found them to be Madam White and Little Green!

As they gained the shore, Madam White called out, "Why didn't you come back earlier? Get on the boat, quick!"

Xu Xuan was about to board when a voice was heard shouting from behind, "What is that foul beast doing here?"

As Xu Xuan turned around, he heard voices saying, "Abbot Fahai is here!"

"You foul beast!" continued the abbot. "This old monk is here to make sure you won't dare come again and do harm to people!"

At the sight of the monk, Madam White rowed the boat away from the shore. Then, she and Little Green tipped the boat over and disappeared into the water.

Xu Xuan bowed to the abbot, saying, "Your Reverence, please save this worthless life of mine!"

"How did you meet that woman?" asked the abbot, whereupon Xu Xuan recounted all that had happened.

After listening to his story, the abbot said, "That woman is an evil spirit. Now, go back to Hangzhou as soon as possible. If she comes to pester you again, you can find me at Clear Mercy Monastery south of the lake. Let me give you a quatrain:

> *"An evil spirit in the shape of a woman,*
> *Her voice rings sweet by West Lake.*
> *Unsuspecting, you fell into her trap;*
> *When in distress, come to me south of the lake."*

Thankfully, Xu Xuan took leave of Abbot Fahai and embarked on a ferry boat with Jiang He. After crossing the river, he went ashore and returned home, but Madam White and Little Green were not there. Now convinced that they were evil spirits, he had Jiang He spend the night with him to keep him company. He felt so miserable that he did not sleep a wink throughout the night. The next morning, he rose early and had Jiang He take care of the house while he went to Li Keyong's house by Needle Bridge and told the squire everything that had happened.

Squire Li said, "On that day during my birthday celebrations, I ran into her accidentally when she went to the lavatory and saw her in her true beastly form. I was scared to death, but I didn't dare tell you about it. Now that things have come to this, why don't you move into my house while you decide what to do next?"

Xu Xuan thanked Squire Li and moved in. Quite unnoticeably, two months slipped by.

One day, he was standing by the door when he saw the local headman going from door to door, soliciting donations of incense, flowers, lanterns, and candles to celebrate the imperial court's amnesty. Emperor Gaozong had designated his heir apparent, who was later to be Emperor Xiaozong, and an amnesty was granted to mark the occasion. Except those convicted of homicide, all prisoners throughout the land were released and allowed to return home. Jubilantly, Xu Xuan intoned a poem:

> *"The emperor be praised for this act of mercy!*
> *The freed convict gains a new lease on life.*
> *I am not fated to die in an alien land*
> *But will resume my life in my hometown.*
> *My ill-starred meeting with the demon brought me woe;*
> *I never dreamed that I'd be cleared of all charges.*
> *On my return, I shall fill the house with incense*
> *To thank the cosmos for a life reborn."*

After intoning the poem, he asked Squire Li to present gifts of money to those high and low throughout the yamen. He then had an audience with the prefect and was given a pass for his return journey to his hometown. He offered his thanks to the neighbors, Squire Li's wife and other members of the Li family, old and young, as well as the two managers. Carrying with him some local products that the ever helpful Jiang He had bought for him at his request, he made his way back to Hangzhou.

As he bowed four times to his brother-in-law Officer Li and his sister, his brother-in-law said in irritation, "How arrogant you can be! Twice I wrote letters of recommendation on your behalf, but you never even bothered to write and tell me that you were married at Squire Li's place. What a false-hearted scoundrel you are!"

"But I'm not married."

"Two days ago, a woman who claimed to be your wife came here with her maid, saying that you couldn't be found anywhere after your trip to Golden Hill Monastery on the seventh day of the seventh month. After learning that you were returning to Hangzhou, they came here and have been waiting for you for two days." So saying, the brother-in-law had a servant summon the woman and the maid. Who should appear but Madam White and Little Green! Xu Xuan was flabbergasted. Not wishing to give a detailed explanation to his brother-in-law and sister, he listened resignedly to a harsh lecture, after which Officer Li told him to retire with Madam White to a room assigned to them.

Seeing that it was now getting dark, Xu Xuan grew afraid of Madam White. Nervously, he fell to his knees, facing her but not daring to go near her, and pleaded, "Please spare my life, whoever you are, goddess or evil spirit!"

"What are you doing, Brother Xiaoyi?" said Madam White. "In all our married years, I've never done you any wrong. Why are you saying such absurd things?"

"Since I've known you, you've twice gotten me in trouble with the law. I went to Zhenjiang Prefecture, and you came after me. The other day, I was just a little late returning from a trip to Golden Hill Monastery, and you had to run after me with Little Green. When you jumped into the river at the sight of the abbot, I thought you had died. What a surprise when you turned up again here, and before I arrived, too! Please have mercy!"

Her fiendish eyes wide open, Madam White said, "Brother Xiaoyi, I did everything out of the best of intentions, little knowing that I would turn out to be the cause of such resentment! We were a loving couple, sharing the same pillow and the same quilt, and yet you had to believe some vicious gossip meant to sow dissension between us. Let me tell you something frankly. If you do as I say, everybody will be happy and every grudge forgotten. But if you betray me, I'll drench the whole town in a bloodbath and toss everyone from wave to wave in the river until all die violent deaths."

Xu Xuan trembled with fear and was speechless for quite a while, nor did he dare take a step forward. Then Little Green spoke in a pacifying tone, "Madam loves you because of your Hangzhou native's good looks and your deep affection for her. Now listen to me and make up with her. Have no more suspicions."

Thus under pressure from both of them, Xu Xuan cried out, "Woe is me!"

Upon hearing the cry, his sister, who was enjoying the cool air in the courtyard, rushed to their door. Believing it to be just another conjugal fight, she dragged Xu Xuan out of the room, whereupon Madam White closed the door and went to sleep alone.

When Xu Xuan was giving his sister a detailed account of everything that had happened, his brother-in-law returned from the courtyard. The sister told him, "They just had a fight. I wonder if she has gone to sleep or not. Could you go take a look?"

Accordingly, Officer Li went up to Madam White's room, but since the lamp had gone out, there was only a faint glimmer inside. So, he wetted the window paper with his tongue and looked in through the hole. Everything would have been all right had he not looked, but since he did, he saw a python with a body as thick as a water bucket sleeping in the bed, its head resting against the skylight so it could take in fresh air. Its shining white scales made the room as light as day. (*Judging from the case of Empress Wu, how do we know that this white snake is not a beautiful woman? Who is to say that a white snake can't change into a beautiful woman?*) In shock, he turned on his heels and fled.

Back in his own room, instead of telling anyone what he had seen, he said, "She's gone to bed. There isn't a sound." But Xu Xuan still hid himself in his sister's room, not daring to show his face, nor did his brother-in-law question him. The night passed without further ado.

The next day, Officer Li took Xu Xuan outside to a secluded spot and asked, "Where did you get this wife of yours? Tell me the truth! Don't hide anything from me! Last night, I saw with my own eyes that she is a big white snake. I didn't say anything at the time because I didn't want to frighten your sister."

Upon learning the entire story, Officer Li said, "In that case, let's go to Mr. Dai, the snake charmer in front of White Horse Temple. He's good at catching snakes."

The two men proceeded to White Horse Temple and saw Mr. Dai standing right there by the gate. "Greetings to you, sir!" they called out.

"What can I do for you?"

"There's a big python in our house," said Xu Xuan. "Could you please go and catch it?"

"Where is your house?"

"It's Officer Li's house on Black Pearl Lane by Reward the Troops Bridge." Taking out a tael of silver, Xu Xuan added, "Please take this for now. We'll have more to offer you by way of thanks after the snake is caught."

Mr. Dai took the silver and said, "You can go home now, gentlemen. I'll come right away." So Officer Li and Xu Xuan returned home by themselves.

Armed with a bottle of medicated wine,[9] Mr. Dai headed straight for Black Pearl Lane and asked for directions to Officer Li's house. Upon being told that it was the very two-storied house up ahead, he went to the door, lifted the portiere, and coughed, but no one came to answer. He kept knocking on the door until a young woman emerged. "Which family are you looking for?" she asked.

"Is this Officer Li's home?"

"Yes."

"I heard that there's a big snake in the house. Two gentlemen just came to ask me to catch it for them."

"How can there be a snake in our house? You're quite mistaken."

"The gentlemen gave me one tael of silver, saying that they'll have a handsome reward for me after the snake is caught."

"But there is no snake," insisted Madam White. "Don't believe the nonsense they told you."

"Why would they play tricks on me?"

Her repeated attempts to drive him away were futile, and Madam White grew impatient. "Do you really know how to catch snakes? I'm afraid you won't be able to get this one!"

"We've had seven or eight generations of snake charmers in our family. Why wouldn't I be able to get this particular snake?"

"You may very well say so," retorted Madam White, "but I'm afraid you'll want to get out of here as soon as you see it!"

"I won't! If I do, I'll let you fine me one ingot of silver."

"Follow me, then."

When they got to the courtyard, the woman turned a corner and disappeared into the house. Bottle of wine in hand, Mr. Dai stood in the empty courtyard. Soon, a chilly wind sprang up. As it blew past, a python with a body as thick as a water bucket thrust fiercely at him. Truly,

> The human means no harm to the tiger;
> The tiger is bent on harming the human.

A terrified Mr. Dai fell backward, smashing his bottle of medicated wine. The python lunged forward as if to bite him, its blood-red mouth wide open, showing its snow-white fangs. He scrambled desperately to his feet and, regretting that his parents had not endowed him with two extra legs, ran all the way across the bridge in one breath. There, he bumped into Officer Li and Xu Xuan.

Xu Xuan asked, "How did it go?"

"Let me tell you what happened." After recounting the event, he took out the tael of silver and returned it to Officer Li, adding, "Had I not been blessed with these two legs of mine, I would have died. Now, you gentlemen save this for someone else." With that, he scurried off.

"Brother-in-law, what are we going to do now?" asked Xu Xuan.

"Well, we know for sure that she's an evil spirit. Now, Zhang Cheng of Red Hill Town owes me a thousand strings of cash. You go there, wait patiently, and rent a room. With you out of its sight, that monster will surely leave."

Xu Xuan saw no alternative but to agree. Upon arriving at home with his brother-in-law, he found the house quiet with nothing astir. Officer Li wrote a letter and put it in an envelope, along with the receipt of the loan, for Xu Xuan to take with him to Red Hill Town.

At this point, Madam White called Xu Xuan to her room. "The audacity!" she said. "Hiring a snake charmer to get me! If you are good to me, I'll be as kind as a Buddha to you. Otherwise, I'll have to make the entire population of the town suffer and die violent deaths!"

Shaking with fright, Xu Xuan dared not utter a word. In low spirits, he took the envelope and went to Red Hill Town, where he found Zhang Cheng. When he tried to take the loan receipt out of his sleeve, he realized it was gone. With a cry of anguish, he turned back, looking for it along the way, but without success. Dejected, he found himself in front of Clear Mercy Monastery, which suddenly reminded him that Abbot Fahai of Golden Hill Monastery had told him that if that evil spirit followed him to Hangzhou to pester him again, he could find the monk at Clear Mercy Monastery. He thought to himself, "Now is the time to do that. What am I waiting for?" Without a moment's delay, he entered the monastery and asked the head monk, "Your Reverence, is Abbot Fahai here?"

"No, he's not here."

These words made him feel even more miserable. He turned around and proceeded to Long Bridge. Stopping at the foot of the bridge, he said to himself, "As the proverb goes, 'When down and out, one falls easy victim to the devil.' Why would I want to hang on to life?" Gazing at the clear water, he prepared to jump into the lake. Truly,

> *If King Yama wants you at the third watch,*[10]
> *He won't let you live till the fourth watch.*

He was about to throw himself into the water when he heard a voice behind him calling out, "Why would a grown man want to kill himself? Don't you know that ten thousand deaths can be easily written off as only five thousand when you count them in pairs? Don't you see the worthlessness of death? Why don't you ask for my help when you find yourself in trouble?"

Xu Xuan turned around and whom did he see but Abbot Fahai! His cassock and alms bowl on his back, his cane in his hand, he had indeed just arrived. Xu

Xuan was not destined to die at this hour after all, for if the abbot had tarried for as long as it takes to eat a bowl of rice, Xu Xuan would have perished. At the sight of the abbot, he bowed deeply, saying, "Please save my life!"

"Where is that cursed beast?"

Xu Xuan told him what had happened, adding, "She's after me again. Please save me, Your Reverence."

The abbot produced an alms bowl from his sleeve and handed it to Xu Xuan, saying, "After you get home, don't let her know you're back, and place the bowl firmly over her head. Press it down hard. Don't panic. You may go home now."

Xu Xuan thankfully took leave of the abbot and returned home. There, he saw Madam White, seated and muttering to herself, "I wonder who poisoned my husband's mind against me. I'll have it out with him when I find out!"

Now, just as a person with a plan waits for the right moment to pounce on the unsuspecting party, Xu Xuan sneaked up on Madam White from behind and put the bowl over her head. As he applied all his weight on the bowl, the woman disappeared, but he kept pushing the bowl down without ever letting up. A voice from inside the bowl pleaded, "How can you be so heartless after we have lived together as husband and wife for all these years? Release the bowl just a little bit!"

Xu Xuan was wondering what to do when he heard the announcement, "There's a monk here who says he's come to subdue an evil spirit."

Xu Xuan immediately asked Officer Li to invite the abbot into the house. "Please save me!" pleaded Xu Xuan.

After muttering goodness knows what words to himself, the abbot gently lifted the bowl, and there for all to see was Madam White, reduced to a length of only seven or eight inches, looking like a puppet, her eyes tightly closed and her body huddled up on the floor. The abbot shouted, "What are you? How dare you pester human beings? Tell me everything!"

"Abbot, I am a python. In a raging storm of wind and rain one day, I went to West Lake to find shelter and joined Little Green there. And then, something unanticipated happened. I met Xu Xuan. Unable to control my desires, I violated the heavenly rules, but I never took a life. Please have mercy on me, Abbot!" (*One can hardly find her equal anywhere!*)

"And what exactly is Little Green?" the abbot persisted.

"She's a carp from the pond under the third bridge in West Lake. She acquired immortality after a thousand years of spiritual cultivation. I met her quite by accident and made her my companion. She hasn't had any fun, not even for one day. Please have pity on her, Abbot!" (*In such a desperate situation, she still remembers to put in a good word for Little Green. A truly kind evil spirit she is!*)

"I'll spare your lives, considering the thousand years of spiritual cultivation that you have undertaken. Now show your true selves!"

Madam White refused. In a rage, the abbot intoned an incantation and shouted, "Guardian of the Buddha-truth [*lokapala*]! Where might you be? Get me the carp, and make it and the white snake show their true forms so that I may render judgment on them!"

In a trice, a fierce wind sprang up in the yard. After the wind had swept past, a carp more than ten feet long fell from mid-air with a heavy thud. It bounced on the ground a few times before shrinking into a small carp one foot in length. By this time, Madam White had also been reduced to her true form as a three-foot-long white snake, staring at Xu Xuan, its head raised high. The abbot put the snake and the carp in the bowl, sealed it with a piece of cloth torn from his cassock, and took it to Thunder Peak Monastery. He laid the bowl on the ground in front of the monastery and ordered men to transport bricks and stones to the site to build a pagoda. Later, Xu Xuan sought donations and with the money thus raised made it into a magnificent seven-story pagoda. For tens of thousands of years, the white snake and the carp were not to be freed from that spot.

Let us retrace our steps and come back to the moment when the abbot laid the bowl on the ground. He intoned the following quatrain:

> *"When West Lake is drained of its water,*
> *When all the rivers and the lakes run dry,*
> *When Thunder Peak Pagoda falls down,*
> *Only then may the white snake see the light of day."*

Abbot Fahai then intoned another eight lines as a warning to posterity:

> *"Be advised! Do not abandon yourselves to lust;*
> *Those who do will be held under its spell.*
> *Evil eschews the pure in heart;*
> *Bane visits not the virtuous.*
> *Consider how Xu Xuan, a victim to his lust,*
> *Found himself in trouble with the law.*
> *Had it not been for this old monk's succor,*
> *The white snake would have swallowed him whole."*

After the abbot finished intoning this poem, the crowd dispersed, but Xu Xuan stayed behind to ask to join the Buddhist order. Honoring the abbot as his mentor, he took the tonsure right there by Thunder Peak Pagoda and became a monk. After several years of spiritual cultivation, he willed his death while sitting in his seat one evening. The assembly of monks in the monastery bought a monk's coffin for him, had his body cremated, and built a tower for his ashes as a monument to his eternal memory. Before he died, he also wrote a poem by way of an admonition to posterity:

The abbot delivered me from the mortal world;
The iron tree burst into spring blossoms.
The wheel of life and death goes round and round;
Reincarnation occurs life after life.
The phenomenal world is elusive,
The formless, in fact, is not lacking in form.
The Form is the Void; the Void is the Form;
Yet the two should be clearly set apart.

6

Du Shiniang Sinks Her Jewel Box in Anger

With the Mongols wiped out, the new capital was born
Midst the grandeur of dragon- and phoenix-shaped hills.
On its east, the vast sea joins the sky;
On its west, the Taihang Mountains stretch afar.
The frontiers well guarded by the nine garrisons,
The emperor revered by all countries,
Peace reigns throughout the blissful land;
The empire shines forever with the sun.

This is a poem in praise of the magnificence of Yanjing, capital of this dynasty. The city is so situated that it is protected by an impregnable mountain pass to the north and is poised for a descent on the central plains to the south. It is indeed a richly endowed and indestructible city, destined to last for ten thousand years.

The dynasty began when Emperor Taizu of the Hongwu reign period [1368–98] wiped out the Mongols and founded the capital in Jinling, which became Nanjing, or the Southern Capital. Later, Emperor Chengzu of the Yongle reign period [1403–24] raised an army from Beiping, put down a rebellion, and moved the capital to Yanjing, which became Beijing, or the Northern Capital. This move transformed the desolate region into a world of opulence and prosperity. After the Yongle reign, the throne passed through nine successions to Emperor Shenzong of the Wanli reign period [1573–1620], the eleventh emperor of this dynasty. With sharp intelligence, an impressive bearing, and a virtuous nature, and richly blessed by fate, he ascended the throne at the age of ten. During the forty-eight years of his reign, he had one invasion repelled and two rebellions suppressed. Which ones? An invasion of Korea by the Japanese *kanpaku* Hideyoshi[1] and two rebellions by Bo Chen'en of Xixia and Yang Yinglong of Bozhou, both local officials of non-Han origin.[2] They were all wiped out, one after another. In awe, distant tribes vied with one another in coming from afar to offer tributes. Truly,

Divine blessings on one brought joy to all;
The four seas tranquil, the empire at peace.

Our story begins with the twentieth year of the Wanli reign period [1592], when the *kanpaku* of Japan invaded Korea. In response to an emergency appeal for help from the king of Korea, our Heavenly Court dispatched troops across the sea to go to his aid. With the endorsement of the emperor, the Ministry of Revenue announced that the National University would be open, for the time being, to any student who could offer tribute, to make up for the shortfall in army provisions. Now, status as a tribute student at the National University had the following advantages: the opportunity to study, eligibility for the imperial civil service examinations and a greater chance of passing them, and, when all's said and done, a none-too-shabby career. Therefore, the sons of officials and rich families gave up attempts to sit for the examinations even at the preliminary level, and once a precedent was set, they all followed suit and bought their way into the National University. The number of tribute students increased to more than a thousand on each campus of the university in the two capitals.[3]

Among the new tribute students was a certain Li Jia, courtesy name Ganxian. A native of Shaoxing Prefecture, Zhejiang, he was the oldest of the three sons of a Provincial Commissioner Li. He started his formal education at an early age but had not yet achieved success at the examinations. He took advantage of the new practice and was admitted to the National University in Beijing. While in the capital, he toured the courtesans' quarters with a fellow student from his hometown, Liu Yuchun, and, there, he met a celebrated courtesan by the name of Du Mei. Being tenth in seniority among the courtesans of the house, she was called by all and sundry Du Shiniang [Tenth Girl].

> *Her body full of grace and charm,*
> *Her skin soft and fragrant,*
> *Her brows the color and shape of distant hills,*
> *Her eyes as limpid as autumn water,*
> *Her cheeks as lovely as lotus petals,*
> *She was the very image of Zhuo Wenjun.[4]*
> *Her lips the shape of a cherry,*
> *She was a veritable Fan Su.[5]*
> *How sad that such a piece of flawless jade*
> *Has fallen by misfortune into the world of lust!*

Now age nineteen, Du Shiniang had lost her virginity when she was thirteen. In those seven years, she had taken on goodness knows how many young men from rich and noble families, who were, one and all, so enamored of her that they were ready to throw away their family fortunes for her sake. There came into circulation among the courtesans' quarters a four-line song that says,

> *With Du Shiniang at the dining table,*
> *Those who hardly drink drain a thousand cups.*

He who gets to see Du Mei the beauty
Turns up his nose at a thousand powdered faces.

Now, young Mr. Li was a romantically inclined young man who had never before encountered a real beauty. Acquaintance with Du Shiniang threw him into such ecstasy that he lavished on her all the love he had in him. With his handsome face, gentle temperament, free-spending habits, and eager attentiveness, he won her heart, and the two grew deeply attached to each other. Having observed the madam's greed and treachery, Shiniang had long wished to leave the brothel and get married, and now, impressed by Li Jia's kindly disposition and his devotion to her, she was quite inclined to marry him. However, Li stood in such fear of his father that he dared not commit himself. Even so, their love deepened. They gave themselves up to pleasure from morning till night, spending as much time together as if they were a lawfully wedded couple and swearing eternal love and fidelity. Truly,

Their love was deeper than the sea,
Their devotion higher than the mountains.

Now, as Madam Du's girl was thus occupied with Li Jia, other patrons with well-lined pockets were denied access to the one whose reputation had drawn them to the establishment. When Li spent extravagantly in the beginning, the madam wore an ingratiating smile, humbly bent her shoulders, and busily danced attendance on him. With the sun and the moon exchanging places day after day, all too quickly, more than a year went by. Li's funds began to run out. As his payments dwindled, much against his wishes, the madam began to give him the cold shoulder. Provincial Commissioner Li, having heard about his son's involvement with a house of ill repute, wrote the young man one letter after another, demanding that he return home, but Li Junior was so enamored of Shiniang's beauty that he postponed his return again and again. Reports of his father's outbursts at home only added to his fear of returning.

The ancients said, "Friendship based on profit falls apart when the money runs out." But since Du Shiniang's feelings for the young man were genuine, the less he had in his pocket, the more passionate her love became. Time and again, the madam urged Shiniang to put Li Jia out, and when her words fell on deaf ears, she turned on the young man herself, hurling insults at him, in attempts to provoke him into leaving. But, being of a gentle nature, he grew even meeker in his responses. (*A good-for-nothing with no pride in him!*) In exasperation, the madam screamed at Shiniang day after day, saying, "In this line of business, we depend on our patrons for a living, sending the old ones out the front door and greeting the new ones at the back. The more activity there is in the house, the higher our pile of money. With that Li Jia making a nuisance of himself here for more than a year now, old patrons are not coming, not to speak of new ones! The way he scares away every soul with any money to offer, he's a veritable incarnation of Zhong Kui![6] Now look at this house! There may still be breath left in us, but there's certainly no kitchen fire going. How low have we sunk because of him!"

Unable to put up with such abuse, Du Shiniang shot back, "Mr. Li didn't come with empty hands. He's been quite generous."

"How times have changed! Just tell him to spare a little money so I can buy firewood and rice to keep the two of you alive. (*The madam does have a point.*) In other houses like ours, the girls are like money-growing trees. They're living in luxury, while I have to be the unlucky one, feeding a white tiger that keeps money out of the house![7] From the moment the door is opened every morning, I busy myself preparing the seven necessities of life [firewood, rice, cooking oil, salt, soy sauce, vinegar, and tea] for the household. Now, where am I supposed to get food and clothes to support that pauper of yours, you little hussy? You tell that pauper, if he's still a man, why doesn't he scrape together a few taels of silver and take you away from here? I'd be happy to get myself another girl."

"Mother, do you mean it?"

Knowing that it was impossible for the penniless Li Jia, who had pawned everything he owned, to come up with any money, the madam said, "I never lie. Of course I mean it."

"Mother, how much do you want from him?"

"If it were anyone else, I'd ask for a thousand taels of silver. But in the case of that penniless wretch, I'll be merciful and ask for only three hundred taels, so that I can find a replacement for you. But there's one condition: he has to pay me in three days. When he gives me the money, I'll give him his girl. He may be a gentleman, but if he can't pay up in three days, whatever the circumstances, I'll beat him and kick him out. When it comes to that, don't hold me to blame!"

Shiniang pleaded, "He doesn't have money with him because he's away from home, although he should be able to raise three hundred taels. But three days is not enough. Could you make it ten days?"

The madam thought to herself, "That miserable wretch has nothing left now but his bare hands. Even if I allow him a hundred days, he won't be able to do anything. Without the money, he won't dare show his face around here again, however cheeky he may be. And by that time, the girl should have no objection to starting over again." Aloud, she promised, "For your sake, I'll allow him ten days. But if I don't see the money on the tenth day, don't blame me for anything I do!"

"If he can't come up with anything on the tenth day, I don't think he'll ever have the nerve to come here again. But if he does deliver the money, you, Mother, wouldn't back out of the deal, would you?"

"I'm already fifty-one years old, and I follow the Buddhist diet ten days out of the month. Why would I even dream of lying? If you don't trust me, let's clap our hands on the deal. If ever I should back out of it, let me become a pig or a dog in my next life!"

> *The sea is not to be measured in scoops;*
> *How laughable the evil crone!*
> *Knowing the student to be penniless,*
> *She demands payment to smash the girl's hopes.*

That night, with their heads against the pillows, Shiniang consulted Li Jia about her marital future. He said, "It's not that I'm disinclined, but it takes at least a thousand taels to get your name deleted from the courtesans' registry book. My pocket being as empty as it is, what can I do?"

"I've talked with Mother. She asks only for three hundred taels, but they have to be paid in ten days. Your own means may be exhausted, but don't you have relatives and friends in the capital you can borrow from? (*Poverty is a test of compassion.*) If you can raise the amount, I'll be yours, and we won't have to bear the old witch's abuses any longer!"

"All my relatives and friends have forsaken me because I refuse to leave this place. Tomorrow, I'll go and tell them I'm packing for the journey home and have come to say good-bye. And then I'll ask for travel money. I may even be able to collect the whole amount." (*If, by a stroke of luck, he does manage to get the money, what next? He still doesn't have a plan for the future. I fail to see what Shiniang sees in this good-for-nothing Li Jia.*)

The next morning, Li rose, washed, combed his hair, and took leave of Shiniang. "Be sure to come back soon," she admonished. "I'll be waiting for good news."

"Don't worry," said he. He left the house and called on friends and relatives. They were delighted to hear that he was there to bid them farewell before starting his journey home. Then he mentioned his lack of funds and asked for a loan. As the proverb puts it, "Talk of money drives friends away." His relatives ignored his request, and not without reason, for they saw him as a dissolute prodigal who had been away from home, wallowing in vice in a brothel for more than a year, while his father was fuming with rage. And now, all of a sudden, he claimed he was going home, but who could be sure he was telling the truth? Should it be but a trick so he could use the supposed travel money to pay the brothel again, his father would surely misconstrue their good intentions when he heard of it. If his father was going to blame them anyway, they'd be well advised not to get involved in the first place. Without exception, everyone said, "I happen to be short of money at this moment. I'm really sorry I'm not able to help you out." No one was generous enough to part with so much as ten or twenty taels.

Li ran around for three days straight without raising the slightest fraction of a tael. He did not dare tell Shiniang the truth and put her off with evasive answers.

When the fourth day also failed to bring him any hope, he felt too ashamed to return to her. (*Just as the madam had predicted.*) But, having made the Du house his home, he had no other place to stay. He had no choice but to ask Liu Yuchun, the fellow student from his hometown, to put him up for the night. Concerned by the miserable look on Li's face, Liu Yuchun asked what was wrong, whereupon Li told Liu all about Du Shiniang's offer of marriage.

Yuchun shook his head and said, "I doubt it, I doubt it. Du Mei is the number one courtesan. If she wants to get out of the business and marry, the madam would ask for no less than ten pecks of pearls and betrothal gifts worth a thousand taels of silver. Why is she asking for only three hundred taels? My guess is that the madam resents the fact that you are keeping her girl without paying anything. This is her way of driving you out. As for the girl, having known you for so long, she can't very well tell you to leave outright, for fear of hurting your feelings. Knowing all too well that you're penniless, she purposely sets the price at three hundred taels as a favor to you and gives you ten days to come up with the money. If you can't deliver, you can't show up at her door any more. If you do, she'll ridicule you and laugh at you and make you feel too humiliated to stay on. Brothels often use this trick to drive out unwanted clients. Now think carefully. Don't be fooled. In my humble opinion, the best thing to do is to make a clean break with them as soon as possible."

Li lapsed into silence, unable to make up his mind. After a good while, Yuchun continued, "Don't make a wrong move. If you do decide to go back home, the travel expenses won't amount to much. There will surely be people willing to help you out. But if you ask for three hundred taels, you're not likely to get it even in ten months, let alone ten days. You know how the world is today. Who will bother to care about other people's troubles? The brothel is deliberately making things difficult for you because they are sure you won't be able to get a loan."

"Right you are, my good brother." Even as he mouthed these words of agreement, Li could not bear the thought of parting with Shiniang. Again, he set about begging for loans here and there, though he did stop going back to the brothel at night. For three days in a row, he stayed with Tribute Student Liu. Six days passed.

Deeply worried by Li's continued absence, Du Shiniang had Si'er, a page boy, go out to look for him, and it so happened that Si'er ran into Li on a main street. "Brother-in-law Li!" called out Si'er. "Mistress is expecting you at home!"

Feeling ashamed, Li answered, "I'm too busy today. I'll come tomorrow."

Determined not to fail Shiniang, Si'er grabbed him and, holding him tightly, said, "Mistress told me to look for you. You must come with me!"

His heart longing for Shiniang, Li submitted and followed Si'er. When he saw Shiniang, he could think of nothing to say.

"How are you coming along in what you set out to do?" asked she. As tears flowed down his cheeks, she continued, "Can there be so little human kindness that you haven't been able to put together three hundred taels?"

Tearfully, Li intoned a couplet, "'It's easier to catch a tiger in the hills / Than to open your mouth and beg for favors.' I've been running around for six days and haven't gotten even one cent. I felt so ashamed to come back to you with empty hands that I stayed away these last few days. It was only because you sent for me that I came in all humiliation. It's not that I haven't tried, but such are the ways of the world."

"Don't let Madam know about any of this. Why don't you stay here tonight? I need to talk to you about something."

Shiniang prepared food and wine, and she and Li enjoyed a hearty meal before they went to bed.

When they awoke in the middle of the night, Shiniang asked him, "So are you truly unable to come up with even a cent? What's to be done about my marital future?"

The young man continued to shed tears, unable to speak.

Gradually, it began to grow light, and the fifth watch struck. Shiniang said, "I've hidden one hundred and fifty taels of loose silver inside my mattress. This is my private savings. Take it. So that's half of the three hundred taels. Now that you only need the other half, you may stand a better chance. There are only four days left. You've got no time to lose." So saying, she rose and gave the mattress to Li.

Beside himself with joy, Li had a page boy carry the mattress for him and follow him all the way to Liu Yuchun's place. There, he told Liu all that had happened during the night. The mattress was then torn open to reveal pieces of loose silver all wrapped up in the padding. They weighed exactly one hundred and fifty taels. Yuchun was astounded. "So, she does mean it! In that case, her sincerity must not be betrayed. Let me try to raise the money for you."

"If this turns out well for us, I'll never forget your kindness."

So Liu Yuchun kept Li Jia at his place, while he went everywhere to borrow money. In two days, he raised one hundred and fifty taels. Handing the money to Li, he said, "I went into debt on your behalf, not for your sake, but because of Du Shiniang's devotion to you."

With the three hundred taels in his possession, Li Jia rejoiced at this heaven-sent good fortune. All smiles, he went merrily to see Shiniang, one day before the ten-day limit was to expire.

"You didn't have a cent the other day," said Shiniang. "How did you come by these one hundred and fifty taels?"

After listening to Li's account of what Tribute Student Liu had done, Shiniang said, her hand raised to her forehead in a gesture of great delight, "So Mr. Liu is the one who has gotten us what we want."

Happy beyond measure, they spent the night together in the house.

The next morning, Shiniang rose bright and early and said to Li Jia, "As soon as the silver is delivered, I'll be free to go with you, but we need to arrange for transportation. Yesterday, I borrowed twenty taels of silver from my sisters. Take them to pay for our travel expenses."

This news was most welcome because Li had been worrying about the lack of travel funds but had not dared to bring up the subject. While they were talking, the madam knocked on the door. "My girl Mei," she called out. "It's the tenth day today!"

Upon hearing this, Li opened the door and said invitingly, "Thank you for coming here, Mother. I was just going to ask you over." With that, he laid the three hundred taels of silver on the table.

The madam, who had not expected him to produce any money, was dumbstruck. Her face hardened, and she looked as if she was going to back out of the deal. Shiniang said, "In the eight years I've been living here, I've made thousands of taels of silver for you. Today is the happy day I leave and get married, and you have given me your word. The three hundred taels are all here, not a fraction of a tael less, nor have we exceeded the ten-day limit. If you go back on your promise, Mr. Li will walk out with the money, and I will immediately kill myself. If that happens, you will lose both me and the money, and regrets will be too late."

Not knowing what to say in reply, the madam fell silent. After much thinking, she resignedly took up a scale and weighed out the silver. "Since things have come to this," said she, "I guess I won't be able to keep you. But if you must go, be off this very instant. Don't even think of taking any of the jewelry and clothes you wear every day." With that, she pushed the two of them out, asked for a padlock, and locked the door.

It was the ninth lunar month of the year, and the weather was growing chilly. Since she had just risen from bed, Shiniang had not yet dressed and groomed herself. In her old clothes, she bowed twice in the madam's direction. Li also bowed. That done, they left the madam's house as husband and wife.

> *The carp broke free from the golden hook;*
> *Flicking its tail, shaking its head, it's gone for good.*

Li told Shiniang to stop for a moment, adding, "I'll get a small sedan-chair for you. Let's go first to Mr. Liu's place before deciding on the next thing to do."

"My sisters have always been very kind to me. I ought to say good-bye to them. Moreover, they loaned me money for travel expenses, and I can't leave without saying thanks." Accompanied by Li, she went to bid her sisters a thankful farewell.

Of the sisters, Xie Yuelang and Xu Susu lived nearest to the Du house and were Shiniang's most intimate friends, so Shiniang went to Xie Yuelang's house first. Surprised to see Shiniang with her hair unadorned and her clothes old and worn, Yuelang asked her what had happened. Shiniang told Yuelang the whole story and introduced Li Jia to her. Pointing at Yuelang, Shiniang said, "This is the sister who helped us out with travel money. You should thank her." Accordingly, Li Jia gave her one bow after another.

Yuelang let Shiniang do her toilette and, in the meantime invited Xu Susu to come over for a reunion. After Shiniang had finished, the two beauties Xie and Xu offered her their kingfisher-feather hair ornaments, gold bracelets, jade hairpins, earrings inlaid with jewels, a brocade blouse, a floral-pattern skirt, a phoenix belt, and a pair of embroidered shoes. With Du Shiniang now aglow in all her splendor, a farewell celebration feast was laid out. When the feast was over, Yuelang offered her own bedchamber to Li Jia and Du Mei for the night.

The next day, another feast, a grand one, was set out, to which all the courtesans of the quarters were invited. Everyone who had warm feelings for Shiniang came to toast and congratulate the couple. The guests played musical instruments, sang, and danced, offering the best of their talents for the joyous occasion, and the drinking and merrymaking lasted until midnight. When Shiniang offered words of thanks, they replied, "Now that you, the very best of us, are going away with your husband, we might never see you again. Let us know when you're going to set out on your journey, and we'll come to see you off."

Yuelang said, "When the date is decided, I'll surely let all of you know. But Sister Shiniang's journey with her husband will be long and arduous and one that they can ill afford. We sisters are duty bound to do something so that she won't have anything to worry about."

The sisters all agreed to the proposal before dispersing. That night, Li and Shiniang again stayed in Yuelang's room.

At the fifth strike of the night drum, Shiniang said to Li, "Where shall we settle down after leaving this place? Do you have any definite ideas?" (*These things should have been worked out before they left the brothel. Why wait until this moment?*)

Li said, "My father, as angry as he is, will surely raise hell if he knows I'm returning home married to a courtesan, and that will make things even worse for you. I've been racking my brains over the matter but haven't come up with a surefire plan."

"The natural bond between father and son can't be broken. But if this is not yet the right time to approach him, why don't we take up temporary residence in a scenic city like Suzhou or Hangzhou? That way, you can go back to your hometown and ask relatives and friends to mediate on your behalf and pacify your father. Only then can you take me to your parents. That would be better for both sides." (*Yes, that is indeed a felicitous solution.*)

"Well said," Li agreed.

The next morning, Li and Shiniang took leave of Xie Yuelang and set out for Tribute Student Liu's place, where they were to stay for a while and pack for their journey. As soon as she saw Liu Yuchun, Du Shiniang fell to her knees and made obeisance. Thanking him for his help in bringing about the marriage, she said, "My husband and I will surely return your kindness."

Yuchun promptly bowed in return and said, "You, madam, are indeed an exceptional woman, who does not let poverty stand in the way of your love. I did nothing more than fan the fire when the wind was favorable. Such a trivial thing is hardly worth mentioning."

The three spent the day at the wine table. On the morrow, they chose an auspicious day for the couple's departure and hired sedan-chairs and horses. Shiniang then had a page boy dispatch a letter to Xie Yuelang, thanking her and bidding her farewell.

As the hour of their departure drew near, there came a stream of sedan-chairs. It was Xie Yuelang and Xu Susu leading all the sisters to see them off. Yuelang addressed Shiniang in the following words: "We cannot bear the thought of letting you follow your husband on a thousand-li journey with an empty purse. We have put together a modest gift. Please accept it. It may come in handy on your long journey." So saying, she had a servant give Shiniang a gold-traced jewel box locked so securely that there was no clue as to its contents. Shiniang neither opened it nor declined the gift but busied herself in saying thanks.

A short while later, the sedan-chairs and horses were ready, and the footmen urged them to be on their way. Tribute Student Liu offered three cups of farewell wine and, along with the beauties, escorted the couple as far as Chongwen Gate, where everyone tearfully said farewell. Truly,

> *They knew not when they would meet again*
> *At this sad moment of farewell.*

To continue with our story, Li Jia and Du Shiniang proceeded to the Lu River, where they were to board a boat. There happened to be a government courier boat returning to Guazhou, so they negotiated the fare and paid for the cabin. Once on board, Li found that he had already spent the last cent in his pocket. Now you may wonder, didn't Du Shiniang give him twenty taels of silver? They couldn't all be gone, could they? Well, having spent all his money in the brothel until he was in rags, Li could hardly resist the temptation of redeeming a few articles of clothing from the pawnshop once he laid his hands on some silver. He had also bought bedding, and the remainder of the silver was just enough to pay for the sedan-chairs and horses.

Noticing his woebegone look, Shiniang said, "Don't worry. My sisters' gift should be of some use."

With that, she took out the key and opened the box.

Li was standing beside her, but he felt too ashamed to look into the box. All he saw was a red silk purse, which Shiniang took out. She threw the purse on the table and said, "Won't you open it and see what's inside?"

When he picked it up, Li thought it was quite heavy. He opened it and found it was filled with pieces of silver amounting to fifty taels. Shiniang locked the box again without mentioning what else it contained. Instead, she said to him, "Thanks to the kindness of my sisters, we have not only enough money for this journey but also some to spare for our stay south of the river."

At this pleasant surprise, Li said, "If it were not for you, I would have been stranded in an alien land and died without even a burial place. I'll never forget your kindness to me."

Henceforth, every time past events came up in conversation, Li would shed tears of gratitude and Shiniang would go out of her way to console him with soothing words. And nothing else of note occurred as they continued their journey.

In a few days, they came to Guazhou. After the courier boat had anchored by the shore, Li hired a passenger boat, transferred their luggage to it, and arranged to set sail early the next morning. It was the middle of the eleventh month of the year, and the moon was as bright as sparkling water.

Sitting at the bow with Shiniang by his side, Li said, "Ever since we left the capital, we've been cooped up in a cabin with people all around us and never had a chance for a good talk. Now, with a boat to ourselves, we can finally disregard all scruples. (*This is not yet the right time for endearments. Small wonder that the relationship was not fated to last long.*) Since we've left the north and are approaching the south side of the Yangzi River, let's drink to our hearts' content to shake off the gloom of the last few days. What do you say?"

"I was thinking along the same lines, because I, too, miss having a good talk and a good laugh. Your bringing this up shows that we are truly of the same mind."

Li fetched wine utensils, spread out a rug on the bow, and sat down shoulder to shoulder with Shiniang. They began passing the cups back and forth. When well warmed with wine, he said to Shiniang, wine vessel in hand, "Your voice is the very best in the courtesans' quarters. When I first met you, my soul took flight every time I heard you sing. With all the troubles we've gone through, we've been in such low spirits that I haven't heard your divine singing in a long time. Now, with the moon shining brightly on the clear water and no one around us in the depths of the night, would you be willing to sing for me?"

Shiniang was so carried away that she cleared her throat and, beating time with her fan, started singing. (*She, too, lacks prudence.*) Set to the tune of "Small Red Peaches," the song was about a scholar offering wine to the moon, from the play *Moon Pavilion,* by Shi Junmei of the Yuan dynasty.[8] Truly,

> *Her voice rose into the sky and stopped the clouds,*
> *Dived down into the deep spring and brought out the fish.*

Now, in another boat, there was a young man called Sun Fu, courtesy name Shanlai, a native of Xin'an, Huizhou, who was from a fabulously rich family that had been in the salt business in Yangzhou for generations. He was twenty years of age and also a tribute student at the National University in Nanjing. A licentious and frivolous man, he frequented houses of ill repute and was a master in matters relating to the pleasures of the flesh.

As coincidence would have it, his boat was also anchored at the Guazhou ferry that night. Drinking alone and feeling bored, he suddenly heard a clear voice singing so beautifully that metaphors of phoenix songs were not enough to capture its beauty. He stood up in the bow and listened for a good while before deciding that its source was the very next boat. He was about to pay a visit when the singing stopped, whereupon he told a servant to slip out and ask the boatman who the singer was. When he was told that the boat had been hired by a Mr. Li but nothing was known about the singer, Sun Fu thought to himself, "Obviously, the singer is not from a decent family. How shall I get to see her?" These thoughts kept him awake throughout the night.

When the fifth watch of the night finally came, he heard a windstorm spring up on the river. By dawn, the sky was overcast with ominous clouds, and flakes of snow whirled frantically in the air. How do we know this? There is a poem in testimony:

> *Trees vanish into the clouds from hill to hill;*
> *All footprints disappear from path to path.*
> *An old man with a straw hat sits in a small boat,*
> *Fishing all alone on a river clad in snow.*

Since he was stuck in the snowstorm and unable to continue with his journey anyway, Sun Fu ordered his boatman to move closer to Li's boat. Sun Fu put on his sable hat and fox-fur coat and pushed open the window as if to watch the snow. At this very moment, Shiniang, having finished her toilette, raised the short curtain of the cabin window with her delicate hands and emptied her basin into the river. As she did so, Sun Fu caught a partial glimpse of her face. Just as he had thought, the woman was a ravishing beauty. He was thrown into such raptures that he kept his eyes fixed upon the same spot, waiting for her to appear again, but to no avail. After reflecting a good while, he leaned against his window and intoned aloud two lines from the poem "Plum Blossoms," by Academician Gao Qi.[9] (*Shi Junmei's song and Academician Gao's poem are the ruin of Du Shiniang's life. Outrageous! Outrageous!*):

> *"On the snow-clad hill sleeps the hermit;*
> *In the moonlit woods walks the beauty."*

Upon hearing someone intoning a poem in a neighboring boat, Li Jia craned his neck out the cabin window to look. With that one glimpse, he fell victim to Sun Fu's scheme. Sun's very purpose in chanting the poem was to entice Li to show his face so that he could take the chance to strike up a conversation. With alacrity, he raised his hands in greeting and asked, "What is your honorable name?"

After saying his name and where he was from, Li directed the same question to Sun Fu, who readily answered. After some small talk about the National University, they gradually warmed to each other. Sun Fu said, "To be stranded here in the snowstorm is a god-sent opportunity for me to have the honor of meeting you, my honorable brother. As there's little to do on the boat, I'd like to invite you to go ashore and have a drink or two in a wineshop, so that I may have the benefit of your conversation. I hope you won't turn me down."

"I've just met you as a total stranger! How can I put you to such trouble?"

"What kind of talk is this? As they say, 'All men within the four seas are brothers.'" With that, Sun Fu had his boatman put down the gangplank, and his page boy held out an umbrella for Mr. Li to cross over to his boat. After an exchange of greetings at the bow, Sun asked Li to precede him as they went ashore.

Before they had gone many paces, a wineshop came into view. They went upstairs, chose a clean table by the window, and sat down. After the waiter laid out a fine spread of wine and food on the table, Sun Fu raised his cup and plied Li with wine. While they were drinking and viewing the snowy scenery, their conversation, polite and innocuous enough at first, gradually turned to houses of ill fame. Being frequenters of such places, they found that they shared the same tastes and, in the excitement of the conversation, became the closest of friends.

Sun Fu dismissed the waiters and said in a subdued voice, "Who is the girl who was singing so beautifully last night in your boat?"

In his eagerness to show off his connoisseurship, Li Jia told him the truth (*His imprudence made him unable to keep a secret.*): "That's Du Shiniang, a celebrated courtesan in Beijing."

"But why does a courtesan now belong to you alone?"

Thereupon, Li acquainted him with all the details of the first time he'd met Du Shiniang, how they had fallen in love, her desire to marry him, and how he had borrowed money to redeem her.

Sun Fu said, "To take a beautiful woman home is a happy event, to be sure, but I wonder if your family will accept her?"

"I'm not worried so much about my wife as about my father. He's very strict. I need to think well before I approach him."

Seeing his chance, Sun Fu pressed further, "If your father refuses to take her in, where are you going to put her? Have you worked out any plans with her?"

With a frown, Li replied, "I have indeed talked about it with her."

"So, your beloved one must have come up with a wonderful idea," said Sun Fu lightheartedly.

"Well, she wants to take up temporary residence in Suzhou and Hangzhou to enjoy the hills and the waters. I'll return home first and ask relatives and friends to put in a good word for me with my father. When my father comes around, I'll take her home. What do you think?"

After reflecting for a good while, Sun Fu assumed a concerned expression and said, "I'm afraid you might take amiss any advice coming from someone you've only just met."

"I do need your advice. Please don't hesitate."

"As an important official in the region, your father must be firmly against improper love affairs. Since he's already scolded you for frequenting places of ill repute, he's not likely to let you marry a loose woman. As for your relatives and friends, who among them would not try to play up to your father? Your pleas to them will surely be rejected. Even if there's someone who doesn't know better and puts in a good word on your behalf with your father, that person will change his tune as soon as he finds out what your father thinks. On the one hand, you'll sow discord in the clan; on the other, you'll disappoint your beloved one. And to enjoy the hills and the waters is not a viable, long-term solution either. What if you run out of money? Wouldn't you find yourself in a dilemma?" (*Rogues like him do have a way with words.*)

Knowing all too well that the bulk of his fifty taels of silver was already gone, Li nodded in agreement when Sun Fu got to that last part.

Sun Fu continued, "I have something more to say, and it's from the bottom of my heart, but you may not want to hear it."

"You are too kind. Please say whatever you want to say."

"Well, I'd better shut up, because as the proverb goes, 'An outsider shouldn't come between those near and dear to each other.'"

"Please go ahead. It's quite all right!"

"Well, as the ancients said, 'Women are as fickle as water.' Prostitutes are much more so. Those who feel true love are greatly outnumbered by those who don't. Since she was celebrated among the courtesans' quarters, she must have lovers everywhere. She may have an old flame south of the Yangzi River and is using you to take her there, so as to be reunited with him."

"I don't think that's the case."

"Even if it's not, young men south of the river are known for their ways with women. If you let her live by herself, you can't say for sure that a man won't climb over the wall or sneak in through some hole, so to speak. And yet, if you take her home, you'll only add to your father's anger. I don't have a good plan for you, but the natural bond between father and son should never be broken for any reason. If you turn against your father and abandon your family because of a prostitute, you'll be considered a debauched and wayward person by all and sundry. In due course, you will be forsaken by your wife, brothers, and friends. How will you be able to justify your existence on earth and under the sky? You'll have to do some solid thinking now!" (*Had these words not been said with an ulterior motive, they would have been good advice.*)

Li was so dismayed upon hearing these words that he moved his seat closer to Sun and asked, "So, what's your advice?"

Sun Fu replied, "I do have an idea. It will be very much in your favor, but I'm afraid you might be too deeply infatuated with her to follow my advice. In that case, wouldn't I have wasted my breath?"

"If you really have a plan to help me rejoin my family, you'll be nothing less than my savior. Why are you afraid to speak?"

"You've been away from home for more than a year. Your father is angry, and your wife is estranged from you. If I were you, I'd hardly be able to eat or sleep. Your father is angry with you because your philandering ways and lavish spending habits have made him afraid that you will surely squander everything once you come into your inheritance. By returning empty-handed now, you'll only make him angrier. (*A stab at Li's heart.*) If you give up your woman and do the right thing under the circumstances, I'll offer you a thousand taels of silver for her. You may present the thousand taels to your father and say that you have been teaching in the capital and saved every possible cent. He will surely believe you. Henceforth, you'll enjoy domestic peace with never a harsh word said against you. In a trice, your woes will be changed to bliss. Please think carefully. I say all this not because I covet the woman's beauty but because I wish to help you in any small way I can."

Li Jia being a man without a mind of his own and in mortal fear of his father, Sun Fu's words struck a deep chord in his heart and dispelled all his worries. He rose and said with a bow, "You have made me see the light. But I can't very well break my ties with her after she has followed me this far on such a long journey. Please let me consult her first. I'll report back to you if she agrees."

"Put it gently to her. If she's really devoted to you, she won't have the heart to cut the ties between you and your father and will surely help you return home." (*Another attempt to poison Li's mind.*)

They continued drinking a while longer. The wind subsided, and the snow stopped when dusk set in. Sun Fu had his servant settle the bill, and, hand in hand, they returned to their boats. Truly,

> Never disclose everything on your mind;
> Never pour out all of your heart.

In the meantime, Du Shiniang had laid out wine and fruit in anticipation of a good time with Li and, after waiting for him in vain throughout the day, was sitting by the light of the lamp when he stepped onto the boat. Shiniang rose to greet him, noticing that he looked preoccupied and slightly irritated. She filled a cup with warm wine and offered it to him with some soothing words, but he shook his head in refusal and went to bed without speaking. None too pleased, Shiniang put away the cups and plates and helped him take off his clothes and lie down against the pillow. "What did you hear today that makes you so upset?"

Li sighed but didn't utter a word. Shiniang repeated the question three or four times but found he had fallen asleep. Full of misgivings, she sat down at the head of the bed, unable to sleep. At midnight, Li woke up with another sigh.

"What is it that you find so hard to say? Why so many sighs?" asked Shiniang.

Gathering the quilt around him, Li sat up and, after several futile attempts to speak, began to weep. Shiniang held him to her bosom and said gently, "It's been two years since I fell in love with you. We've gone through all kinds of difficulties together to get where we are. Along the thousands of li we've covered on our journey, you never felt sad, but now that we're on the point of crossing the Yangzi River to start a happy life, why are you suddenly looking so miserable? There must be a reason behind this. Husband and wife are supposed to share life and death. You can tell me whatever's on your mind. Don't hide anything from me."

Yielding to her insistence, he said, with tears in his eyes, "When I was penniless and stranded away from home, you, in your kindness, chose to be with me. No favor can be greater than that. But I've been giving the matter a lot of thought. You see, my father, being an important official in the region, is a man who clings to conventions, and he's a very rigid and demanding person, too. I'm afraid he'll be so angry that he'll drive us out of the house. If so, when will our itinerant life ever come to an end? Our love will not last, and the bond between father and son will be destroyed. Earlier today, a friend, Mr. Sun from Xin'an, invited me to drink with him and discussed this with me. My heart aches as if it's been stabbed with a knife!"

Alarmed, Shiniang asked, "So, what are you going to do?"

"Since I'm the one involved, I don't see the situation as clearly as an onlooker would. Mr. Sun has come up with a good plan for me, but you may not go along with it."

"Who's this Mr. Sun? If his idea is as good as you say, why wouldn't I go along with it?"

"He's Sun Fu, a salt merchant from Xin'an and a dashing young man. He heard you sing last night. That's why he asked about you. I told him your background as well as the reason for our not going home. He offered me a thousand taels of silver if you would marry him, so that I'll have something to give my parents and you'll have a husband. But the thought of leaving you makes me want to cry." With that, his tears fell like rain.

Shiniang withdrew her hands from him. With a scornful laugh, she said, "What a great hero, the fellow who designed this plan for you! You get your one thousand taels of silver and rejoin your family, I get a man, and both of us will be spared the tribulations of life on the road. What a perfect plan—what began as an affair of passion now ends in proper decorum! All right, where's the money?"

Holding back his tears, Li answered, "The money's still with him because I didn't have your consent."

"Go give him my consent first thing tomorrow morning. Don't miss the chance! But a thousand taels of silver being quite a handsome amount of money, they must be weighed out and handed to you before I step over to the other boat. Don't let that brute of a merchant take advantage of you."

The night drum struck the fourth watch. Shiniang rose, lit the lamp, and began her toilette. "Today," said she, "I'm sending off the old and greeting the new. This is a special occasion!" She applied powder, rouge, and fragrant hair oil with great care and put on hair ornaments and an embroidered gown. There she stood in all her radiance, her perfume sweetening the air, her beauty dazzling to behold.

By the time she had finished her toilette, the sky was beginning to brighten. A page boy sent by Sun Fu stood at the bow of the boat, waiting for a reply. Glancing quickly at Li, Shiniang saw a faint glow of joy on his face. She urged him to go quickly and give his reply and reminded him to have the silver weighed out as soon as possible. (*If he really could not bear the thought of leaving her, he would have acted otherwise.*)

So Li Jia went to Sun Fu's boat and replied in the affirmative. Sun Fu said, "Weighing out the silver is not a problem, but I need her jewel box as a pledge."

Li reported back to Shiniang, who said, pointing at her gold-traced jewel box, "Take it."

A jubilant Sun Fu immediately sent the thousand taels of silver to Li's boat. Shiniang personally inspected them and found them to be of standard purity and not the slightest fraction of a mace short in weight. With one hand holding on to the side of the boat, she beckoned to Sun Fu with the other, a sight that sent him into raptures. Then she said, revealing pearly white teeth between her ruby lips, "May I have the jewel box back for just a moment? Mr. Li's travel permit is in it. I must return it to him."

Believing that he had already caught Shiniang in his trap, Sun Fu had his page boy put the jewel box on the bow. Shiniang took out her key and unlocked it to reveal a stack of small drawers. At Shiniang's bidding, Li drew out the first drawer. Lo and behold, it was filled with pieces of expensive jewelry worth hundreds of taels of silver. She picked them up and tossed them into the river, to the astonishment of Li Jia, Sun Fu, and everyone else on the two boats.

She then told Li to pull out another drawer, which was seen to contain jade flutes and golden pipes. Yet another drawer was filled with jade and gold objects of art worth thousands of taels of silver. Shiniang tossed them all into the water in full view of the wall of spectators now gathered on the shore. "What a pity!" they exclaimed in unison, wondering what on earth could have made this woman do such a thing.

The last drawer was pulled out to reveal a small box. When it was opened, there, for all to see, was a large handful of luminous pearls as well as emeralds, cat's-eyes, and other precious objects, the likes of which none had ever seen and the value of which none could determine. Amid thunderous cheers from the onlookers, Shiniang was about to throw them into the river when Li Jia, overcome with bitter remorse, flung his arms around her and broke into wails of grief. When Sun Fu came over to try to calm her, Shiniang pushed Li aside and unleashed an explosion of furious words on Sun Fu. "Mr. Li and I went through a lot together before we got here. But you cajoled him with clever words out of lecherous motives and destroyed a marriage of love in one day. You are my worst enemy. If my spirit survives my death, I'll certainly bring a complaint against you to the gods. As for the pleasures of the pillow, you don't have a ghost of a chance!"

Turning to Li Jia, she went on, "In my years as a courtesan, I put away some private savings to support myself in the future. After we met, you and I took many a vow of lifelong love and fidelity. Before we left the capital, I had my sisters give me what were in fact my own possessions. The treasures hidden in the jewel box were worth no less than ten thousand taels of silver. I meant to add some grandeur to your return, so that your parents might act out of compassion and accept me as a member of the family. With the remainder of my life committed to you, I would have had no regrets in life and in death. Little did I know that you trusted me so little that you followed some evil advice and abandoned me before the journey was even completed. You have betrayed my devotion to you. I opened the box and showed its contents in public so that you'll know that a mere thousand taels of silver are of little importance to me. I am not unlike a jewel box that contains precious jade, but you have eyes that fail to recognize value. Alas, I was not born under a lucky star. Having just freed myself from the tribulations of a courtesan's life, I find myself abandoned again. All those present will testify, by the evidence of their eyes and ears, that I have not failed you in any way. It's you who have betrayed me!"

There was not a dry eye among the onlookers, all of whom cursed Li for being the fickle ingrate that he was. Ashamed and exasperated, Li shed tears of remorse and was about to apologize to Shiniang when she threw herself into the middle of the current, the jewel box in her arms. The horrified onlookers cried out for her rescue, but with a heavy mist hanging over the raging waves, not the slightest trace of her could be seen. How tragic that a celebrated courtesan as pretty as a flower and as fair as jade fell prey to the fish of the river!

> Her three souls returned to the Water Palace,
> Her seven spirits wafted to the underworld.

Gnashing their teeth and raising their fists, the crowd swarmed menacingly toward Li Jia and Sun Fu. In fear, Li and Sun called for their boats to get under way and fled in different directions. For Li Jia, Sun Fu's thousand taels of silver were a constant reminder of Shiniang, and he was haunted day and night by guilt and shame. His depression worsened into mental derangement, from which he never recovered. For his part, Sun Fu had sustained such a shock that he fell ill and, while confined in his bed, saw Du Shiniang at his side. She gave him tongue-lashings day and night for more than a month until he gave up the ghost. His death was generally explained as retribution for what had happened on the river.

In the meantime, Liu Yuchun finished his studies at the National University in the capital, packed up his belongings, and started his journey home by boat. When he reached the town of Guabu, he stopped and was washing his face by the side of the boat when his brass basin fell into the water. He sought out a fisherman to retrieve it, but what came up was a small box.

Yuchun opened it and saw that it was filled with bright pearls and other price-less jewelry. He gave the fisherman a handsome reward and kept the box by his bed so that he could examine the contents and admire them at his leisure. That very night, he dreamed he saw a woman approaching him, treading upon the waves of the river. He looked closely at her and recognized her to be Du Shiniang.

When she had drawn near, she curtsied and told him about Li's act of treachery, adding, "You generously helped me out with one hundred and fifty taels. I meant to repay you for your kindness after I settled down. Little did I expect that things would not turn out that way, but I haven't forgotten my debt of gratitude to you. This morning, I gave you that little box by way of the fisherman as a small token of my gratitude. I shall never see you again." At this point, Yuchun woke up with a start and realized that Shiniang had died. For days on end, he heaved one sigh after another.

In later times, when commenting on the account we have given above, people had this to say: Sun Fu, in scheming to gain a beauty and lightly throwing away a thousand taels of silver, was by no means a decent sort; Li Jia, in failing to appreciate Du Shiniang's devotion, was nothing but an imbecile on whom it was not worth wasting one's breath. But Shiniang was a true heroine of all time. She could very well have found a worthy husband and had a blissful marriage, and yet, she picked Li, whose character she misjudged. As a result, a bright pearl, a piece of fine jade, was thrown in front of a blind man. How tragic that love turned to hate and went into the flowing river! There is a poem that says in lament,

> Those who don't know what love is, hold your tongue!
> "Love" is a word too deep to understand.
> If its meaning can be grasped in full,
> Feel no shame when you're called a lover.

7

The Oil-Peddler Wins the Queen of Flowers

Young men vie in boasting of their conquests
Over the choppy sea of romance.
Money without looks breeds no tender feelings;
Good looks without money get one nowhere, either.
Even those with money and looks
Must keep paying little thoughtful attentions.
Only a dashing young man eager to please
Can beat all others and win the beauty's heart.

This lyric to the tune of "Moon over West River" captures the essence of life in the courtesans' quarters. As the saying goes, "The girls love a good-looking face; the madams love the sight of cash." Among the patrons, those with Pan An's looks[1] and Deng Tong's money[2] naturally win the good graces of all and sundry and become kings of the establishment. However, there is also another attribute called "attentiveness," which is to a girl as the lining is to a garment or the upper is to a shoe. One who otherwise doesn't have much to be said about him will soar in the girl's estimation if he dances attendance on her, goes to great lengths to cover up her flaws, humbly attends to her needs in weather hot or cold, and caters to her likes and steers clear of her dislikes. (*A list of do's and don'ts to keep in mind.*) The object of such affection will find it unthinkable not to love him back. This is what attentiveness can do. In the courtesans' quarters, it is such patrons who get the best deals. What they may want in looks and money is easily made up. A case in point: When Zheng Yuanhe was reduced to begging and lived in a poorhouse sponsored by a Buddhist temple, Li Yaxian [a courtesan whom he had known in his better days] saw him on a snowy day and took pity on him in his penniless and emaciated state.[3] She bundled him in embroidered robes, fed him fine food, and married him. Was she enamored of his money and his looks? No! It was only because Zheng Yuanhe had been affectionate, considerate, and attentive that Yaxian had lost her heart to him. Consider the time when Yaxian had craved horse-tripe soup in her illness. Zheng Yuanhe killed his fancy horse whose mane was fashioned to look like five flower petals, and with the tripe made soup for her. This alone was enough to make her remember his love. Later on, Zheng Yuanhe came out first in the imperial examinations and Li Yaxian was granted the title of Lady of Qianguo. So the beggars' song "Lotus Petals" led to government policies that were to stand the test of time, and the poorhouse gave way to a marble mansion. A "brocade quilt" covered up Yaxian's past, and their story gained wide circulation in the courtesans' quarters. Truly,

> *When luck goes, even gold glitters no more;*
> *When luck comes, even iron takes on luster.*

Our story takes place in the Song dynasty. Emperor Taizu [r. 960–75], who founded the great Song dynasty, and the six succeeding emperors—Emperor Taizong [r. 976–97], Emperor Zhenzong [r. 998–1022], Emperor Renzong [r. 1023–63], Emperor Yingzong [r. 1064–67], Emperor Shenzong [r. 1068–85], and Emperor Zhezong [r. 1086–1100]—all favored culture and the arts over military activities. The empire and its people enjoyed peace and prosperity. However, after Emperor Huizong the Daoist [r. 1101–25] assumed the throne, he placed his trust in evil ministers like Cai Jing [1047–1126], Gao Qiu [d. 1126], Yang Jian [d. 1121], and Zhu Mian [1075–1126], and spent his days reveling in the fancy palaces and gardens built for his pleasure, to the neglect of government affairs. As resentment seethed among the populace, the Jurchens, seeing their chance, invaded the empire and brought chaos to this land of splendor and beauty. Then Emperor Huizong and his son Emperor Qinzong [r. 1126] were captured, and Emperor Gaozong [r. 1127–62] crossed the Yangzi River on a clay horse and started the Southern Song dynasty in the south, thus dividing the country in half.[4] It was only then that the turmoil subsided. Goodness knows how much misery the people went through in those few decades. Truly,

> *They hung on to life amid armor and horses;*
> *They made their homes among spears and swords.*
> *Killing was like a child's game;*
> *Looting became a way of life.*

Let me now tell of a man named Shen Shan who lived in Peace and Happiness Village outside the city gate of Bianliang [present-day Kaifeng in Henan]. He and his wife, née Ruan, owned a grain store, selling mostly rice but also wheat, beans, tea, wine, oil, salt, and other sundry goods. They made a comfortable living. In their forties now, they had only one child, a daughter named Yaoqin [Zither Inlaid with Jade] who was as pretty as she was talented from childhood on. At age seven, she was sent to the village school, where she learned to read a thousand sentences per day. At age ten, she was able to write poems. Her poem "In the Boudoir," which came to be widely circulated, is as follows:

> *Quietly the red curtains come off the golden hooks;*
> *Coldly stands the incense burner in the painted tower.*

She moves her pillow but hates to awaken the embroidered lovebirds;
She trims the lamp but is loath to break the pair of wicks.

Twelve years of age at this point in our narration, Yaoqin excelled in music, chess, calligraphy, and painting, and her dexterity in needlework exceeded everyone's expectations. All these accomplishments came not from practice but from her innate talents. Shen Shan, who had no male issue, wanted to have a live-in son-in-law to support him and his wife in their old age. But the girl was too talented and versatile for him to find a suitable match. And so he declined the many offers of marriage proposals that came his way. As bad luck would have it, the ferocious Jurchen troops laid siege to the city of Bianliang. Even though there was no lack of loyal troops all over the land ready to do battle, the prime minister was determined to make peace and gave the order not to fight. Thus emboldened, the Jurchen invaders took the capital and kidnapped the incumbent emperor and his father. The terror-stricken civilians outside the city abandoned their homes and, helping along the elderly and the children, took to the road and fled for their lives.

Shen Shan took his wife, Ruan-shi, and their twelve-year-old daughter and joined the stream of refugees carrying bundles and parcels on their backs.

They hurried along like frightened stray dogs;
They pressed on like fish that escaped the net.
Thirsty, hungry, they bore all manner of hardships;
Where would they have a home to call their own again?
They prayed to heaven, earth, and their ancestors,
Not to let them run into the Jurchens.
Truly, better be a dog in days of peace
Than a human in times of war!

While they were thus pushing on, they did not see any Jurchens but ran into a group of defeated Song soldiers. At the sight of so many refugees carrying baggage on their backs, the soldiers cried out purposely, "The Jurchens are here!" And they set things on fire as they went. (*This often happens in times of war and separation. Army discipline is therefore of first importance.*) As it was growing dark, the refugees ran helter-skelter in too much panic to watch out for one another. The soldiers took advantage of the situation to rob and loot. Those who resisted were killed. Indeed, to chaos was added chaos; to misery was added misery.

Yaoqin of the Shen family tripped and fell in the onrush of the imperial troops. After she rose to her feet, her parents were lost to sight. She dared not call out loud but hid herself among grave mounds by the roadside, and there she stayed throughout the night. When she ventured out for a look the next morning, all she saw was windblown dust and a road strewn with corpses. Those who had traveled with her the day before were nowhere to be seen. She missed her parents so much that she burst into bitter tears. She wanted to look for them, but without knowing which way to go, she finally headed south, weeping as she went along.

After walking for about two li in agony and hunger, she saw an adobe hut. Thinking there must be someone inside, she headed straight for it to ask for a drink of water. But it turned out to be an abandoned and dilapidated hut. The residents had taken to the road as refugees. Yaoqin sank to the ground to sit against the wall and burst into another flood of tears.

As an ancient saying goes, "No coincidence, no story." It so happened that a man named Bu Qiao, a neighbor of the Shens, went by the wall. Not the sort to abide by his lot, he was a loafer used to sponging off people for meals and cash. Called by all and sundry Big Brother Bu, he was walking all alone at this moment because he had also been separated from his companions by the onrush of the soldiers, and had come over when he heard the sobs. At a time when she had no one to turn to for help in her distress, Yaoqin was as happy to see this neighbor as if she had seen a member of her own family, because she had known him since her childhood. Holding back her tears, she stood up to greet him.

"Uncle Bu," said she, "have you seen my parents?"

Bu Qiao thought, "The soldiers robbed me of my bundle yesterday and I have no money left. Now isn't this a rice bowl sent from heaven? This girl is a rare commodity worth hoarding." Lying through his teeth, he said, "Your parents were heartbroken because they couldn't find you. They said to me before they moved on, 'If you see our daughter, be sure to bring her to us,' and they promised me a nice reward." However smart Yaoqin was, she was in desperate straits, and, as the saying goes, "A trusting gentleman is easily fooled." Without the slightest suspicion, Yaoqin went with Bu Qiao. Indeed,

> Knowing he was not the right companion,
> She followed him in a desperate moment.

Bu Qiao gave her some of his provisions and said to her, "Your parents didn't stop for the night. If we don't catch up with them along the way, we won't be able to see them until we cross the river and get to Jiankang [present-day Nanjing]. While we're on the road, I will call you 'daughter' and you will call me 'father'. Otherwise, people will think I keep lost children, and that won't look good."

Yaoqin agreed. Henceforth, as they traveled by land and by water, they addressed each other as "father" and "daughter." Upon reaching Jiankang, they heard that Jin Wuzhu, the fourth son of the Jurchen emperor,[5] was leading his troops across the river toward Jiankang, which meant that the city would soon be plunged into turmoil. Then news came that Prince Kang had assumed the throne and was staying temporarily in Hangzhou, which he had renamed Lin'an. So Bu Qiao took Yaoqin to Runzhou [present-day Zhenjiang] by boat and passed through

Suzhou, Changzhou, Jiaxing, and Huzhou, until finally arriving at Lin'an, where they found lodging at an inn.

It was to Bu Qiao's credit that he had brought the girl over three thousand li from Bianliang to Lin'an. By this time, he had spent his last few pieces of loose silver. Even the outer layers of his clothes went to the innkeeper to pay the bill. He was now left with only Yaoqin, a live commodity that he was determined to sell. After being informed that a procuress by West Lake, Madam Wang the Ninth, was looking for a new girl, he led the madam to the inn to show her his merchandise and strike a deal. Impressed by Yaoqin's good looks, Wang offered fifty taels of silver. Bu Qiao pocketed all the silver and escorted Yaoqin to the Wang establishment.

Being the crafty man that he was, Bu Qiao said these words to Madam Wang, "Yaoqin is my very own daughter. Now that she is unfortunately with you in this kind of a house, you need to teach her patiently. She'll surely give in. Don't rush things." To Yaoqin, he said, "Madam Wang is a close relative of mine. I'm putting you under her care for now, so that I can take my time looking for your parents. I'll come back for you as soon as I've found them."

Having heard this, Yaoqin merrily went to Madam Wang. (*This is the way most swindlers operate.*)

> How sad that such a jewel of a girl
> Ended up in a house of ill fame.

Having thus acquired Yaoqin, Madam Wang had her change into new clothes, inside and out, and put her up in a room in a discreet inner chamber. She served the girl nice meals to help her regain health and showered her with honeyed words to win her heart. Yaoqin thought that she might as well stay put for now. A few days went by without any news from Bu Qiao. Longing for her parents, she asked Madam Wang tearfully, "Why doesn't Uncle Bu come to see me?"

"What Uncle Bu?"

"Mr. Bu who took me here."

"He said he was your father."

"But he is a Bu. I am a Shen." She then gave a detailed account of how she had become separated from her parents while fleeing from Bianliang, how she had run into Bu Qiao on the road, how he had taken her to Lin'an, and what he had said to fool her.

"So, that's what happened," said Madam Wang. "Now that you are all alone by yourself and can't very well go outside, like a crab without legs, let me tell you something. That man Bu sold you to me for fifty taels of silver. This is a brothel. I make a living out of my girls. I already have a few, but none of them is any good. I like you for your good looks. I've been treating you like a daughter of my own. After you come of age, I'll make sure that you live in comfort for the rest of your life."

Realizing that she had been tricked by Bu Qiao, Yaoqin burst into sobs. Madam Wang tried hard to pacify her, and it was a long time before Yaoqin finally calmed down. Madam Wang then changed Yaoqin's name to Wang Mei [Beautiful] and had everyone in the establishment call her Sister Mei. She was taught to play musical instruments and to sing and dance, all of which she did to perfection. By age fourteen, she had grown into a ravishing beauty. Rich young men in the city of Lin'an, laden with gifts, descended upon the Wang establishment to see her fair face. Those interested in literature and art, hearing about her talent, also came every day, asking for her poems and calligraphy, and her fame spread far and wide. Instead of Sister Mei, she became known as "The Queen of Flowers." A song to the tune of "Hanging Branch" in praise of her came to circulate among the young men of West Lake:

> *Who among the girls has Wang Mei's beauty?*
> *She writes, she paints, she makes poems,*
> *She plays the flute and the zither,*
> *She sings and dances—all with the greatest ease.*
> *The West Lake is often compared to Xishi*[6]
> *But even Xishi was in no way her equal!*
> *Those lucky enough to touch her body*
> *Find the experience worth dying for.*

With her kind of fame, there were men who made offers for her first night as soon as she reached fourteen years of age, but Wang Mei refused, and Madam Wang dared not go against her wishes, for the madam treasured her as if she were made of gold and therefore obeyed her as she would obey an imperial decree. Another year went by, and Wang Mei was now fifteen. Among the courtesans' quarters there is this convention: The first patron of a thirteen-year-old girl, too young to start working in the profession, is said to be a "tester of the flower." This happens because the madams are too greedy to care if the girl suffers, and the patron wins only false fame rather than real pleasure. At age fourteen, the flower "blooms" and begins to menstruate. This is the right time for the male and the female to give and take. At fifteen, the flower is ready to be "picked." A girl of fifteen in an ordinary home is still considered very young, but in the courtesans' quarters, a fifteen-year-old is considered to have already passed her prime. Since Wang Mei had not yet taken a patron at age fifteen, the young men of West Lake came up with another song to the tune of "Hanging Pearl":

> *Wang Mei is like a quince, pretty but only for show;*
> *At fifteen, she hasn't been with a man.*
> *What good is a courtesan in name only?*
> *If not a "girl of stone,"*[7] *she must be in fact a "he!"*

If her you-know-what is in good condition,
How can she put up with the itching?

Having heard such words, Madam Wang tried to talk the girl into taking a patron, afraid that her business would suffer. Wang Mei adamantly refused, saying, "If you want me to take patrons, you must bring me my parents. They have to agree first."

Madam Wang was exasperated but didn't have the heart to come down hard on her. (*This madam is not a bad sort.*) And so life went on as before. Quite some time later, an immensely rich Squire Jin Er offered three hundred taels of silver for Sister Mei's first night. Tempted by such an impressive amount of money, Madam Wang devised a plan. She told Squire Jin to do thus-and-so if he wanted to have his way. Squire Jin took the advice. On the fifteenth day of the eighth lunar month, Jin invited Wang Mei to West Lake to watch the tidal bore. Once she was in his boat, he and three or four of his accomplices engaged her in finger-guessing games and did everything they could to make her pay forfeit by drinking. When they had gotten her quite drunk, they took her to Madam Wang's house and put her in bed. The weather being warm, she had few pieces of clothing on. As she lay there unconscious, Madam Wang personally undressed her. Squire Jin was thus free to do whatever he wanted with the now stark-naked girl. That member of his being of none too brave a size, Squire Jin applied some saliva, softly pushed apart her thighs, and drove it in. By the time Sister Mei woke up from the pain, Squire Jin had already had his way with her. She tried to struggle herself free, but her limbs were too weak. The man took his pleasure of her until his lust abated, just as "the green darkens and the red fades [with the departure of spring]." Truly,

The flowers wilted in the rain after blooming;
The eyebrows lost their charm in the mirror.

As the night drum struck the fifth watch, Sister Mei woke up from her wine-induced sleep and realized that the madam had schemed to take her virginity. Lamenting that she who was blessed in looks but not in fate should be subjected to such brutality, she rose to go to the toilet. Then she put on her clothes, lay down on a speckled-bamboo couch by the bed, and turned her face toward the wall to hide her tears. When Squire Jin came up to seek intimacy, she scratched him right in the face, leaving trails of blood on his cheeks. Very much put out, he waited miserably until daybreak to bid the madam good-bye and was out the door before the madam could try to keep him.

The established practice in cases of first-night patronage is for the madam to go to the girl's room early the next morning to offer her congratulations. Other courtesans would follow to do the same. Then a celebration feast would be laid out, and the feasting would continue for several days. The patron would stay on for a month or two or at least fifteen to twenty days. No patron had ever left so early the very next morning, as did Squire Jin. In amazement, Madam Wang threw some clothes over her shoulders and went upstairs, only to see Sister Mei lying on the couch, her face awash in tears. In her eagerness to coax the girl into practicing her profession, Madam Wang apologized over and over again, but with Sister Mei keeping her mouth tightly shut, she could do nothing but go back downstairs. Sister Mei wept the whole day without touching any food or drink. From that day on, she refused to go downstairs or receive visitors on plea of illness.

Madam Wang was exasperated. If she were to rough Sister Mei up, the girl with her fiery temper, would most likely turn more bitter against her rather than submit. But if she were to let Sister Mei have her way, she would have no money to rake in. And if the girl was determined not to take on patrons, even keeping her for one hundred years wouldn't serve any useful purpose. So the madam debated with herself for several days in a row without coming up with a plan.

All of a sudden, she thought of a sworn sister of hers called Madam Liu the Fourth, with whom she had frequent mutual visits. This Madam Liu had the gift of the gab and was friends with Sister Mei. Why not invite her over and have her talk to the girl? If the girl could be brought around, she would thankfully make generous offerings to the gods. Right away, she sent a male servant to invite Madam Liu over.

The two women sat down in the front hall, and Madam Wang poured out her heart to her guest. Madam Liu the Fourth said, "I'm a woman Sui He and a female Lu Jia.[8] I can talk an arhat into falling in love and Chang'e the moon goddess into thoughts of marriage. Just leave everything to me!"

"If so," said Madam Wang, "I'll kowtow to you, even though I'm older than you are. Now drink more tea so you won't talk yourself thirsty."

"I was born with a sea of saliva that won't run short even if I talk nonstop from now on until tomorrow!"

After a few more cups of tea, Madam Liu went around to the room in the back of the house but found the door tightly shut. With a gentle tap, she cried, "My dear niece!"

Recognizing Auntie Liu's voice, Sister Mei opened the door. After an exchange of greetings, Madam Liu sat down at the guest's end of the table and Sister Mei sat down by her side. Noticing that spread out on the table lay a scroll of fine silk on which was drawn a yet uncolored sketch of a woman's face, Madam Liu said in praise, "Good job! What clever hands you have! Ninth Sister is so lucky to have a girl as smart and pretty and skillful as you are! Even if one searches through the whole city of Lin'an with an offer of thousands of taels of gold, one wouldn't find another girl like you!"

"Surely you jest," said Sister Mei. "Now, what wind brought you here today, auntie?"

"I've often wanted to come and see you. It's just that I'm too busy with household chores. Well, I heard that you've had your first patron. What a happy occasion! I took some time off today and came here to offer Ninth Sister my congratulations."

At the words "first patron," Sister Mei blushed furiously. She lowered her head and said nothing. Aware of the girl's shyness, Madam Liu hitched her chair forward and, taking Mei's hand into her own, said, "My child! Girls in this line of business can't be as tender as soft-shelled eggs. How can you ever make big money if you're so shy?" (*What a skillful talker!*)

"Why would I want money?"

"My child! You may not want money, but wouldn't your mother want to get back all that she spent in bringing you up? The ancients said, 'Live on the mountain, live off the mountain; live by the water, live off the water.' Sister Ninth has quite a few girls, but which of them is as good as you are? Of all the melons in the garden, you are the seed melon. And Sister Ninth treats you best. You are a smart girl. You should know better. I heard that you refuse to take on patrons after what happened that night. What's the meaning of that? If everybody is like you, who's going to feed mulberry leaves to this family of silkworms? For each favor that your mother does you, you need to make a good showing for her sake, rather than go the other way around and draw unkind words from the other girls." (*Every argument of hers appeals to the emotions. She's gradually getting there.*)

"They can say all the unkind things they want, for all I care!"

"Good gracious! Unkind words may not mean much to you, but do you know what this line of business is all about?"

"What?"

"We owners of the businesses live off the girls. If we get a nice girl by a stroke of luck, it's as if a large family has acquired a piece of fertile land or valuable property. When the girl is still small, we wish the wind would blow her into puberty. After she's had her first patron, it's as if the crops are ready for reaping. And we expect the money to come in every day. A good, famous house of pleasure is a busy one where new patrons are led in through the front door as old ones are escorted out through the back door, where Mr. Zhang brings in rice and Mr. Li brings in firewood."

"How shameful!" said Sister Mei. "I will not do such things!"

Covering her mouth, Madam Liu the Fourth giggled and said, "Will not do such things indeed! You think it's up to you? It's the madam who calls the shots in the family. If the girls don't do as she says, she can flog them any time she wants until they are more dead than alive. They will then do whatever she tells them to. Sister Ninth has never made life hard for you because you are smart and pretty, and you've been pampered since childhood. She respects your feelings and sensibilities. She just told me a lot of things, saying you don't know what's good for you, that you can't tell which one weighs more—a goose feather or a millstone. She was so upset she wanted me to talk you around. If you don't change your stubborn ways, you'll only get her back up. If she turns against you, yells at you, and beats you, where do you think you can go? To the sky? If there's a first time, there's going to be more. If you have to be beaten every day into accepting patrons, wouldn't you be cheapening yourself? You would otherwise be worth a thousand pieces of gold, you know! And you'll become a laughing stock among the sisters, too. As I see it, now that the water bucket has already fallen to the bottom of the well and can't be pulled up again, you might as well throw yourself happily into your mother's arms and just enjoy yourself."

"I'm from a decent family, in this place of sin by a quirk of fate. If you, Auntie, could help me marry and get out of this life, you'll be doing a better deed than building a nine-story stupa, but if you want to make me ingratiate myself with the patrons and lead new ones in and escort old ones out, I'd rather die than comply."

"My child! To marry and get out of this business is what any girl with any pride would want to do. How can I say no to that? (*Maneuvering tactfully to get to her point.*) But there are different ways of doing it."

"What different ways?"

"There are the real getting-out, the false getting-out, the miserable getting-out, the happy getting-out, the well-timed getting-out, the last-resort getting-out, the once-and-for-all getting-out, and the short-lived getting-out. My child, be patient and listen. What is the real getting-out? Generally speaking, if a bright young man marries a beautiful girl and a beautiful girl marries a bright young man, that's a good match, but the journey to happiness never goes smoothly, as they say. What happens most often is that one may seek but doesn't find the right match. If, by a stroke of good luck, a man and a woman meet, fall in love, can't tear themselves apart, want to marry, and won't let go of each other even in death, like a pair of moths, that's the real getting-out.

"What's a false one? A patron may love one of the girls, but the girl doesn't love him back. She doesn't want to marry him but, with the promise of marriage, lures him into spending money like water on her. By the time the promise is to be delivered, she turns him down on one pretext or another. There are also foolhardy men who know perfectly well that the girls don't love them but they take them home as wives anyway. They pay the madam so handsomely that she will make sure the girls comply. After the girls reluctantly enter the household, they will sulk and deliberately violate household rules. In minor cases, they make scenes. In more serious cases, they brazenly commit adultery until their husbands find it impossible to keep them. After six months to a year, the girls will be let go to pick up their old profession. So, marriage is used just as a pretext to make money. These are cases of a false getting-out.

"What's a miserable getting-out? Well, when a patron loves a girl but the girl doesn't care for him, the man will use his power to bully her. Afraid of getting involved in any trouble, the madam gives him her consent, and the girl goes in tears against her own will. Once she joins the rich family with its strict rules, she can't even hold her head high. She's somewhere between a concubine and a maidservant and wishes herself dead as her life drags on day after day. This is a case of a miserable getting-out.

"What's a happy getting-out? A girl on the lookout for a husband gets to know a patron of gentle temperament from a rich family, whose wife, kind but childless, hopes that the girl would join the family and bear children. If she does bear children, she will become a mistress of the family. So she gets to enjoy a peaceful life and a higher status after childbirth. This is a happy getting-out.

"What's a well-timed getting-out? Well, the girl has had her fill of romances. So, while her reputation is at its highest and her suitors numerous, she picks one whom she finds most satisfactory and marries him. By leaving this business while the going is still good for her, she beats a timely retreat so that she won't be cold-shouldered later on. This is a well-timed getting-out.

"What's a last-resort getting-out? The girl has no wish to marry her way out of the profession but does so nonetheless because she is forced to by the authorities, or because she is bullied or duped into doing so, or because she is in more debt than she can ever repay. And so in desperation she marries whomever happens to be available, to get herself a safe haven. This is a last-resort getting-out.

"What's a once-and-for-all getting-out? Having gone through everything that comes with this profession, the girl now reaches a certain age. It so happens that she meets a patron who is older and more mature, and they hit it off. She pulls in the ropes, so to speak, and lives with him to a ripe old age. This is a once-and-for-all getting-out.

"What's a short-lived getting-out? The girl and a patron fall passionately in love and she marries him on the spur of the moment without any long-term commitment. Then, either because his parents reject her or his wife is jealous of her and makes a few scenes, she is sent back to the madam's house for a refund. Or the man falls on hard times and can't support her anymore. So, unable to bear the hardships of such a life, she picks up her old profession again. This is a short-lived getting-out." (*A thorough and detailed exposé of the different ways to marry and get out of the business. Madam Liu and Granny Wang form a perfect pair in this line of profession.*)[9]

"I certainly would like to marry my way out of here," said Sister Mei. "How do I go about it?"

"My child, I have a surefire plan for you."

"If you can teach me how to do it, I'll never forget your kindness."

"As they say in this profession, a girl is not clean until she marries. Now, your body has already been sullied anyway. Even if you marry tonight, you won't pass as a virgin. (*Getting closer to the point.*) Of all mistakes, none is greater than to be in this place. This is your fate. Your mother has gone to such trouble for your sake. If you don't help her out for a few years and make a thousand taels of silver for her, how will she ever let you go out the door? And there's another thing: if you want out, you must pick a good man. You can't just go off with some disgusting guy. But if you don't take on patrons, how do you know which one is a good candidate and which one is not? (*By now, even a person made of iron will follow Madam Liu's baton wherever it leads.*) If you stand your ground, your mother will have no choice but to sell you off as a concubine to anyone willing to cough up the money. That's also a way out, but if the man is old or ugly or an illiterate country bumpkin, wouldn't you be doomed for life? That's even worse than if you throw yourself into the river, because at least you'll be making a splash and onlookers will cry out 'What a pity!' As I see it, you'd better follow your mother's wishes and receive patrons. With your talent and your looks, ordinary men won't dare ask for you. And men from royal and eminent families don't exactly bring you disgrace, do they? First, you should enjoy the romances this life has to offer while you're young; second, help your mother build up some family fortune; and third, have some private savings, so as not to have to ask for other people's help in the future. In five to ten years, if you meet someone who understands you and gets along with you well, let me be the matchmaker and marry you off in style. By that time, your mother won't stop you. Wouldn't that be nice for both of you?"

Sister Mei smiled but said nothing.

Detecting a slight thaw in the girl's position, Madam Liu said, "I mean well in everything I say. If you follow my advice, you'll have much to thank me for in the future." With that, she got up to go.

Madam Wang the Ninth, in the meantime, had been hiding by the door, listening to everything being said. Sister Mei bumped straight into her when walking Madam Liu out of the room. Painfully embarrassed, the girl shrank back into her room. (*A vivid detail that captures the girl's mind.*) Madam Liu followed Madam Wang the Ninth back to the front hall, where they sat down.

"She's a most stubborn girl," said Madam Liu, "but after I talked my head off, that piece of iron began to melt. Now you must quickly find her another patron. She'll surely take him. I'll then come to offer my congratulations."

Madam Wang the Ninth said her thanks over and over again and set out a fine meal in Liu's honor. They didn't part company until they were roaring drunk.

Later, another song to the tune of "Hanging Branch" about this episode came to circulate among the young men of West Lake:

> *Madam Liu the Fourth, what a tongue you have!*
> *No diplomat measures up to you!*
> *You leave no loopholes in your tittle-tattle.*
> *You sober up the drunk and stupefy the wise;*
> *Even a girl with the most fiery temper*
> *Yields to you and has a change of heart.*

To resume our story, upon further reflection, Sister Mei found much sense in Madam Liu's words. Henceforth, she began to take on patrons readily, and the patrons came in droves, keeping her busy and driving up her price. A night with her cost as much as ten taels of silver. Even so, the men fought with one another for their turns. Madam Wang the Ninth was beside herself with joy at the stream of silver coming in. Sister Mei, on her part, kept her eyes open for a candidate who was just right for her, but this was something that would take time. Truly,

> It's easier to acquire a priceless treasure
> Than to find a man after her own heart.

Our story forks at this point. By Clear Waves Gate of the city of Lin'an, there lived a Zhu the Tenth, owner of an oil shop. Three years earlier, he had adopted a boy, also a refugee from Bianliang, named Qin Zhong. The boy's mother having passed away long ago, his father, Qin Liang, had sold him when he was thirteen and gone to Upper Tianzhu Monastery to serve as an acolyte.

Zhu the Tenth had no children of his own. Being advanced in years and having just lost his wife, he treated Qin Zhong as his own son and changed his surname to Zhu. So Zhu Zhong began to learn the trade. In the beginning, things went well for the father and son as they went about their business, but then Mr. Zhu Senior began to be afflicted with a backache and had to lie in bed or sit most of the time. Unable to work, he hired a man called Xing Quan to help out in the shop.

Time flew by like an arrow. Quite unnoticeably, four years elapsed. Zhu Zhong was now a handsome young man of seventeen. Though old enough to wear a hat, he remained a bachelor. A maidservant of the family, called Orchid, now over twenty years of age, had her eye on Young Master Zhu and repeatedly made advances to him. But Zhu Zhong was an honorable and well-behaved young man. Besides, he found Orchid disgusting and ugly. This was a case of "The flowers falling into the water, seeking love/ But the water flowing on, untempted." Young Master Zhu being unresponsive, Orchid turned her eyes to Xing Quan, a bachelor in his late thirties. The two immediately hit it off. Finding Young Master Zhu too much of a hindrance in their many amorous adventures, they conspired to drive him out. So Xing Quan and Orchid worked in coordination to carry out their plan. To Mr. Zhu the Tenth, Orchid said in affected demureness, "The young master made passes at me several times. What a dirty man!" Mr. Zhu the Tenth could hardly suppress his jealousy because he, too, had had an affair with Orchid.

Xing Quan, on his part, stole some pieces of silver belonging to the shop and said to Zhu Senior, "Young Master Zhu gambles. What a good-for-nothing! He's stolen several times from the shop."

At first Zhu the Elder didn't believe what he heard, but after the two complained a few more times, the old addlehead who didn't know better called Zhu Zhong to him and gave him a good lecture. Being a smart young man, Zhu Zhong knew that this was the doing of Xing Quan and Orchid. He wanted to defend himself but gave up the idea, because if the old man did not believe him, he would only stir up a lot of trouble and offend them without doing himself any good. Then an idea came to him. He said to Zhu the Tenth, "With the business as slow as it is, you don't need two people in the shop. Mr. Xing can take care of the shop. I'll be glad to take up a carrying pole and a load of oil to peddle on the streets. Every day, I'll turn in every penny I make. Wouldn't that be another source of income for the shop?"

Zhu the Elder had a mind to say yes, but Xing Quan said, "He doesn't really want to peddle oil. The fact is, he has now saved up a tidy sum from years of stealing and he's mad at you for not finding him a wife. He doesn't want to work here anymore and is looking for a way out, so that he can get himself a wife and set up his own household."

With a sigh, Zhu the Elder said, "I treat him like my own son, but he is full of ill will towards me. Heaven will not protect such people. Oh well, he's not my own flesh and blood after all. There's no bond between us. I'll just let him be!" He told Zhu Zhong to leave but gave him three taels of silver, along with his clothes for every season and his bedding. This was an act of generosity to the credit of Zhu the Tenth. Knowing the latter would not relent, Zhu Zhong kowtowed four times to him and bade him farewell with bitter sobs. Truly,

> Prince Xiaoji died of words of slander;[10]
> Shensheng of Jin met the same fate.[11]
> Such tragedies befall even birth sons,
> Let alone adopted ones, however innocent.

As a matter of fact, Qin Liang [the boy's birth father] had joined Upper Tianzhu Monastery as an acolyte without telling his son about this. Now, after leaving Zhu the Tenth, Zhu Zhong rented a small room by All Peace Bridge, put down his baggage, bought a padlock, locked up the door, and took to the streets in search of his father. After several days went by without any news, he saw nothing for it but to give up the attempt. In all the four years he had lived with Zhu the Tenth, in his utter devotion to his adoptive father, he had not saved one penny for himself. The three taels of silver he received upon dismissal was all the money he had, but what line of business could he go into with such meager capital? He turned his thoughts this way and that before finally settling on oil, the only business he knew well. Being familiar with the oil dealers in the area, he thought that peddling oil would be a secure way for him to make a living. Right away, he bought the necessary equipment and gave the balance to an oil shop for a supply of oil. The owner of the shop knew Young Master Zhu to be good and honest, and was indignant that this young man, who had been working in Mr. Zhu's shop for all these years, was now reduced to peddling oil on the streets, all at the instigation of Clerk

Xing. Determined to help, the shop owner offered the purest of his oil, measuring out more than he charged the young man for. With these advantages, Zhu Zhong, in his turn, gave his clients good deals. Therefore, he sold his oil faster than others and turned a profit every day. Being a frugal man, he saved up some money with which he bought himself some housewares and clothes, but not more than was necessary. The only thing preying on his mind was the whereabouts of his father. He thought, "I've been called Zhu Zhong for so long that nobody knows that my surname is actually Qin. If Father comes looking for me, he won't have a clue as to who I am." And so he changed his surname back to Qin. (*Remember well the two surnames, Zhu and Qin, that have been changed back and forth.*)

Storyteller, when those of the upper classes with bright career prospects want to change back to their original surnames, they need to request permission from the imperial court or notify the Ministry of Rites, the Imperial Academy, the National University, and other departments, so that the registry books can be updated and the corrections made public. But how is a lowly oil-peddler to make his change of name known to the public? Well, this one had his own way of doing it. He painted on one side of each of his oil buckets a large character "Qin" and, on the other side, the two characters for "Bianliang." The bucket thus became an eye-catching mark of his identification. He came to be called "Qin the Oil-peddler" by all and sundry in the marketplaces of Lin'an.

One day in the second lunar month, when the weather was neither too hot nor too cold, Qin Zhong heard that monks of Zhaoqing Monastery were having a prayer service that was to last nine days and nights. Since they would be using a lot of oil, Qin Zhong carried his load there to make a sale. Having heard about Qin the Oil-peddler, who sold good-quality oil at a low price, the monks bought oil exclusively from him. For nine days in a row, Qin Zhong did his business only with this monastery. Indeed,

> Pettiness doesn't bring in gains;
> Honesty doesn't lead to losses.

On the ninth day, which was a glorious day, after having disposed of his oil at the monastery, Qin Zhong was carrying his empty load and walking along the water's edge through crowds of sightseers when he saw, some distance off, Ten-Scene Dyke with its pink peach blossoms and green willows. On the lake floated painted pleasure boats amid the music of flutes and drums. There was more to admire than his eyes could take in. Feeling tired after all this walking, he went back to an open space to the side of Zhaoqing Monastery, put down his load, and sat down on a rock to rest. Nearby stood a house facing the lake with a gilded gate and a clump of thin bamboo showing through the vermilion-colored balustrades inside. The interior of the house was not visible, but the doorway and the courtyard were certainly well kept. He saw three or four men wearing hats coming out and a girl behind them seeing them off. Upon reaching the gate, the men folded their hands and said good-bye, whereupon the girl turned back into the house. Qin Zhong fixed his eyes on her and found her to be the prettiest and the most lithe and graceful girl he had ever seen. He stood transfixed. Being as innocent as he was, he had no idea that this was a brothel. As he was wondering what kind of people lived in this house, a middle-aged woman and a young maidservant emerged from within. They leaned against the gate and looked around.

Her eyes falling upon the oil load, the middle-aged woman said, "Aya! I've been meaning to buy some oil, and here comes an oil peddler! Why don't we buy some from him?"

The maid went in and reemerged with an oil bottle. It was not until she was by the side of the oil load and cried out "Oil-Peddler!" that Qin Zhong became aware of her. "Oh, I have no oil left," he replied. "If your mistress needs oil, I'll deliver to her tomorrow."

Being somewhat literate, the maid recognized the character "Qin" written on the oil buckets and told the woman, "The oil peddler's surname is Qin."

Having heard that there was a Qin the Oil-Peddler known for his honest ways of doing business, the woman said to Qin Zhong, "I need oil every day in the house. If you are willing to deliver, you can count on me as a regular client."

"Thank you so much, ma'am. I won't fail you."

After the woman and the maid went back into the house, Qin Zhong thought, "I wonder who this woman is to the young lady. It'll be a stroke of predestined good luck if I can deliver oil to this house every day and get a look at the young lady. I don't care whether I make a profit or not." He was about to shoulder the load and set off when he saw two carriers of a blue-curtained sedan-chair, followed by two page boys, running as fast as they could toward the house. Upon reaching the gate, the carriers put down the sedan-chair and the page boys disappeared into the house. Qin Zhong said to himself, "How strange! I wonder whom they're picking up." Soon two maids came out, one carrying a scarlet felt bag, the other carrying a speckled-bamboo visiting-card box with carved designs. They handed both objects to the sedan-chair carriers, who put them under the seat. Then the girl he had seen before came out of the house, followed by the two page boys, one carrying a zither case and the other holding in his arms several scrolls with a jade flute dangling from his wrist. After the girl mounted the sedan-chair, the carriers raised it and went the way they had come. The maids and the page boys followed on foot. After having thus laid his eyes a second time on that girl, Qin Zhong felt even more intrigued. His load hanging from the pole over his shoulders, he went away slowly.

After a few steps, he caught sight of a wineshop by the river. He was not a drinker, but today, both delighted and saddened by the sight of the girl, he put down his load, entered the wineshop, and sat down by a small table. The waiter asked, "Are you treating friends or are you drinking by yourself?"

"I'm drinking alone. Give me three cups of your best wine and a couple of dishes of fresh fruit but no meat."

While the waiter was pouring out the wine for him, Qin Zhong asked, "Who lives in that house with the gilded fence gate?"

"That's Young Master Qi's property, now occupied by Madam Wang the Ninth."

"I just saw a young lady go off in a sedan-chair. Who's she?"

"She's Sister Wang Mei, a famous courtesan. Everybody calls her Queen of Flowers. She's a native of Bianliang but got stranded here. She's good at playing musical instruments, singing and dancing, chess, calligraphy, and painting. She takes only rich clients. It costs ten taels of silver to spend one night with her. Those who can't come up with the money have no chance. She used to live outside Yongjin Gate, but the house was too small. So about six months ago, her friend Young Master Qi lent her this house with its garden."

When Qin Zhong heard that she was also a native of Bianliang, a feeling of fellowship welled up in him, and his heart grew doubly fonder of her. After a few more cups, he paid his bill and picked up his load. As he walked along, he thought, "What a shame that such an out-of-this-world beauty should have ended up in a brothel!" Then he laughed at himself, "If she were not in this line of business, an oil-peddler like me would never have gotten to see her." Pursuing these thoughts, he indulged in another flight of fancy and said to himself, "A man has only one life to live, and grass dies in autumn. I would die content if I could hold such a beauty in my arms for one night." He went on thinking (*His thoughts do go everywhere.*) and said, "Bah! How can I have such fanciful ideas when I make only a few pennies a day out of my oil load! This is like a toad in a ditch craving the flesh of a swan. Impossible! She takes only rich patrons. She won't take an oil-peddler like me, even if I have the money." Then he thought again, "I've heard that the madams are only after money. They'll even accept a beggar if he can pay. I am a man with an honest business. If I can pay, why would they reject me? But where am I going to find the money?"

And so he indulged in these wild thoughts as he walked along, talking to himself. Isn't it a wonder that there are such fools in this world? A peddler who had started his business with only three taels of silver wanted to spend ten taels for a night with a celebrated courtesan. Isn't this an impossible dream? Well, as the ancients said, "Where there is a will, there is a way." He racked his brains and came up with a plan: "Starting from tomorrow, I'll save up whatever profit I make. Even if I put aside only one penny a day, I'll have three taels and six maces in one year. Another two years, and I'll be able to do it. If I put away two pennies a day, it'll take me only one and a half years. If I can put away more, one year will do." (*So long as one works hard at it, an iron pestle can be ground down to a needle.*) Preoccupied with these thoughts, he arrived at home before he knew it. His head was filled with such a jumble of thoughts all along the way that after he opened the lock on his door and went inside, he was overwhelmed by a feeling of misery at the sight of his own bed. Without even bothering to eat supper, he went to bed, but thoughts about the beauty kept him tossing and turning all through a wakeful night.

> *The one as fair as flowers and the moon*
> *Made his fancy run away with him.*

When daybreak came at last, he rose, filled his oil buckets, made breakfast, ate it, and locked the door. Carrying his load, he headed straight for Madam Wang's house. After going through the gate, he dared not barge into the house but craned his neck for a look inside. Madam Wang had just risen from bed and, her hair disheveled, was telling a male servant what food to buy. Recognizing the voice, Qin Zhong cried out, "Madam Wang!"

Turning her eyes toward the door, Madam Wang the Ninth said with a smile at the sight of Qin the Peddler, "What an honest young man! You kept your word." She summoned him in with his load of oil and had a bottle of about five catties filled up, for which she paid him a price she thought was fair. Qin Zhong did not haggle. Greatly pleased, Madam Wang said, "This bottle of oil can only last us two days. If you can come every other day, I won't buy from anyone else."

Qin Zhong promised and left with his load, regretting not to have seen the Queen of Flowers. He thought, "It's a good thing Madam Wang is now my regular customer. If I don't see her this time, there'll be a second time. If I still don't get to see her the second time, there'll be a third time. But there's one problem. To carry the load over such a long distance for Madam Wang alone isn't the right way to do business. Zhaoqing Monastery is on my way. Even though there's no prayer service there today, I'm sure they use oil for everyday purposes also. Let me go over and ask them. If the monks in the various halls can all buy from me, one trip to Qiantang Gate will be enough for me to dispose of all my oil."

It so happened that when Qin Zhong went to the monastery with his load to ask, the monks of the various halls were just thinking of Qin the Peddler. His timing was most opportune. All the monks bought oil from him in varying amounts and they arranged to have him make deliveries every other day. That day being an even-numbered day, they agreed that, henceforth, Qin Zhong would ply his trade elsewhere on odd-numbered days but make a special trip through Qiantang Gate on even-numbered days. Once outside the gate, he would first head for Madam Wang's house, ostensibly to sell oil, but actually to see the Queen of Flowers. He didn't get to see her every time. When he didn't, he would miss her sorely, but when he did, he would long for her even more. Indeed,

> *The sky and earth will end some day;*
> *But his love will live on forever.*

After many deliveries to Madam Wang, everyone in the house, old or young, came to know Qin the Peddler. Time flew by. Quite unnoticeably, another year had elapsed. Every day he put by pieces of the finest silver worth three pennies, or two pennies, or at least one penny. After he put together a certain amount, he would have the small pieces melted and made into a larger piece. As the days and months went by, his silver grew into a pile, which he wrapped up with a piece of cloth. Having saved them in a piecemeal fashion, he had no idea of the exact amount. One odd-numbered day with a pouring rain, he took the day off and stayed at home. The sight of the parcel of silver filled him with joy. He thought, "With all this time on my hands today, let me have the silver weighed out to get an exact figure." Holding an oilcloth umbrella, he went to the silversmith's shop across the street to use their scales.

This silversmith was a snob. He thought, "How much silver can an oil-peddler have to need my scales? Let me give him a small five-tael weight. He may not even need the largest cord." (*A petty man.*)

Qin Zhong untied the knot of his parcel to reveal all his loose pieces of silver. Generally speaking, a pile of loose pieces of silver may appear to be worth more than one ingot of equal weight. The silversmith being a petty man without having seen much of the world, his facial expression changed as he saw so much silver. Thinking to himself, "As they say, you can't judge a man by his looks, nor measure the sea with a pitcher," he hastened to set up the scales and took out many weights of varying sizes. Qin Zhong put his parcel onto the scale pan and saw that it weighed exactly sixteen taels, or one catty. Qin Zhong said to himself, "If I take off the three taels of capital, I still have more than enough for one night at that house." Then again, he thought, "I can't pay with these loose pieces of silver. They'll look down on me. While I'm in the silversmith's shop, why don't I have them made into nicer-looking ingots?"

Right away, he had some loose pieces weighing ten taels melted and made into a fine large ingot. A few pieces weighing one tael and eight maces were made into a small ingot. Then he picked a small piece from the remaining four taels and two maces and paid the silversmith. With a few maces, he bought himself a pair of white socks and a pair of shoes with fortified copper soles, and had a new square hat made. Back at home, he washed and starched his clothes and scented them over and over again with a few benzoin joss sticks.[12] On a chosen fine day, he rose bright and early and fitted himself out for the occasion.

> He may not be a rich patron,
> But he does cut a dashing figure.

All spruced up now, Qin Zhong put some silver in his sleeve, locked the door, and, in high spirits, headed straight for Madam Wang's house. Upon gaining the door, however, he was again gripped with a sense of his inadequacy. He said to himself, "I've always been the oil peddler to them. What am I going to say today as a patron?" Before he could make up his mind, the door opened with a creak, and out came Madam Wang.

At the sight of Qin Zhong, she said, "Young Master Qin, why aren't you doing business today but all dressed up like this? Where are you going?"

Now that things had come to this, Qin Zhong forced himself to step forward and make a bow. Madam Wang returned the courtesy.

"I am here to see you, madam."

Being an old hand in the business, the madam had the sharpest eyes. Noticing the young man's outfit and hearing his stated purpose of the visit, she thought, "He must be fancying one of my girls, and wants to spend some time or a night with her. Granted that he's no fat cat, whatever comes into my basket can be served on the table, be it veggies or crabs. Even if what money he brings in is enough for only a handful of green onions, it'll be better than nothing." Switching on an obsequious smile, she said, "Young Master Qin must be thinking of doing this old woman a favor."

"I have an impertinent request but I just can't bring myself to say it."

"It's all right. Let me hear it. Let's go to the sitting room. Feel free to say what you've got to say."

As an oil-peddler, Qin Zhong had been to the house a hundred times, but this was the first time his bottom had ever made acquaintance with a chair in that sitting room.

Once in the sitting room, Madam Wang had the young man take the seat of honor. She herself took the host's seat and called out for tea. Before long, a maid came in with tea. Recognizing Qin the Peddler, she lowered her head and giggled at the way the madam was treating him. Madam Wang said sharply to her, "What's so funny? Have you forgotten your manners?"

The maid stifled her giggles, collected the used teacups, and left. Only at this point did Madam Wang ask, "Young Master Qin, what is it you want to say to me?"

"Nothing much, really. It's just that I'd like to invite a sister of this house to a cup of wine."

"Just wine and nothing else? You must be thinking of spending some time with her in bed, too. You're not a wild one. Why this sudden interest in girls?"

"I've had this wish for quite some time now."

"You know all the girls in this house. Which one do you have in mind?"

"None other than the Queen of Flowers."

The madam's face hardened, for she thought the young man was making fun of her. "What a thing to say! You can't be teasing me?"

"I'm an honest man. I mean what I say."

"Even a night-soil bucket has ears [handles]. Haven't you heard that Sister Mei is expensive? Even if you sell off your oil business, you won't be able to come up with enough money for half a night. (*The procuress has a lot of nerve.*) Why don't you just pick a cheaper one?"

In mock surprise, Qin Zhong drew his head into his shoulders, stuck his tongue out, and said, "My goodness! You can't be bluffing? May I venture to ask, how many thousands of taels a night for your Queen of Flowers?"

His jocular tone dissolved Madam Wang's anger. Breaking into a smile, she said, "How can I ask for that much? It's ten taels of the finest silver, plus dinner treats and other expenses."

"I see. That's not a problem." He retrieved from his sleeve a large, smooth, and shining ingot of high-grade silver and handed it to the procuress, saying, "This one weighs a full ten taels and is of the finest quality. Please take it." Then he produced a small ingot and gave it to her as well, adding, "This two-tael piece is for a simple dinner. Please do me this favor. I'll never forget you. I'll have more gifts for you in the future."

The madam hated the thought of parting with the silver, especially that larger ingot, but she was also afraid that he might regret later on for having spent all he had on an impulse. She felt obliged to remind him, "It's not easy for someone in your business to come by ten taels. Think well before you do anything."

"I have made up my mind. Please don't worry."

The madam slipped the two ingots of silver into her sleeve and said, "All right, I'll do it, but it won't be an easy job."

"Aren't you the mistress of the house? Why do you say it won't be an easy job?"

"Sister Mei associates only with sons of the nobility, and with the rich and the powerful. She 'talks and laughs with great scholars and associates with no illiterates.'[13] How can she not know that you are Young Mr. Qin the peddler? How will she condescend to take you?"

"Could you please tactfully put it to her? If you can pull this off, I'll never forget your great kindness!"

Impressed by his determination, Madam Wang the Ninth knitted her eyebrows and hit upon a plan. With a smile, she said, "I've got a plan for you, but I don't know if this is in your fate. If I succeed, don't jump for joy. If I don't, don't hold me to blame. Sister Mei went to a dinner party at Academician Li's house yesterday and hasn't come back yet. Today, she's scheduled to go on a tour of the lake with Young Master Huang. Tomorrow she's invited by Hermit Zhang and others to a meeting of their poetry club, and the day after tomorrow, she'll be taken up with Minister Han's son, who made the arrangements a few days ago. You can come back for a look the day after that. Another thing: In the next few days, don't deliver oil to this house, so as to prepare everyone for your change of status. Also, you don't look like an upper-class patron in your cotton clothes. Next time you come, wear silk, so that the maids won't recognize you, and it'll be easier for me to cover up for you."

"I understand." With that, Qin Zhong bade her good-bye and went off. He suspended his business for three days and went to a pawnshop and bought a silk robe that was far from new, though not shabby. He put it on and walked leisurely around the neighborhood to practice ways of behaving like a gentleman. Truly,

> *Before he learned much about the brothel,*
> *He first practiced Confucian manners.*

Let us skip those three days but come to the fourth day. Qin Zhong rose at first light and went to Madam Wang's house. He was so early that he found the gate still closed. He had a mind to go for a walk, but, wearing such fancy clothes, he dared not go to Zhaoqing Monastery for fear of the monks' disapproval, and went instead for a walk by Ten-Scene Dyke. When he returned quite some time later, the gate was open, but a horse carriage was parked in front and many servants were sitting idly by. However unsophisticated he was, he had enough sense not to go in. Quietly, he signaled to the groom and asked, "Whose horse carriage is this?"

"We are sent by the Han establishment to pick up the young master."

Qin Zhong realized that Mr. Han had stayed overnight and had not yet left. So he turned away again and went to a restaurant, where he ordered some tea and food. He sat a while longer before returning to the Wang house for another look. Finding the horse carriage gone, he walked in. Madam Wang came up to greet him and said, "I'm sorry, but she's busy again today. Mr. Han just took her to East Manor to see the early plum blossoms. He's a regular customer. I can't say no to him. I heard that he'll take her tomorrow to Soul's Retreat Monastery for a few games of chess with a chess master. And Young Master Qi has asked for her a few times. Since he owns this house, I can't turn him down, either. Every time he comes, he stays for three to five days. Even I can't tell for sure how long he's going to stay. Now, Young Master Qin, if you really want her, you'll have to be patient and wait a little longer. Otherwise, I can give you back every penny of what you gave me the other day."

Qin Zhong said, "I'm just afraid that you won't be able to pull this off. Better late than never. I'll gladly wait even if it takes ten thousand years." (*Number-One lover.*)

Madam Wang said, "In that case, I'll surely be able to do it for you."

Qin Zhong was about to leave when the madam said again, "Young Master Qin, there's one more thing. Don't be too early next time you come to check with me. Let's make it sometime late in the afternoon. I'll surely let you know if she's free or not. Remember to be as late as possible. I have good reasons for saying so. Don't misunderstand me."

"I wouldn't dare! I wouldn't dare!"

That day, Qin Zhong did not do any business. The following day, he rearranged his load and plied his trade away from the Qiantang Gate area. Every evening, after his business of the day was over, he would dress up and go to Madam Wang's house for a reply, but to no avail. More than a month went by without any progress.

On the fifteenth day of the twelfth month, after a heavy snowstorm had cleared up and the west wind had dropped, the accumulated snow iced over in the bone-chilling air, but at least the ground was dry. After spending the better part of the day plying his trade, Qin Zhong put on his finer clothes as usual, and went again to hear a reply. Madam Wang greeted him and said, her face wreathed in smiles, "Today is your lucky day. Your chances are ninety-nine out of a hundred."

"What's that one out of a hundred?"

"Well, she's not in."

"Is she coming back?"

"Marshal Yu invited her to enjoy the snow scene. The feast is laid out in a boat on the lake. Marshal Yu is over seventy now, and is surely not in for that kind of thing. He said he would have her sent back at dusk. You can go to the bridal chamber, have a cup of warm wine, and wait for her."

"Would you please take me there, then?"

Madam Wang led Qin Zhong through many twists and turns to a bungalow of three spacious and airy rooms. The one on the left was a room for the maids, now unoccupied. It was furnished with a bed, a couch, and a table and chairs for the use of guests. The one on the right, the Queen of Flower's bedroom, was locked. On each side of the bungalow was a small side room. Hanging over the seat of honor in the living room in the middle was a landscape painting by a famous artist. On a side table stood an antique bronze incense burner with ambergris incense sticks aglow. On the tables on both sides were placed some antiques. On the wall were posted many scrolls of poetry. Feeling ashamed that he was not an educated man, Qin Zhong dared not look at them closely. He thought, "Even the living room is so nice. The bedroom must be really elegant. If I can get to enjoy all this luxury tonight, ten taels is not too much." (*Right.*)

Madam Wang offered him the seat for the guest of honor and sat down herself in the host's seat. Presently, some maids came in with a lit lamp and a big square table on which they laid out six bowls of seasonal fruit and a partitioned box filled with assorted delicacies. The aroma of the food and the fine wine assailed the nostrils. A wine cup in her hand, the madam said, "My girls are all occupied today. You'll have to put up with me as a drinking companion. Please drink to your heart's content."

With little capacity for wine and something weighing on his mind, Qin Zhong drank only half a cup of wine and, after a while, said he was not going to drink anymore.

The madam said, "Young Master Qin, you must be hungry. Eat something and then drink some more."

A maid laid down in front of Qin Zhong two bowls of snow-white rice, one for him to eat right away and the other for his second helping, along with a bowl of soup with mixed ingredients. Madam Wang, with her large capacity for wine, did not need the rice but went on drinking to keep him company. After finishing one bowl of rice, Qin Zhong put down his chopsticks. The madam said, "It's going to be a long night. Please eat some more," whereupon Qin Zhong helped himself to another half bowlful of rice. Then the maid came over with a lantern and said, "Your bath is ready, sir."

Qin Zhong had already taken a bath before he came, but, not daring to turn down the offer, he went to the bathroom and washed himself again with soap and perfumed water before putting his clothes back on and returning to his seat. Madam Wang ordered that the food be taken away and the wine be warmed up in a chafing dish. By this time, dusk had deepened into evening and the bells in Zhaoqing Monastery had been struck, but Sister Mei had still not returned.

> *Where is the fair one enjoying herself?*
> *He wears his eyes out awaiting her return.*

As the saying goes, "Waiting tries one's patience." Qin Zhong was quite distraught over the girl's absence. With the procuress talking her head off and plying him with wine, two more hours went by. Then a commotion was heard outside. The Queen of Flowers was back. As soon as a maid came to announce her arrival, Madam Wang hastened to rise and go out to greet the girl. Qin Zhong also stood up from his seat. Sister Mei, very much the worse for drink, was being helped into the house by a maid. Upon gaining the door, she stopped in her tracks at the sight, through her bleary eyes, of the litter of cups and plates in the brightly lit room. "Who's been drinking here?" she asked.

"My child," said the madam, "this is the Young Master Qin I've been telling you about. He's such an admirer of yours, he keeps sending gifts over. But you've been busy, so he's been waiting for more than a month now. Luckily you are free tonight. So I've kept him here for you."

"I've never heard of any Young Master Qin in Lin'an. I don't want to see him." With that, she turned to go. Spreading out her arms, Madam Wang blocked her way and said, "He is a good man, and very sincere. Trust me."

Sister Mei had no choice but to turn back into the room. As she stepped into the room, she raised her head and saw Qin Zhong. She found his face familiar, but, in her drunken condition, she couldn't recall his name on the spur of the moment. "Mother," said she, "I know this man. He's not an upper-class gentleman. I'll be laughed at if I take him."

"My child, this is Young Master Qin, owner of a fabric shop at Yongjin Gate. You must have seen him when we were living there. That's why he looks familiar to you. Don't mistake him for someone else. I was so impressed by his sincerity that

I gave him my promise, and I can't very well go back on it. Why don't you just let him stay tonight, if only for my sake? I know I'm in the wrong. I'll make it up to you tomorrow." While saying this, she pushed Sister Mei forward by her shoulders. Hardly able to fight back, Sister Mei had to go into the room and greet the patron. Truly,

> *A procuress' tongue has the sharpest bite;*
> *A procuress' hand just never lets go.*
> *Thousands of plans you may have in your head,*
> *But the best one is to bend to her will.*

Qin Zhong had heard every word but pretended to have heard nothing. After greeting him with a curtsey, Sister Mei sat down on one side and scrutinized him suspiciously. After sitting in gloomy silence for a while, she asked a maid for some warm wine. When the wine was brought to her and she began to fill a large cup with it, Madam Wang thought she was going to offer the cup to Qin Zhong, but, in fact, she drank it all up herself.

"My child, you're already drunk. You mustn't drink anymore."

Turning a deaf ear to her pleas, Sister Mei said, "I'm not drunk!" After more than ten cups in a row, which further added to her drunkenness, she felt her legs giving way under her. She had a maid open the door of her bedroom and light the lamps. Without bothering to remove the jewelry from her hair or untie her sash, she kicked off her embroidered shoes and lay down in bed fully clothed. Feeling apologetic for the girl's behavior, Madam Wang said to Qin Zhong, "My girl is used to throwing temper tantrums. She's a little upset today for some reason, but it has nothing to do with you. Don't take offense!"

"Oh I won't!"

The madam refilled Qin Zhong's cup a few more times. It was only at his firm insistence that she stopped. When walking him into the bedroom, the procuress whispered into his ear, "She's drunk. Be gentle." Aloud, she called out, "My child! You should get up and take off your clothes before going properly to sleep!"

Being already fast asleep, Sister Mei made no response. The madam had to take her leave. After clearing away the cups and plates and wiping the table, the maid said, "Young Master Qin! You can retire now."

"Could you give me a pot of hot tea?" said Qin Zhong.

The maid made a pot of strong tea and delivered it into the room. She then closed the door after her and withdrew into one of the side-rooms for the night. Qin Zhong saw that Sister Mei was fast asleep, lying on top of her brocade quilt with her face to the wall. Afraid that one in a drunken state would be susceptible to cold, he wished to do something but didn't want to disturb her lest she wake up. He saw that over the bedstead hung a scarlet silkfloss-padded and brocade-covered quilt. Noiselessly he took it down and spread it over her. He then picked the lamp wick until the lamp shone brightly, took off his shoes, got into bed with the pot of hot tea, and nestled up against her. With his left hand holding the teapot against his bosom and his right hand on Sister Mei, he dared not close his eyes even for one instant. Truly,

> He did not enjoy the clouds and rain,
> But he did nestle against fragrant jade.

In the middle of the night, Sister Mei woke up and felt the power of the wine getting the better of her. Feeling on the verge of vomiting, she struggled up to a sitting position, her head hanging low, and she retched over and over again. Qin Zhong also rose quickly. Realizing that she was about to vomit, he put down the teapot and stroked her back. After a while, Sister Mei could not hold out any longer. In less time than it takes to tell, she let go of herself and threw up. Afraid that the quilt would get soiled, Qin Zhong spread out the sleeve of his robe under her mouth. Unaware of his move, Sister Mei vomited with abandon. With her eyes closed, she then asked for tea to rinse her mouth with. Qin Zhong got down from the bed, quietly took off his robe, and laid it on the floor. Finding the teapot still warm, he filled a bowl with the savory strong tea and handed it to her. After finishing two bowls of the tea in quick succession, she lay down, feeling slightly better but still exhausted. Turning her face toward the wall, she went back to sleep. Qin Zhong rolled up his robe tightly around the soiled sleeve and put the bundle by the side of the bed. He then got onto the bed again and held her in his arm as before.

Sister Mei did not wake up until daybreak. Turning over, she saw a man sleeping by her side. "Who are you?" she asked.

"My name is Qin."

Vaguely recalling what had happened in the night, she said, unsure of herself, "I must have been dead drunk last night."

"No, you were not all that drunk."

"Did I throw up?"

"No."

"That's better," said she. But, after a few moments of thinking, she continued, "I remember I did. I also remember drinking some tea. Can I have dreamed everything?"

It was only then that Qin Zhong said, 'Yes, you did throw up. Because you had a drop too much, I had taken precautions by holding a teapot against my bosom to keep it warm for you. Then, when you threw up and asked for tea, I offered you some. You obliged me by drinking two cups."

Appalled, Sister Mei said, "But that was filthy stuff! What did I vomit into?"

"I was afraid that the quilt would be soiled, so I held up my sleeve for you."

"Where is your robe now?"

"I rolled it up and put it over there."

"Too bad your robe is ruined."

"I'm only too lucky to have something from you on my clothes."

Hearing these words, Sister Mei thought, "What a sweet man!" And she became more than a little favorably disposed toward him.

It being broad daylight by now, Sister Mei got off the bed to relieve herself. Looking at Qin Zhong, she suddenly realized that he was Qin the Oil Peddler. "Tell me the truth," said she. "Who are you? Why were you here last night?"

"I wouldn't dare to say anything but the truth to you, Queen of Flowers. Yes, I am Qin Zhong, often in this house to deliver oil." He then proceeded to tell her how he was smitten when he first saw her walking patrons to the gate and later mounting a sedan-chair, and how he had saved money to be with her. "Now that I've spent a night by your side, the happiness of it will suffice for three lifetimes. I can't be more content."

These words touched Sister Mei even more deeply. "I was too drunk last night to take care of you," said she. "Don't you regret that you got nothing for your money?"

"You are a fairy from heaven. My only worry is that I may not have served you well. I'm already happy enough that you are not angry with me. How would I dare to ask too much?"

"You have a business to take care of, so why don't you use your savings to support your family? This is not the kind of place for you."

"I'm a bachelor. I have no wife or children."

After a pause, Sister Mei continued, "Will you come back again?"

"My happiness last night is enough to comfort me throughout the rest of my life. How would I dream of the impossible?"

Sister Mei thought, "Such a good man is hard to come by. He's so honest and kind and considerate. He says only nice things about me and overlooks my faults. He's one in a thousand. Too bad he is of low class. If he were from a respectable family, I'd gladly marry him." While she was in the midst of these thoughts, the maids brought in water for them to wash their faces with, along with two bowls of ginger soup. Qin Zhong washed his face but he needed not comb his hair because he hadn't undone his hair the night before. After a few sips of the ginger soup, he said he was ready to go.

"Why don't you stay a while longer?" said Sister Mei. "I want to talk to you."

"I admire you so much, Queen of Flowers, that I'd be more than happy to be with you for as long as I can. But one must know one's place. I was impudent enough to have come here last evening. If others get to know this, I'm afraid your reputation will suffer. I'd better go as soon as possible."

With a nod, Sister Mei dismissed the maids. She then hurriedly opened her make-up box and took out twenty taels of silver. Handing them over to Qin Zhong, she said, "Last night was tough for you. This money is for your business. Don't tell anyone about it."

Qin Zhong stoutly declined her offer.

"Money comes easily to me," said she. "This little trifle is just to show my gratitude to you for your kindness last night. Don't turn me down. Any time you're short of money for your business in the future, I'll help you out. As for that soiled robe, I'll have a maid wash it clean before returning it to you."

"That worthless piece of clothing doesn't deserve your attention. I'll wash it myself. And I can't take your money."

"Nonsense!" So saying, Sister Mei stuffed the silver into his sleeve and turned him around. Realizing that he would not be able to prevail, he saw nothing for it but to accept. After making a deep bow, he put the rolled-up robe under his arm and walked out the door. When he passed by Madam Wang's room, a male servant saw him and exclaimed, "Ma'am! Young Master Qin is leaving!"

Sitting on her chamber pot at the time, Madam Wang cried out, "Young Master Qin! Why are you leaving so early?"

"I have a few things to take care of," replied Qin Zhong. "I'll come to thank you another day."

Let us not follow Qin Zhong as he left but stay with Sister Mei, who was moved by his sincerity and felt deeply sorry for this man whom she hardly knew. For the rest of the day, she turned away all visitors and stayed in her room to recover from her hangover. Of the entire legion of her patrons, her thoughts were with Qin Zhong alone throughout the day, as attested to by the following song to the tune of "Hanging Branch":

> My sweet foe is no frequenter of brothels,
> But a petty trader, a decent man.
> Tender, gentle, you know my heart and mind;
> You are neither hot-tempered nor fickle.
> I try to dismiss you from my heart,
> But my thoughts keep wandering back to you.

Let us follow another thread of the story and come back to Xing Quan, who was living in Zhu the Tenth's house. Xing was having an affair with Orchid, and, with Zhu confined to bed in his illness, they threw all caution to the winds. After several outbursts of anger from Zhu, the two of them worked out a plan. One night, taking advantage of the darkness, they took all the money of the shop and fled none knew whither. Zhu did not learn about this until the next morning. He had neighbors help him draw up a list of stolen items and go on a search for the two missing persons, but all to no avail. He deeply regretted having been misled by Xing Quan into dismissing Zhu Zhong. As the saying goes, "It takes time to know a person." Having heard that Zhu Zhong was now living in a rented place by All Peace Bridge and peddling oil for a living, he had a mind to take the young man back, so that he could have someone to look after him in his old age and to take care of the funeral after his death. But afraid that Zhu Zhong might still be bearing a grudge against him, he asked some neighbors to talk the young man into coming back home, and to advise him to remember only good things about people and banish bad memories. As soon as he heard these words, Qin Zhong packed his belongings and returned to Zhu the Tenth's house. Upon seeing each other, they burst into bitter sobs. Zhu gave all his savings to Qin Zhong. Throwing in his own savings of more than twenty taels of silver, Qin Zhong renovated the shop and resumed his position behind the counter.

Because he had returned to Mr. Zhu's house, he changed his name back to Zhu Zhong from Qin Zhong. Within a month, Mr. Zhu Senior's illness took a turn for the worse. Medicine failed to work, and he died. Zhu Zhong thumped his chest and wailed in grief as if the deceased were his own birth father. He took care of the funeral and held seven memorial services in all, one on every seventh day after the death. The Zhu family's ancestral grave site was located outside Clear Waves Gate. Zhu Zhong went about all the ceremonies strictly in accordance with etiquette and won praises from the neighbors for his kindness. After the rituals were over, the shop was reopened for business. This oil shop was one of long standing. Business had always been good, but because Xing Quan had been stealing from the shop to fatten his own pocket, the shop had lost many clients. However, now that Young Master Zhu was the owner of the shop, who would not come to patronize? Therefore the business grew to be even more prosperous than before.

Working all by himself, Zhu Zhong was anxious to find an experienced person to help him out. One fine day, a middleman called Jin Zhong led into the shop a man around fifty years old. It turned out that he was none other than Shen Shan (*Good plot*.), who had lived in Peace and Happiness Village outside the city of Bianliang. He was the one who had lost his daughter, Yaoqin, in their flight south when the government troops scattered the crowd of refugees. He and his wife spent the next few years of their lives on the road, fleeing in panic from one place to another. Having recently heard that Lin'an was a prosperous city where most of the refugees from the north had taken up residence, they made their way there to look for their daughter, but no clue was found. Their travel money all spent, they were reduced to their wits' end as the innkeeper kept pressing them to leave unless they paid the bills for room and board. Quite by accident, they heard Jin Zhong the middleman mention that the Zhu family oil shop needed an assistant. Shen Shan had been owner of a grocery store, and oil retailing was very much in his line. In addition, Young Master Zhu was a fellow native of Bianliang. So he had Jin Zhong take him to the shop. Zhu Zhong asked him some questions and was overcome with emotion upon learning that they were from the same place.

"Since you have nowhere else to go," said he, "you and your wife can stay with me, a fellow townsman. You can take your time looking for your daughter before deciding what to do next." Right away, he offered Shen Shan two strings of cash to pay the innkeeper with. Shen's wife Ruan-shi was also brought over to Zhu Zhong. After an exchange of greetings, Zhu Zhong had an unoccupied room cleaned up for the elderly couple to stay in. Much to Zhu Zhong's delight, the husband and wife did their best to help him out in every way they could in the shop and around the house.

Time flew like an arrow. Quite unnoticeably, more than one year elapsed. As Young Master Zhu remained a bachelor, many people were willing to offer their daughters to him and forgo the betrothal gifts, because they were impressed by his financial status as well as his honesty and sincerity. However, remembering the beauty of the Queen of Flowers, Zhu Zhong had no interest in those of mediocre looks and was determined not to marry until he found a girl with outstanding qualities. And so he dragged his feet as time wore on day by day. (*A clear explanation of why Zhu Zhong remains a bachelor.*) Truly,

> One who has sailed the vast seas
> Is not impressed by just any body of water.
> One who has been to the Wu Mountains
> Is not easily awed by just any cloud.

Let us come back now to Sister Mei in Madam Wang's establishment. Enjoying her reputation, she indulged in pleasure day and night. Indeed, she had more exquisite food and clothing than she could ever desire. And yet, every time things didn't turn out right, every time her patrons went too far or fought with one another over her or passed her over for some other girl, and every time she got ill or woke up in the middle of the night after a wine-induced sleep to find no one there to take care of her, she would recall Young Master Qin's kindness and regret that there was no way for her to see him again. Well, her life as a courtesan being predestined to come to an end around this time, a change in her fortunes was about to occur. One year later, something happened.

In the city of Lin'an, there lived a Young Master Wu the Eighth, whose father Wu Yue was the incumbent prefect of Fuzhou. Young Master Wu had recently returned home from his father's duty station with a liberal amount of gold and silver. With a penchant for gambling and drinking, he was also a frequenter of houses of pleasure. Having heard of the fame of the Queen of Flowers but never laid eyes on her, he sent over invitations time and again, but Wang Mei did not want to take him because she had heard unfavorable comments about his character. More than once she turned him down on one excuse or another. He also went several times in person to Madam Wang's house with his good-for-nothing friends to see her, but in vain.

It being the season of the Clear and Bright Festival,[14] every family went out to sweep their family graves and enjoy the sights and sounds of spring. Sister Mei was tired after all the spring excursions day after day. Moreover, she still owed some patrons quite a number of poems and paintings she had promised them. So she instructed the servants to turn away all visitors. Behind closed doors, she lit some joss sticks of superior quality and laid out the four treasures of the scholar's study.[15] She had barely picked up her brush-pen when she heard a commotion outside. It was Mr. Wu, followed by more than ten fierce-looking lackeys, here to take her on an outing to the lake. Because Madam Wang had turned him away each time, he and his men broke everything they saw and smashed their way from the main hall to Sister Mei's room, which they found to be locked. The truth of the matter was that the courtesans' way of rejecting patrons was for the girl to stay in her room with her door locked from the outside, and the patron would be told that she was not there. A naïve patron would be taken in by the trick but Young Master Wu, being a frequenter of houses of ill repute, was not to be deterred. He had his lackeys wrench off the padlock and kick open the door.

Sister Mei dodged but was not quick enough. Wu saw her, and, before she could protest, had two of his men drag her, one by each arm, out of her room. While Wu was spouting a stream of curses, Madam Wang wanted to go up and apologize to him to calm him down, but seeing that things had taken an ugly turn, she shrank back to get out of his way. All the members of the establishment hid themselves out of sight. And so Mr. Wu's lackeys dragged Sister Mei out the gate and tore with all speed down the streets, with total disregard for her small bound feet. Young Master Wu triumphantly brought up the rear. The two lackeys did not let go of Sister Mei until they got to the bank of West Lake, where they put her down into a boat.

Since joining the Wang establishment at age twelve, Sister Mei had enjoyed a pampered life in the lap of luxury. Never had she been subjected to such violence. Once in the boat, she covered up her face and burst into loud sobs, her face turned toward the bow of the boat. Young Master Wu did not relent but sat in anger in his chair facing the lake, in the pose of the valiant Guan Yunchang,[16] with his lackeys standing behind him. After giving the order for the boat to get on its way, he lashed out at Sister Mei, "Cheap little hussy! Little whore! You don't appreciate a favor when you see one! If you cry again, you'll be beaten up!"

Fearlessly, Sister Mei went on crying. Upon reaching the Mid-Lake Pavilion, Wu ordered some food set out in the pavilion. He himself went up first into the pavilion, saying to his men, "Bring that little hussy up for a drink with me."

Sister Mei clung to the railing of the boat and adamantly refused to budge, while crying at the top of her voice. Very much out of countenance, Wu drank a few cups of wine listlessly by himself, had the place cleaned up, and went back down into the boat. As his hands reached out for Sister Mei, she stamped her feet and wailed even more loudly. In a rage, Wu had his men pull off her hairpins and ear-rings. Her hair disheveled, she ran up to the bow and made as if to throw herself into the water, but the servants held her back. Mr. Wu said, "You think you can get away with your antics? Even if you die, it'll just be a matter of a few taels of silver as far as I'm concerned. Big deal! But I don't want to have a death on my hands. The moment you stop crying, I'll let you go back. I won't be hard on you."

Upon hearing that he would let her go, the Queen of Flowers stopped crying. By Wu's order, the boat moved to a quiet spot by Clear Waves Gate, where Sister Mei's embroidered shoes and foot-bindings were taken off, to reveal a pair of golden-lotus feet shaped like white bamboo shoots. After instructing his men to help her ashore, Wu said crossly, "Whore! Walk home if you can! I can't spare anyone to escort you." (*What a brute!*) With that, the boat was poled away from the shore toward the middle of the lake. Truly,

> *All too many burn zithers and cook cranes;*
> *All too few show kindness to the fair sex.*

Her feet now bare, Sister Mei could not take even one step. She thought, "With my talents and my looks, I got to be so humiliated only because I was driven to this profession. None of my rich and powerful patrons comes to my aid when I need them. Even if I make it back, how can I get on with my life in such humiliation? I'd be better off dead, and yet such a death would be worthless. All this reputation of mine will be for nothing. The way I am now, any village woman is far more fortunate than I am. This is all Madam Liu the Fourth's fault. It was her glib tongue that got me into this pass. The proverb says, 'Pretty face, sorry fate.' But no beauty since ancient times had a fate as sorry as mine!" Her grief deepening with these thoughts, she broke out into another violent fit of sobbing.

As coincidence would have it, it so happened that Zhu Zhong passed by at this moment. He had just paid his respects to Zhu the Tenth's grave by Clear Waves Gate and was heading for home on foot after having loaded the sacrificial offerings onto the boat. Upon hearing sobs, he went up for a look. However unkempt she was now, her one-of-a-kind beauty shone through. How would he fail to recognize her? (*Good detail.*) Much taken aback, he said, "Queen of Flowers, what happened to you?"

Hearing a familiar voice through her sobs, Sister Mei stopped crying to take a look. Lo and behold, it was that affectionate and considerate Young Master Qin. Feeling as if she had seen someone from her own family, she poured her heart out to him and told him everything.

Zhu Zhong's heart ached. With tears in his eyes, he pulled out from his sleeve a white silk kerchief more than five feet in length, tore it in half, and gave her both pieces to bind her feet with. He then wiped off her tears and gathered up her hair, all the while comforting her with soothing words. (*For someone truly in love, these actions are not disgusting.*) After Sister Mei had had her cry, he hastened to hire a curtained sedan-chair for her. Walking on foot, he escorted her all the way to Madam Wang the Ninth's house.

Having heard nothing about the girl's whereabouts, Madam Wang had been running around, making inquiries. It was at this anxious moment that she saw Young Master Qin escorting her girl back. She was overcome with joy at the return of her precious pearl. She had not seen Qin Zhong with his load of oil for a long time, and had heard from various sources that he had inherited Mr. Zhu's shop. In easy circumstances now, he was not the same man as before, and so she looked at him in a new light. (*Such is human nature. Procuresses are not the only ones to be snobbish, although those who are may be justifiably regarded as being as bad as a procuress.*) She asked why the girl was in such a state and, upon learning what an ordeal she had gone through and that Young Master Qin was the one who saved her, bowed deeply to him in gratitude and set out wine in his honor. The hour being late, Qin Zhong drank only a few cups before he stood up to leave, but Sister Mei was not about to let go of him. She said, "I've always liked you and hoped to see you again. I'm certainly not going to let you go this time without doing something for you."

Madam Wang also persuaded him to stay, to his great delight. That evening, Sister Mei played her musical instruments, sang, and danced, trying to please him to the best of her ability. (*A scholar dies for one who appreciates his worth; a woman makes herself pretty for one who strikes her fancy.*) Qin Zhong was thrown into raptures and almost danced for joy, feeling as if he were in a dream, roaming the fairyland. When night came and the wine was finished, the two of them went to bed in each other's arms. Their game of clouds and rain was as blissful as could be.

> *He was a young man in his prime;*
> *She a girl skillful in the art of love.*
> *He had dreamed about this for three long years;*
> *She had wished for this moment for one full year.*
> *She thanked him for his patronage last time,*
> *Which deepened all the more her gratitude now.*
> *He thanked her for obliging him tonight,*
> *Which added to the love he had in his heart.*
> *The courtesan overturned her powder box;*
> *The silk handkerchief was stained.*
> *The oil peddler knocked over his oil jar;*
> *The quilt became wet and soiled.*
> *The village boy who foolishly squandered his money*
> *Now became a figure of romance.*

The clouds and rain over, Sister Mei said, "I have something from the bottom of my heart to say to you. Don't turn me down."

"I'll do anything you want me to do, even if I have to go through boiling water and raging fire. How could I ever turn you down?"

"I want to marry you," said Sister Mei.

Qin Zhong laughed. "Even if you marry ten thousand men, I won't be able to make the list. Don't tease me. You'll only make the gods cut my life short."

"I mean it. How can you say I'm teasing you? I was fourteen when the madam got me drunk and made me take my first patron. Ever since then, I've wanted to marry and get out of this business. But because I had met too few people to tell the good from the bad, I was afraid I might marry the wrong man and ruin my future. Later, even though I took on many patrons, they were all big spenders and libertines. They buy pleasure with money. They care nothing about me. Of all the men I've met, you are the only trustworthy one. I've also heard that you are still single. If you don't look down on me because of my lowly profession, I will be more than happy to serve you as your wife for the rest of my life. If you turn me down, I will strangle myself with a three-foot-long piece of white silk and die at your feet to prove my sincerity. This will be better than dying at the hands of that bumpkin yesterday and getting laughed at for a worthless death." So saying, she started to weep.

Qin Zhong said, "Don't feel so bad. You are too kind. To have your love is more than anything I can ever wish for. Far be it from me to turn you down. But with my limited means, much as I want to, I won't be able to afford you at your high price."

"That's all right. To tell you the truth, in preparation for marriage to get out of this business, I have saved up some things which I've deposited elsewhere. So you don't have to pay a penny for my redemption." (*Thanks to Madam Liu the Fourth's advice.*)

Qin Zhong said, "Even if you redeem yourself with your own money, how are you going to put up with my way of life, after having lived in such grand style for so many years?"

"I'll be content with plain cotton clothes and simple food. I won't have regrets."

"You may be willing to do so, but I'm afraid the madam won't have it."

"I'll come up with something," said Sister Mei. The two of them talked until daybreak about what to do.

The truth of the matter was that Sister Mei had deposited many trunks and boxes with some patrons she knew well, such as the sons of Academician Huang, Secretary Han, and Marshal Qi. Now she took them back one by one, saying that she had a need for them. (*Sister Mei has the potential to do great things.*) Secretly she had Qin Zhong keep these possessions in his house. Then she went to Madam Liu's house in a sedan-chair and told the latter about her plan to marry.

"I did talk to you about this once," said Madam Liu. "But you're still too young to marry. And whom do you have in mind?"

"Auntie, never mind who he is. I did as you said. This is a case of a real getting-out, a happy one and the once-and-for-all kind. It's not a false one, nor a short-lived one. (*A wonderful reply, echoing Madam Liu's own words.*) If you, Auntie, could bring this up to Mother, she'll surely agree. I have nothing much to offer you, Auntie, but here are ten taels of gold for you to make some hairpins with. Please talk to Mother on my behalf. If you can talk her around, I'll have more gifts for you, the matchmaker."

At the sight of the gold, Madam Liu smiled until her eyes all but vanished. "You are like my own daughter. And this is a good thing, too. How can I take money from you? I'll just keep it for you for the time being. You can leave this job to me. I'm only afraid that your mother won't let you go off lightly because you are her money tree. She'll probably ask for a thousand taels of silver. Is your man willing to pay that much? I'd better see him and settle things with him first."

"Auntie, you don't have to concern yourself with this. Just look on it as if I'm paying for my own redemption."

"Does your mother know you are here?"

"No."

"All right. You stay here for lunch. I'll go talk to her. If she changes her mind, I'll come back to let you know."

In a hired sedan-chair, Madam Liu the Fourth went to see Madam Wang. After Madam Wang showed her in, she asked about what Young Master Wu the Eighth had done. After hearing Madam Wang' s account, Madam Liu said, "For those of us in this business, it's better to have girls of the middling sort, because they bring in money but don't cause trouble. They don't pick and choose their patrons, and they bring in business every day. But this girl has got too much of a name for herself. She's like a piece of dried fish that has fallen onto the ground: all the ants will swarm up to take a piece of her. Business is good, but there's also a down side to it. She's expensive all right, but she brings you only hollow reputation. Those rich young patrons come with their lackeys who stay the whole night, and that's a lot of work for you because every one of them has to be served well. One slip, and they'll curse you with their foul mouths and break your furniture on the sly. You can't very well complain to their master about them. You just have to swallow the humiliation. (*What a glib tongue! This is only the beginning of much more to come.*) And then, there are those patrons with literary interests and those members of poetry societies and chess clubs, and, several times each month, those girls on the government roster have to provide free entertainment services. With all the rivalry going on among the rich young men, if you give Sister Mei to Mr. Zhang, you offend Mr. Li. When one man is pleased, the other will surely complain. The row kicked up by Young Master Wu was frightening enough. If something had happened to her, you would have lost your capital, and you can't very well sue an official's family. There's nothing for it but to put up with the insult. Thanks to the gods' blessings, nothing much happened to you this time. It was like a thunderstorm that has blown over. But if something unfortunate happened, regrets would have been too late. (*A roundabout way of getting to her purpose: make the madam free*

Sister Mei from the cage.) I heard that Young Master Wu the Eighth is up to some mischief and still wants to pick a quarrel with you. That girl of yours has quite a temper. Her refusal to play up to the patrons is the first source of trouble."

Madam Wang said, "Yes, this is exactly what I worry deeply about. This Young Master Wu is not just anybody. He's no lowly sort. It was just because that girl would rather die than receive him that she got into all this trouble. She used to listen to me when she was small. Now that she has built a name for herself, with all those rich young men praising her, coddling her, and spoiling her, she does things her own way all too often. She gets to decide whether to take a patron or not. If she happens to be unwilling, even a team of nine oxen won't be able to pull her around."

"Girls with some status all act like this," said Liu. (*Another push.*)

"Now, listen. If there's an offer for her, I'd rather sell her off and be done with it, so that I won't have to live in fear anymore."

"Wonderful!" said Liu. "With the money you get for her, you can buy five or six girls. If lucky, you may even get ten. It's such a good deal! Why don't you go for it?"

"I've been doing some thinking. Those with money and power hate to part with their money. Instead, they are always out to get a good deal. As for those willing to cough up some money, that girl is so picky she turns them down with that high and mighty air of hers. If there's a good offer for her, could you please make the match? If she's not willing, I'll have to ask you to talk to her. She doesn't listen to me. She believes only in you. You can talk her around."

Bursting into laughter, Madam Liu said, "The purpose of my visit is precisely to make a match for her. How much would you ask for her?"

"Sister, you are a sensible person. In our line of business, we buy cheap, but have you heard of any cheap sales? Also, Sister Mei has been well known for years throughout Lin'an. Who hasn't heard of the Queen of Flowers? She can hardly be let go with just three or four hundred taels. A thousand taels is the minimum."

"I'll do the asking. If I can get that much, I'll come back to let you know. If not, I won't be back." Before leaving, she asked, feigning ignorance, "Where is she?"

"Oh, don't even get me started on this! Ever since that day when she was roughed up by Wu the Eighth, she's been afraid that he'd come again to make more trouble. So she's been going around in her sedan-chair from house to house to complain. The day before yesterday, she went to Marshal Qi's house; yesterday, to Academician Huang's. I have no idea where she went today."

"Since you've made up your mind, she'll have to do as you say. In case she says no, I'll talk to her. But if I produce a buyer, be sure you don't put on airs."

"I won't go back on my word," said Wang, who then walked her guest to the gate. Madam Liu said good-bye and mounted her sedan-chair. Truly,

> She had the tongue of a diplomat;
> She was endowed with the gift of the gab.

If all tongues wag like a procuress's,
Huge waves can rise from a puddle.

After returning home, Madam Liu said to Sister Mei, "I told your mother thus-and-so, and she has agreed. As long as she sees the money, this will be done."

"I've got the money," said Sister Mei. "Tomorrow, please be sure to come to see me and close the deal. Don't let it cool off, so that we won't have to start the whole thing over again."

"A promise is a promise," said Liu. "I'll surely be there."

Sister Mei bade Madam Liu good-bye and went home. She did not breathe a word to anyone about the matter.

Around noon the next day, Madam Liu made an appearance, as promised. Madam Wang asked, "Any news?"

"It's as good as settled. I just haven't spoken to the girl yet."

Madam Liu then went to Sister Mei's room. After an exchange of greetings and amenities, Liu asked, "Is the client here? And where's the you-know-what?"

Pointing at the head of her bed, Sister Mei replied, "Everything's in those leather trunks." Whereupon she opened all five or six of them and took out thirteen or fourteen packages, each containing fifty taels of silver. Together with her jewelry items, they amounted to a thousand taels.

Madam Liu was flabbergasted. Her eyes spitting fire, her mouth drooling, she thought, "How can such a young girl be so crafty! How did she manage to put aside so much? Don't those girls of mine take patrons just as she does? But they don't come anywhere close! They don't make as much, of course, but even if they have a few pennies in their purses, they spend them on dried melon seeds and candies, and have me buy fabric for them when their foot-bindings wear out. Sister Wang is the lucky one. She already made a fortune out of this girl over the years, and now here comes along this windfall as the girl gets out. And the money is right here in the house, too, so Sister Wang is spared the trouble of going out to get it." But the words remained unsaid.

Taking Liu's silence to mean that she was trying to make things difficult for her and hit her up for a reward, Sister Mei hastened to take out four lengths of fine silk, two hairpins inlaid with jewels, and a pair of jade hairpins with phoenix patterns. Laying them out on the table, she said, "These are a token of my gratitude to you for what you've done for me."

Merrily, Liu went to Madam Wang and said, "Your girl is buying her own way out. You get the full amount, not a penny less. This is better than having a patron redeem her. Otherwise, you would have to thank the middlemen with feasts and a ten or twenty percent commission." (*Madam Liu never fails to make her point drive home. There's hardly anything she can't sell.*)

When Madam Wang heard about all the riches contained in the girl's leather trunks, her face fell. You may well ask why. Well, of all people in this world, procuresses are the most ruthless. They are not satisfied until their girls surrender everything they make. If the madams hear of any girl with private savings stashed away in a trunk, they would wait until the girl is away to break the locks and ransack the boxes and trunks until they empty them of everything of worth. (*An aside as a lull in the thickening plot.*) In this case, Madam Wang had never dared provoke Sister Mei because the girl had fame, and her patrons were all rich and powerful men who brought in money for the procuress, and because the girl was a little eccentric. Madam Wang had never even set foot in Sister Mei's bedroom. How could she have known that the girl had that kind of money!

Guessing from Madam Wang's dark brows what was in her mind, Madam Liu hastened to say, "Sister Ninth, you're not going to have second thoughts, are you? Those are her private savings. They didn't rightfully belong to you anyway. If she'd spent them, they'd be all gone now. Or, she might have been stupid enough to subsidize a patron who strikes her fancy, for all you know! It's a good thing that she has been frugal. Also, if a girl doesn't have any money of her own, can you drive her out naked when she marries? You'll have to deck her out from head to toe, so that she can hold her head up in her new family. Now, Mei has come up with all these things without ever having to trouble you the least bit. This money is yours, every penny of it. Even after she gets out, she'll still be a daughter to you. If she makes a good living, she'll surely come back with gifts to see you at festivals. After she marries, she'll still be without parents. You can be a grandmother to her children. Won't that be quite nice for you?" These words so pleased Madam Wang that she gave her consent then and there.

Madam Liu went and brought over the packages of silver, which she weighed one by one before handing them over to Madam Wang. She also appraised the jewelry piece by piece. She said to Madam Wang, "I deliberately marked down the price. If you sell them, you should be able to make dozens of taels extra." Though they were both procuresses, Madam Wang was more simpleminded and hung on every word of Liu's.

After witnessing Madam Wang put away everything, Madam Liu had Mr. Wang write a note permitting the girl to marry, and transmitted it to Sister Mei.

"While you're here, Auntie," said Mei, "I'd like to say good-bye to Father and Mother and stay in your home for a couple of days before I choose a lucky day for the wedding. Would you be willing to do that?"

Having accepted the many gifts from Sister Mei, Madam Liu was afraid that Madam Wang the Ninth would back out of the deal. She would be only too happy to get the girl out of the house and be done with it. "Yes, of course," said she in reply.

Right away, Sister Mei began to pack up her toilette boxes, leather trunks, and bedding, but left untouched everything that belonged to the procuress. Her packing finished, she followed Liu out of her room and bade farewell to the madam and her husband and all the other girls. Madam Wang the Ninth gave a few sobs, as befitted the occasion. Sister Mei told the servants to carry her baggage and merrily mounted a sedan-chair with Madam Liu. Upon arrival at Liu's house, Madam Liu put up Sister Mei, along with her baggage, in a nice and quiet room, and Madam Liu's girls all came to offer their congratulations. That evening, Zhu Zhong sent Shen Shan to Madam Liu's house to ask how things were going and learned that Sister Mei had already gotten out. On a chosen auspicious day, the wedding took place amid the music of *sheng* pipes, *xiao* flutes, and drums, with Madam Liu as the matchmaker giving the bride away. Zhu Zhong and the Queen of Flowers spent the night in boundless joy in the bridal chamber decorated with carved candles.

> *Their romance of the past*
> *Did not reduce their joy as groom and bride.*

The following day, when Shen Shan and his wife came to greet the bride, all three of them were dumbstruck upon seeing one another. After some questions and answers, the three of them fell on one another's shoulders and cried. Only then did Zhu Zhong realize that the elderly couple were in fact his parents-in-law. He offered them seats of honor and, together with his bride, bowed to them anew. The neighbors who heard about this were all amazed. On that very day, a feast was laid out in celebration of the doubly happy occasion. All drank and enjoyed themselves thoroughly before the party broke up. Three days later, Sister Mei had her husband prepare some nice gifts and offered them to her former patrons to thank them for their kindness in allowing her to deposit her trunks and boxes, as well as to let them know that she had gotten out and married. This goes to show that she was not a person to leave things at loose ends. She also offered gifts to Madam Wang the Ninth and Madam Liu the Fourth, who were filled with gratitude. After a month had gone by, she opened her trunks and boxes to reveal gold, silver, and silk from the Wu region and brocade from the Shu region, which all came to more than three thousand taels in value. She handed all the keys to her husband for him to acquire land and property and expand the family possessions. The oil shop came to be run by her father, Mr. Shen. In less than a year, the business boomed and the family grew rich enough to hire servants and live in grand style.

Out of gratitude for the blessings of the gods of heaven and earth, Zhu Zhong decided to donate a three-month supply of candles and oil to the various monasteries in the area. He observed a Buddhist diet, took a bath, and went to the monasteries to pay homage. He started from Zhaoqing Monastery and went on to the monasteries of Soul's Retreat, Faxiang, Clear Mercy, and Tianzhu. Let us focus our attention on Tianzhu Monastery. Dedicated to the Bodhisattva Guanyin, it consisted of the Upper Tianzhu, the Middle Tianzhu, and the Lower Tianzhu monasteries, with all their crowds of worshipers, but they were located in the mountains and were inaccessible by boat. Zhu Zhong had some men carry one load of candles and three loads of clear oil while he himself took a sedan-chair. He went to the Upper Tianzhu first, where the monks greeted him and led him into the main hall. Mr. Qin, the old acolyte, lit the candles and took care of the incense.

In changed circumstances now, Zhu Zhong had taken on a dignified look, a far cry from the way he had looked in his childhood. Small wonder that Mr. Qin Senior did not recognize his very own son. He did feel intrigued by the big characters "Qin" and "Bianliang" on the oil buckets. What a coincidence that those very two oil buckets had been brought to Upper Tianzhu Monastery!

After Zhu Zhong had finished burning joss sticks, Mr. Qin Senior brought in tea on a tray and the abbot served the tea to the guest.

Mr. Qin Senior said, "May I venture to ask the benefactor the reason for those three characters on the buckets?"

Detecting a Bianliang accent, Zhu Zhong hastened to ask, "Why do you ask, sir? Might you be a native of Bianliang, also?"

"Yes, I am indeed."

"What is your name? Why did you join the Buddhist order in this temple? How many years have you been here?"

Mr. Qin Senior told him his name and where he was from. "I came here years ago to flee from the soldiers. I had no means of livelihood, so I gave up my thirteen-year-old son, Qin Zhong, for adoption by a Zhu family. It's been eight years now. I'm so old and frail that I haven't gone down the mountain to make inquiries about him."

Zhu Zhong flung himself upon the acolyte and cried bitterly. "I am Qin Zhong, your son," said he. "I used to peddle oil for the Zhu family and I wrote those three characters on the buckets in order to seek you out. Who would have thought that we would meet here! This is indeed a blessing from heaven!"

The monks all marveled at this reunion of father and son after eight years of separation. That night, Zhu Zhong stayed in Upper Tianzhu Monastery with his father and they filled each other in on what had happened to them in these years. The next day, Zhu Zhong changed his name back to Qin Zhong on the prayer sheets of Middle Tianzhu and Lower Tianzhu monasteries. After the incense-burning services in both places were over, they turned back to Upper Tianzhu Monastery. Qin Zhong wanted to have his father live with him so that he could support and look after him. But, having joined the Buddhist order many years before, Mr. Qin Senior had become used to a vegetarian diet and did not want to go and live with his son.

"After an eight-year separation," said Qin Zhong, "I should make up for lost time and provide for you, Father. In addition, I've just married. My wife should also pay her respects to her father-in-law." Mr. Qin Senior felt obliged to consent. Qin Zhong yielded his sedan-chair to his father. He himself walked all the way home. Once in his house, Qin Zhong took out new clothes for his father to change into, had him take the seat of honor in the main hall, and bowed with his wife, Shen-shi, to him. His parents-in-law, Mr. Shen and Ruan-shi, also came to greet Mr. Qin. A grand feast was laid out later in the day. Mr. Qin declined offers of meat and had vegetables and wine only. The next day, the neighbors came with gifts of money to congratulate them on the wedding, the bride's family reunion, the reunion of the father and son, and the resumption of Young Master Qin's original family name. It was thus a four-fold joyous occasion. The feast of celebration lasted for several days.

Mr. Qin Senior was not willing to stay on. He wished to go back to Upper Tianzhu Monastery to lead a quiet Buddhist life. Qin Zhong did not want to go against his father's wishes. With two hundred taels of silver, he had a separate house built for his father there. Once every month, he had supplies of daily necessities sent over and every tenth day he personally went to see his father. Once every three months, he took his wife Shen-shi along to see him. Mr. Qin Senior lived to be over eighty years of age, until one day he sat down solemnly and passed away. In accordance with his will, he was buried on that very mountain, but this happened later and is not part of our story.

Now let us come back to Qin Zhong and Shen-shi. They had two sons. Husband and wife lived together to a ripe old age, and the two sons later gained fame as scholars. Even to this day, when praising a lover who is affectionate and considerate, those in the houses of pleasure will refer to him as "Young Master Qin" or "Oil peddler." There is a poem in testimony:

> When spring is here and the flowers are in bloom,
> Bees and butterflies busily cull their essence.
> Pity those sons of wealthy families,
> Who lost to the oil-peddler in romance.

The Leather Boot as Evidence against the God Erlang's Impostor

Past tender green willow branches,
In lingering chill as soft as water,
Amid a drizzle as fine as dust,
Blows a gust of east wind, bringing
Wrinkles to gauze and ripples to water.

Fairy maidens, spirits of flowers and the moon,
Play pipes and flutes to cheer the new season.
With toasts to the long life of the sovereign,
With what the Nine Clouds cups have to offer,
Comes eternal drunkenness on the scents of spring.

The above lyric, to the tune of "Green Willow Tips," was written by a scholar of the Song dynasty founded by Emperor Taizu [r. 960–76].[1] The eighth emperor who succeeded the throne, Emperor Huizong [r. 1101–25], also known as the Venerable Daoist Emperor of Xuanhe of the Jade Hall of Purity in the Highest Layer of Heaven, was in fact a reincarnation of Li Yu [937–78] from south of the Yangzi River, last king of Later Tang. What had happened was that in an interior hall of the palace one day, his father, Emperor Shenzong [r. 1068–86], came upon the portrait of King Li when viewing the portraits of emperors and kings of past dynasties. Li Yu's gracefulness and otherworldly appearance so impressed him that he let out one sigh of admiration after another. Later, he had a dream in which he saw King Li enter the palace, a dream that was soon followed by the birth of Emperor Huizong. Enfeoffed as Prince Duan in his childhood, Emperor Huizong cut a dashing and romantic figure very early on and proved himself capable in every endeavor he undertook. Upon the death of his older brother, Emperor Zhezong [r. 1086–1101], Prince Duan succeeded to the throne with the support of the court ministers. Thereafter, peace reigned throughout the land and the imperial court had little to do.

With his love of gardens, Emperor Huizong ordered a grand construction project in the first year of the Xuanhe reign period [1119–26]. A park with a pond was to be built in the northeastern corner of the city, and the site was named the Silver Hill of Longevity. Emperor Huizong put Liang Shicheng [d. 1126], the eunuch, in charge of the construction and ordered Zhu Mian [1075–1126] to collect and offer to him prized and rare flowers, trees, bamboos, and ornamental rocks from the area south of the lower reaches of the Yangzi River and the Sichuan and Liangguang regions.[2] He called the project the Organized Transportation of Flowers and Rocks.

It took several years, all the savings of the treasury, and the best craftsmen of the land to build the park, which, when completed, also came to be called Ten-Thousand-Year Hill. It was filled with exotic flowers, beautiful trees, and rare birds and animals. The grandeur of the towers and terraces defies description. There were Jade Flower Hall, Peace Preservation Hall, Jasper Forest Hall, Great Serenity Chamber, Celestial Purity Chamber, Wonders Chamber, Rolling Hills Chamber, Rosy Clouds Pavilion, Phoenix on Clouds Pavilion, and, indeed, more attractions than can be enumerated. The six court ministers, Cai Jing [1047–1126], Wang Fu [1079–1126], Gao Qiu [d. 1126], Tong Guan [1054–1126], Yang Jian [d. 1121], and Liang Shicheng, known as "the Six Villains of Xuanhe," often toured the grounds. There is a poem in testimony:

> *The forest of jade buildings stood amid*
> *The mottled shade of bamboos and pine trees.*
> *Those touring the grounds by imperial grace*
> *Thought that they were treading on clouds.*

Southwest of Peace Preservation Hall, there stood True Jade Hall in which resided Lady An, the emperor's most beloved consort, and a splendid place it was. The gate was adorned with elaborately carved golden heads of beasts that held ringed knockers in their mouths. Along with the dainty jade railings, they dazzled the eye and quickened the pulse. Cai Jing and his cohorts, as guests of the emperor at the banquet table there, had left poems on the walls, as the following lines attest:

> *To Peace Hall in all its autumn splendor*
> *The emperor invited mortal souls.*
> *To the wining and dining in True Jade Hall*
> *Was added the pleasure of viewing Lady An.*

But this is not a story about how Lady An enjoyed the special favor of the emperor. Instead, I shall tell of another imperial consort, a certain Lady Han Yuqiao. She was only fifteen when she was selected into the palace. With her jade pendants tinkling and her silk skirt swaying as she walked, she had skin as fair as glistening snow and a face as charming as a lotus blossom. However, since the emperor gave Lady An undivided attention, Lady Han never had a chance to be with the emperor.

Our story begins on a spring day when the enchanting scenery saddened our beauty, Lady Han, and gave her chills as she lay on her red mattress under her green quilt. When the moon shone on the jade terrace, her sorrow made her deaf to the notes of pipes and flutes. When insects chirped by her white walls, her grief kept her awake under her quilt embroidered with lovebirds. She grew weary of doing her morning toilette and languished from the torment of her spring desires. With one sigh after another, she became ill, as attested by the following lyric:

> She let the east wind blow her youth away,
> While the tears never ran dry on her face.
> Early or late, cold or warm, rain or shine,
> Every spring takes away some beauties' lives.
> Only drifting fallen flowers hang on to spring.
> The sweet grass confuses the dancing butterflies;
> The green willows talk to the orioles in vain.
> One has made the love potion,
> But the lover is gone.
> She finds herself in a trance,
> As if dancing in rapture,
> As if waking with a start from a dream.

She gradually wasted away like a shriveling willow or a fading flower. An imperial physician took her pulse and gave her a prescription, but the medicinal broth she took might just as well have been splashed onto a rock.

One day, Emperor Huizong summoned Marshal Yang Jian of the palace guards to a side hall and gave the marshal these instructions:[3] "Since you are the one who offered Lady Han to me, you take her to your home now and take good care of her. She can come back to the palace after she regains her health. The imperial caterers will continue to deliver her food every day, and the imperial pharmacy will provide her with medicine. Let me know as soon as her condition begins to improve."

Yang Jian kowtowed in acknowledgment of the order and immediately had palace attendants as well as his private attendants transport Lady Han's trunks, cases, household utensils, and miscellaneous items to his residence. She was then carried there in a curtained sedan-chair with an entourage that included two waiting women and two maids. The marshal went inside first to tell his wife about the matter so that she could come out and greet the guest. The residence was then divided into two sections, and the western quarters were cleaned up for Lady Han to live in. A padlock was put on the gate, through which only physicians and household servants were allowed access. The marshal and his wife went to visit Lady Han once every day. For the rest of the time, the gate remained locked. A bucket stood to one side, for the delivery of food, beverages, and messages. Truly,

The green grass by the steps bespeaks spring;
The orioles behind the leaves sing in vain.

In about two months, Lady Han regained the color in her cheeks, and her appetite grew slightly. In delight, the marshal and his wife laid out a feast, partly to celebrate her recovery and partly to bid her farewell.

After five rounds of wine and two courses of dishes, the marshal's wife said, "We're so glad you've regained your health. This indeed calls for celebration. Let's report to the emperor soon and pick a day for you to return to the palace. What do you say?"

Lady Han clasped her hands in a gesture of respect and said to the marshal's wife, "My ill-starred fate brought me so much sorrow that I had to be confined to my sick bed for two months. Now that I am beginning to feel better, I would like to stay here for a while longer. Please do not report to the emperor yet. But I feel bad to have to impose on your hospitality like this and put you to such inconvenience. I will surely remember to repay your kindness some day."

The marshal and his wife felt obliged to humor her.

Two months later, Lady Han set out a feast in return of the hospitality and engaged a storyteller for the occasion. One of the stories narrated was about a Lady Han in the palace of Emperor Xuanzong [r. 847–59] of the Tang dynasty. (*Another Lady Han! Indeed, without coincidences, there would be no stories.*)

Never having enjoyed any attention from the emperor either, this Lady Han, in despair, wrote a poem on a red leaf, which then floated away on water that drained from the palace ditch. The poem said,

Why does the water flow in such haste?
There is nothing to do all day deep in the palace.
Heartily I thank the red leaf
On its way to the world of the mortals.

It so happened that outside the palace, a young man called Yu You, who was in the capital to sit for the examinations, picked up the red leaf, wrote a poem in reply, and put it into the ditch again to let it float back into the palace. Later, the young man passed the examinations and won instant fame. Upon learning about what had happened, the emperor ordered that Lady Han be married to Yu You. The husband and wife lived in conjugal bliss to a ripe old age.

At this point in the storyteller's narration, a sudden thought struck Lady Han, and she heaved a sigh. Without saying anything out loud, she thought, "If I could be so lucky, I wouldn't have lived my life in vain!"

The feast over, the table was cleared, and all retired to their own quarters. At about midnight, Lady Han felt her head aching, her face hot, her limbs weak, and her body numb. Tormented by her irrepressible desires, she fell ill again. This time, her condition was worse than before. Truly,

An all-night rain wrecks a hut already leaking;
A head wind slows down a boat already late.

The marshal's wife came to see her in the morning and said, "Luckily, we haven't yet told the emperor that you could be taken back. While you're here, you'd better forget all cares, set your mind at rest, and recuperate well. Don't worry about returning to the palace."

Lady Han said thankfully, "I'm so grateful for your kindness. But I'm already beyond cure. If heaven is too far away, I'm certainly getting nearer to the world down below. Since I can't repay your great kindness in this life, let me do that as a dog or a horse in my next reincarnation!" With that, her breathing became weak and labored. It was a heartbreaking sight.

Feeling saddened, the marshal's wife said, "Don't say such things. Heaven looks after the virtuous. Once this bad spell in your fate is over, you'll surely recover. Now, if the medicine isn't working, I'm afraid that taking more of it will only do harm to your body. I wonder if you owe the gods any unfulfilled pledge from your days in the palace? Maybe the gods are angry with you, for all we know."

"Since I entered the palace, I've been too preoccupied by my sorrows to make any pledges to the gods. But now that I'm so ill and medicine isn't working, I'll be only too happy to go to a nearby temple and make a vow, if the god of that temple is responsive to prayers. If I can pull through, I'll fulfill my vow."

"I do have some information for you, madam," said the marshal's wife. "In this area, there is the Temple of the Immortal Master of the North Pole and the Clear Source Temple of the god Erlang. They are most responsive to prayers. Why don't you set an incense altar and pray for their protection? If you recover, I'll be glad to go with you and make sacrificial offerings of gratitude. What do you say?"

Lady Han nodded her assent, whereupon the servants brought over an incense altar. Unable to rise, Lady Han leaned against her pillow and, her hand on her forehead, prayed, "I, Han-shi, have never enjoyed the emperor's attention since I entered the palace at an early age. I am therefore ill and am staying in the Yang residence. If the gods will protect me and let me get well, I will embroider two long streamers and offer them, along with other items, to your temples to express my gratitude."

The marshal's wife also held joss sticks and prayed for Lady Han. She then bade Lady Han farewell, but we shall speak no more of this.

Strangely enough, after the vow was taken, Lady Han's condition began to improve gradually and she was fully recovered after a month of convalescence. Beside themselves with joy, the marshal and his wife again set out a feast to celebrate her recovery.

The marshal's wife remarked to Lady Han, "The gods indeed answered your prayers. This is ten thousand times better than medicine. Now you must not go back on your word and fail to honor your promise."

"I wouldn't dream of being so ungrateful. After I've finished embroidering the streamers, would you be willing to go with me to the temples to fulfill my vow?"

"Yes, of course. I'll accompany you there."

After the feast was over, Lady Han took out some money for the purchase of sacrificial items, and her embroidery project of four streamers got under way. As the ancients put it so well:

> *A pig's head gets cooked tender with a fire going;*
> *Official business gets done with money talking.*

With money, even the most bizarre and preposterous things in this world can get done. In a matter of days, the embroidery was finished and, when raised high with bamboo poles, the streamers dazzled the eyes. At the chosen auspicious hour on the chosen auspicious day, palace attendants as well as the marshal's household servants carried joss sticks and the offerings to the gods, and escorted the two ladies to the Temple of the Immortal Master of the North Pole first. Upon learning about the arrival of Marshal Yang's family, the head priest of the temple rushed out to meet them and ushered them into the main hall. There, a prayer was read aloud and the streamers were hung up. Lady Han clicked her teeth [as a token of piety] and paid homage to the god. Then they made a tour of the temple, after which the head priest served tea. The ladies had a servant offer a reward of money. They then mounted their sedan-chairs and returned home in the same grand procession as before.

The night went by without ado. The next morning, they rose and proceeded to the temple of the god Erlang. And this visit led to some mysterious events. Indeed,

> *Bear this in mind: words are like fishlines and hooks;*
> *They pull out trouble right in front of your face.*

Let us not encumber our story with unnecessary comments but come to the moment when the ladies were touring the temple after the head priest read aloud the prayer and burned the joss sticks.

When the marshal's wife was in a side hall, Lady Han stepped forward, gently lifted the gilded yellow silk curtain over the altar, and peered inside. All would have been well if she had not taken that peek, but she did, and she gave quite a start. Behold:

> *On his head, a scarf with golden flowers;*
> *Over his body, a brown embroidered gown.*
> *Around his waist, a Lantian jade belt;*[4]

On his feet, black boots with designs of flying phoenixes.
Although made of clay and wood,
His was a dashing figure, with bright eyes and white teeth.
If he had breath, he would have spoken.

Lady Han's eyes glazed over and her heart galloped. Unbeknownst to herself, her innermost thought slipped out through her tongue, "If I am meant to have a bright future, I wish I could marry a husband who looks just like you. If so, my life's wish would be fulfilled."

Before the words were quite out of her mouth, the marshal's wife drew near, asking, "What were you praying for, madam?"

With alacrity, Lady Han said, "I didn't say anything!"

The marshal's wife did not press further. They continued with their tour until late in the afternoon. Then they went home and retired to their own rooms, and there we shall leave them. Indeed,

> *To know what lies in the depths of the heart,*
> *Listen to what comes out of the mouth.*

Back in her own room, Lady Han took off her regalia, tied up her hair, and put on casual wear. She then rested her chin on her hands and fell into a reverie, her mind filled with the image of the god Erlang. All of a sudden, an idea flashed into her mind. She told her servants to set up an incense altar in a secluded spot in the garden. She then prayed to heaven, saying, "If I am meant to have a bright future, please let me marry a husband who looks just like the god Erlang. That will be so much better than living a miserable life in the palace." With these words, tears streamed down her cheeks. She bowed and prayed and bowed again, indulging in nothing less than wild flights of fancy.

Then, the least expected thing happened: after her prayer session was over, she was preparing to go back to her room when, suddenly, a loud bang came from the depths of the flowers and a godlike figure appeared in front of her. Behold:

> *With his dragon-like brows, phoenix-like eyes,*
> *White teeth and bright red lips,*
> *He had an otherworldly grace*
> *And possessed breathtaking looks.*
> *He must be from the immortals' abode;*
> *His diet must consist of rosy clouds and dew.*

A closer look revealed him to bear exactly the same features as the statue of the god Erlang in the temple. He also held a slingshot in his hand in the stance of Zhang Yuanxiao, the fertility god.

Lady Han was alarmed and delighted at the same time—alarmed because there was no knowing whether the advent of a celestial god portended disaster or blessing, and delighted because the god, all smiles, began to talk.

Lady Han stepped forward, solemnly dropped a curtsy, and, opening her rouged lips and revealing her pearly teeth, said, "Since you did me the honor of descending to this place, please go into my room and let me pay my respects to you."

The god Erlang affably went with her into her room and sat down in all complacency. Her salutations completed, Lady Han stood before him, ready to be of service.

"You were good enough to make generous offerings to me, madam," said the god Erlang. "I was taking a stroll in the divine realm just now when I heard your fervent prayers. I learned that you were in fact an immortal living by the Jasper Pool. Because you had not rid yourself of the desires of the flesh, the Jade Emperor banished you temporarily to the royal palace in the mortal world, to enjoy all the wealth and glamour that the human world has to offer. When your banishment term expires, you will return to the realm of the immortals. You will know then that you are no mortal being."

Joy flooded Lady Han's heart. Again she prayed, "Honorable god, I do not wish to go back into the palace. If I am meant to have a bright future, I would like to marry a good man who looks just like you and live with him for the rest of my life. Only then would I be worthy of the spring flowers and the autumn moon. I don't care a thing about wealth and glamour."

With a smile, the god Erlang said, "That can be easily done. I'm only afraid that you may not be firm enough in your determination. If such is your marriage destiny, you will surely get to meet your intended, however great the distance." That said, he rose and jumped onto the windowsill. With a bang, he was gone.

It would have been all right had Lady Han never laid her eyes on him, but she did, and she was smitten by his looks. As if in a trance, she went to bed without even removing her clothes. Truly,

> *In joy, the night goes by all too quickly;*
> *In loneliness, the hours drag on; dawn never comes.*

She tossed and turned in bed, hardly able to suppress her amorous desires. She talked to herself one moment, thinking aloud, and fell into silence again the next moment. "When the god was here a while ago," said she, "there were such tender feelings as we looked into each other's eyes. Why did he leave all of a sudden? Maybe as a god, he has more wisdom and moral integrity than mortal beings. My passion was ill-placed!" Then she gave herself up to her thoughts again and said, "In all his grace and affability, that god looked just like a mortal being. How could my beauty not have any effect on him? Or did I let him go in a momentary lapse of attention? I should have shown him more affection, enough to melt even a man made of iron or rock. Now that I missed this chance, I may never get to see him again!"

Unable to snap out of these thoughts, she waited for dawn to come before deciding on the next course of action. But when night did give way to morning, she drifted off to sleep and did not rise from bed until just before noon. For the rest of the day, she was listless, and when the long-awaited darkness of the evening fell at last, she again set up the incense altar in the garden and prayed as before, "If I could get to see the god once again, I would consider myself most fortunate." (*An infatuated fool.*)

Even as she spoke, the god Erlang appeared before her with another loud bang. Lady Han's heart leaped for joy. All her sorrows vanished like melting ice and crumbling tiles. She advanced one step, dropped a curtsy, and said, letting her excitement get the better of her, "May I ask you, honorable god, to go into my room? I have something to say to you in confidence."

Gleefully the god Erlang took her hand and went with her into her chamber. After her salutations were over, the god Erlang sat down in the middle of the room, with Lady Han standing respectfully before him.

"You have the qualities of an immortal, madam," said he. "So you may sit."

Lady Han sat down across from him. She then had servants bring in wine and fruit. There, in her room, she and the god drank one cup after another and she confided in him her innermost feelings. As they say,

> Spring adds flavor to tea;
> Wine adds fire to lust.

Eager for intimacy, Lady Han said, "If you don't despise my unworthiness, please briefly put aside your heavenly official business and enjoy some moments of the pleasures of the human world."

The god Erlang agreed readily enough. They went to bed, hand in hand, and engaged in a game of clouds and rain. Lady Han did her part with abandon. They tarried until it was almost dawn. The god Erlang rose, told her to take good care of herself, and promised that he would visit her again. He dressed, picked up his slingshot, leaped up onto the windowsill and, with a loud bang, disappeared without a trace.

The idea that this was a god visiting the mortal world had taken full possession of Lady Han's mind, and she was in a transport of joy. Afraid that the marshal and his wife would urge her to go back to the palace, she pretended to be much more gravely ill than she was and hardly ever put on a smile. But when evening came, she radiated with joy. After the god arrived, they would drink three cups of wine before starting their amorous sport in bed, and he would leave by dawn. This went on for some time.

One day, the weather having turned colder, Emperor Huizong ordered that autumn clothes be distributed around the palace. Suddenly he thought of Lady Han, whereupon he sent a palace attendant to Marshal Yang's residence to deliver a message as well as a silk robe and a jade waistband. Lady Han set up her altar and thanked the emperor. The palace attendant said to her, "I'm so glad that you are well, my lady. His Majesty misses you so much that he sends you a silk robe and a jade waistband. If you have recovered, please return to the palace as soon as possible."

Lady Han treated the attendant to dinner and said, "I have a favor to ask of you. My illness is only half gone. Could you please relay my plea to His Majesty and ask him to give me more time? I would be ever so grateful."

"That shouldn't be a problem," said the palace attendant. "His Majesty won't mind the absence of one lady. After I go back, I'll just say that Your Ladyship hasn't fully recovered and needs to take good care of herself."

Lady Han thanked him, and the court attendant bade her farewell.

In the evening, the god Erlang said to Lady Han upon arrival, "I'm glad that the emperor still cares about you. May I see the silk robe and jade waistband he gave you?"

"How did you know about this, honorable god?"

"Nothing under heaven escapes my eyes. How can I not know about this triviality?"

At these words, Lady Han all too readily showed him the objects.

"One must not keep any treasure in the mortal world to oneself," said the god Erlang. "I happen to need a jade waistband. Should you be willing to part with it, that'll be an act of charity and gain you merit in heaven."

"All of me now belongs to you, honorable god. With such a predestined bond between us, please feel free to take the jade waistband."

The god Erlang thanked her and they made merry in bed. He rose before dawn and, slingshot and jade waistband in hand, leaped up onto the windowsill, and was gone with a loud bang. Indeed,

> If you don't want people to know what you did,
> You shouldn't have done it in the first place.

Even though Lady Han and the Yang family were living apart in two separate sections of the residence, the marshal had put her quarters under tight watch because of Lady Han's status as an imperial consort. No unauthorized persons would presumably dare venture into that well-guarded area. However, it had often been observed that lights in the west wing were on all night through, and subdued voices and movements had been heard. And Lady Han was seen to be glowing in high spirits, her face wreathed with smiles. After long and hard debates with himself, the marshal finally said to his wife, "Have you noticed anything out of the ordinary about Lady Han?"

"I did have some suspicions, but then I thought this place is so well guarded that nothing can happen. So I dismissed those suspicions of mine. Now that you bring this up, we can easily do something about it. Tonight, let's have a few of the smarter servants climb onto the roof to find out what's going on, so that we don't do her any injustice."

The marshal said, "Good idea." Right away, he summoned two able servants and told them to do thus-and-so, adding, "Do not use the door. Just put the garden ladder against the wall. When all's quiet, climb over to Lady Han's bedroom and watch what goes on there. Then come back and report to me. This is no small matter. Do be careful." Thus instructed, the two men left, and the marshal waited for their report.

In less than four hours' time, the two servants came back to report what they had witnessed. They had the marshal dismiss all other servants before they proceeded to tell him that there was a man in Lady Han's room, sitting there and drinking. "Lady Han kept addressing him as 'Honorable god,'" they said. "Well, we've been doing some thinking: The walls are high, and security is tight. Even if there's some criminal lurking around, he couldn't have gotten there without wings. That man may very well be some kind of god."

The marshal gave a start. "How extraordinary! How can there really be such a thing! You two must not lie, because this is no trifling thing."

"Everything we said is true."

"Now, this whole thing is just between you and me," said the marshal. "You must not let a word of this get out."

The two servants promised and took off. The marshal relayed the information to his wife and added, "I'll have to see with my own eyes to believe what they said. I'll go tomorrow night to see for myself what that god looks like."

The marshal waited until the next evening before he summoned the same two servants and said to them, "One of you will go with me there, and the other one will wait here. Don't tell anyone about this." Having given these instructions, the marshal and one of the servants went on their mission. They tiptoed their way to Lady Han's window and peeped into it. Sure enough, there sat in the room a god that fitted the two servants' description. The marshal was about to cry out, but, afraid that he might not be able to get himself out of an awkward situation, he swallowed his anger and returned to his own quarters after reminding the two servants not to breathe a word to anyone.

Back in his room, the marshal confided in his wife, adding, "It must be Lady Han's youthful wild desires that drew some evil god here. He's sullying an imperial consort, no less. This is surely not the work of a human being. We'll have to engage a priest to do an exorcism. You talk to her. I'll go to find a priest."

Thus instructed, the marshal's wife went to the west wing early the next morning. Lady Han greeted her and offered her a seat. After tea was served, the marshal's wife dismissed all the servants. Seated face to face with Lady Han, she said in a confidential tone, "I'd like to have a word with you. Whom do you talk to every night in your room? You've been heard, and rumor has reached my ears. This is no trifling thing. You must tell me everything. Don't hold anything back."

At these words, Lady Han blushed and said, "I haven't been talking to anyone at night in my room, although I do chat with my maidservants to while away the time. I have no visitors."

Thereupon the marshal's wife told her about what her husband had seen the night before, sparing no details. Lady Han was dumbfounded, completely at a loss as to what to do.

"Don't be alarmed," said the marshal's wife gently to comfort her. "The marshal is out looking for an exorcist. Soon enough, we'll know if he's human or a ghost. You must be careful at night. But don't be afraid." Having said that, the marshal's wife departed, leaving Lady Han sweating with fear. Darkness had barely fallen when the god Erlang appeared, his slingshot tightly in his grip.

In the meantime, the exorcist engaged by the marshal had already begun his conjuration in the front hall. He was the famous Priest Wang, disciple of Sage Lin of Lingji Palace. When report came at dusk about the god's arrival, Priest Wang threw on his robe and, sword in hand, marched majestically toward Lady Han's room.

"What evil spirit are you?" he roared as he burst into the room. "How dare you violate an imperial consort! Don't move! Try a taste of my sword!"

Quite unruffled, the god Erlang said, "The temerity!" Behold:

> *His left hand as if holding up Mount Tai,*
> *His right hand as if carrying a baby,*
> *His slingshot drawn to look like the full moon,*
> *He sent pellets that flew like shooting stars.*

One pellet hit Priest Wang right in the forehead. As blood flowed down, the priest fell backward, his precious sword cast aside. Witnesses of the scene quickly raised him and helped him into the front hall. In the meantime, the god leaped onto the windowsill and, with a loud bang, was gone. How did it all end? Indeed, when the truth was known,

> *Even the sky and the earth were frightened;*
> *Even the gods and the ghosts were startled.*

Witnessing how the god Erlang had beaten the priest, Lady Han was all the more convinced that he was a genuine god who had descended into the world of the mortals. She set all her fears to rest.

Realizing by this time that the priest was not any good, the marshal saw nothing else for it but to pay him for the trouble he had taken and send him away. Then he engaged a Priest Pan of the Five Mountains Temple, a priest who specialized in the Five Thunder Heavenly Zenith Orthodox method of exorcism. Meticulous in his work, he was also wise and resourceful. He came as soon as he learned that he was wanted by the marshal. After the marshal acquainted him with all the details of what had happened, Priest Pan said, "Have someone take me quietly to the west wing. I need to see the place he frequents to know if he's man or ghost."

"Of course," said the marshal.

Thereupon, Priest Pan took leave of the marshal and went first to look all around Lady Han's bedroom in the west wing. Then he asked to be introduced to Lady Han. After examining her complexion, he turned to the marshal and said, "With all due respect to you, sir, judging by her complexion, I don't see any sign of evil spirits. This is all the doing of a man who knows sorcery. I know how to deal with him. I don't need magic charms or holy water, and there's no need to beat drums or ring bells. The moment he appears, this humble priest will catch him as easily as catching a turtle in a jar. My only concern is that he may have guessed what's going on and won't show up. In that case, there will be nothing I can do."

"I couldn't be happier if he doesn't show up again," said the marshal. "Please stay, sir, and let's have a chat."

Storyteller, if that brute was indeed onto what lay in store for him and had the good sense to do what was best for him under the circumstances, he should never return, like a kite with a broken string. Wouldn't it be nice for him to have enjoyed a good time without tarnishing his name and go on to try his luck elsewhere? As they say, "Do not repeat a trick that got you too good a deal. Do not go again to the place where you made undeserved gains."

To get on with our story, we do not know yet whether that god Erlang was a man or a ghost. Anyway, having tasted the joys of his conquest, he came again that night, little knowing what was good for him.

Lady Han said to him, "I had no idea what was going to happen last night, and I'm sorry for having given you offense. I'm so glad that you're not hurt. Please do not take it ill."

"I am a true god from heaven, here because I have a predestined celestial bond with you, madam. One of these days, I'll deliver you from your mortal frame and fly with you to heaven in broad daylight. That idiot be cursed! Even if he had a thousand soldiers, he couldn't have gotten near me!"

Lady Han was all the more impressed and their union of delight was doubly affectionate.

In the meantime, the marshal had received information about the visit. The marshal, in his turn, notified Priest Pan, who then asked the marshal to send a maidservant to Lady Han's room, ostensibly to wait on them, but in fact to steal the slingshot, so as to render the god Erlang helpless. After the maidservant went off, Priest Pan tightened his clothes around him and, dispensing with the usual exorcist's robe and sword, he only took up a cudgel and told two servants to guide him some distance off, holding torches to light him on his way.

"If you're afraid of his pellets, you can hide yourselves in advance," he said to them. "I will then proceed alone, to see if his pellets can even get near me."

The two men laughed in their sleeves and commented to each other, "What a talker! One of the pellets will surely get him!"

In the meantime, the maidservant had gone to Lady Han's room, ostensibly to offer services. She maneuvered to get near the god. While he was busily exchanging toasts with Lady Han, the maidservant stole his slingshot and put it away. By this time, Priest Pan had arrived at the door. The servants guiding him announced, "This is the place!" Immediately they scurried away as fast as their legs could carry them, leaving the priest there all by himself.

Priest Pan raised the door curtain and swept the room with his eyes. At the sight of that god sitting in the room all cool and poised, Priest Pan gave a shout, began wielding his cudgel, and aimed a front blow at the god Erlang. In haste, Erlang reached for his slingshot, but it was not there. "I've been had!" he cried. He quickly drew back and got onto the windowsill. In less time than it takes to narrate, Priest Pan's cudgel hit him in the back of his leg and brought down an object. With a loud bang, the god Erlang disappeared into the flower bushes.

Priest Pan picked up the fallen object and saw by lamplight that it was a black boot sewn with four pieces of leather. He took it and reported to the marshal. "This humble priest believes that he must be a sorcerer. This has nothing to do with the real god Erlang. (*Knowing that the real god Erlang had nothing to do with this made it easier to take action. If one mistake led to another, goodness knows how many innocent people would be wronged and how many criminals would go unpunished.*) Now how are we going to catch him?"

"You've worked hard enough, sir. You may go now. I'll make arrangements for an investigation." With that, he paid Priest Pan and thanked him. Of Priest Pan, we shall say no more.

The marshal went off by sedan-chair to the residence of Preceptor Cai and entered the study.[5] He gave a whole account of the happenings and added, "We can't let things go on like this. That brute will laugh at us. What a disgrace that'll be!"

"That can be easily taken care of," said the preceptor. "I'll have Prefect Teng of Kaifeng take on this case. Give him this boot as a clue and assign a few able officers to investigate and hunt the culprit down. Then deal with him according to the law."

"Thank you for your advice," said the marshal.

"Sit here for a while," said the preceptor, who then ordered Clerk Zhang to go with all speed to bring Prefect Teng over. After an exchange of civilities upon his arrival, the servants were dismissed. The preceptor and the marshal said, "How can we allow such trespasses in the very capital of the empire? You, Prefect Teng, must give the case your utmost attention and not be negligent in any way. This is no trifling matter. And take care not to 'stir the grass and alarm the snake,' so to speak. Otherwise he'll slip away."

The prefect was so frightened that he turned deathly pale. Without delay, he said, "You can count on me."

Taking the boot with him, he said good-bye to the preceptor and the marshal and returned to his yamen. Immediately he summoned Inspector Wang, who was on duty that day, dismissed the attendants, and acquainted him with all the details of the case. "I give you three days to bring to me the one wreaking havoc in Marshal Yang's residence. But don't make a big fuss over it. Do a thorough job, and you'll be rewarded well. If not, you'll have a lot to answer for!" And with that, he dismissed Inspector Wang.

Inspector Wang took the boot into his own office and assembled all the officers. He sighed. Behold:

> *His eyebrows double locked in deep furrows;*
> *His heart laden with ten thousand worries.*

Among the officers was a Ran Gui, popularly known as Big Ran, whose operations covered three major cities of the empire. A most brilliant, quick-thinking detective, he had helped Inspector Wang solve goodness knows how many baffling cases, and Inspector Wang thought the world of him. Noticing the inspector's furrowed brows and worried look, Big Ran did not press him but kept up a steady chatter about things having little to do with the case.

Seeing that none of his men appeared to take him seriously, Inspector Wang produced the boot and threw it on the table, saying, "Life is hard for us officers! How can our magistrate be so muddle-headed? A boot cannot talk, and yet he gives us three days to bring him the owner of this boot—the man who's been wreaking havoc in Marshal Yang's house. Don't you find this ridiculous?"

The officers took turns examining the boot. When it was passed to Big Ran, he took little notice of it but kept saying, "This is a tough job! A tough job! The magistrate is indeed muddle-headed. Inspector, I don't blame you for feeling frustrated!"

Surprised at such complaints from Ran, the inspector said, "Big Ran, even you are saying this is a tough job. We can't call it quits just like that, can we? You're making things harder for me. What am I going to say to the magistrate? Like everyone else, you get paid by this office, and yet you say nothing but 'it's a tough job!'"

"An ordinary case like burglary or theft would be easy to tackle," said the men. "But if it's a sorcerer we're dealing with, how are we going to get him? If it's easy to get him, that Priest Pan would have done so long ago. Even he could do nothing more than knocking a boot off him. We have only our own bad luck to blame for being assigned this mysterious case. This is hopeless."

If Inspector Wang's worries had registered five on a scale of one to ten, they went all the way up to ten after he heard these arguments, which all sounded valid to him. But, calmly, Ran Gui said, "Inspector, let's not be discouraged yet. Isn't he just a human being like us? He doesn't have three heads and six arms. If we can find some telltale signs, we will be able to track him down." He turned the boot over and over in his hands, his eyes taking in every detail.

The other men burst out laughing. "Big Ran, there you go again! There's nothing exotic about this boot. It's made of leather dyed black, sewn together with thread, and lined with blue cloth. And it has been shaped with a shoe last and stiffened with water."

Big Ran did not say a word but continued to examine the boot closely by lamplight. There were four finely stitched seams. Noticing that one seam split open slightly at the tip of the boot, Big Ran poked his little finger at the place and as he did so, there popped two stitches, and the leather curled upward. When he looked inside the boot under the lamp, he saw a layer of blue lining. A closer look revealed a piece of white paper. He slipped two fingers in, took out the note, and read it. It would have been a different story if he had not read it, but he did, and he rejoiced as someone who had found gold or a treasure trove in the middle of the night. Inspector Wang's face also burst into a smile at this godsend. The others all went forward to look at the note. It said, "Made by Ren Yilang, the shoemaker, on the fifth day of the third month in the third year of the Xuanhe reign period."

The inspector said to Big Ran, "This is the fourth year of the Xuanhe reign. So the boot was made just a little over a year ago. If we can get this Ren Yilang, we stand a good chance of solving the case."

"Let's not alarm him today," suggested Big Ran. "Let's wait until tomorrow morning and then send two men to him to say that the magistrate has a job for him. Once he's here, tie him up. He'll surely tell us the truth."

"I just knew you would come up with something good!" exclaimed the inspector.

They stayed awake throughout the night, drinking. None of the men dared to leave. At the crack of dawn, two men set out with the speed of the wind to get Ren Yilang. In less than four hours, the unsuspecting Ren Yilang was brought to the detective's office. As soon as Ren was in the office, the officers suddenly turned fierce and trussed him up, shouting, "A fine thing you did! How dare you!"

Trembling, Ren Yilang said, "Can't we talk nicely? What did I do to make you tie me up like this?"

Inspector Wang said, "What do you have to say for yourself? Wasn't this boot made in your shop?"

Ren Yilang took the boot and peered at it intently. "Yes, Inspector," he said. "This boot was indeed made by me. Let me explain. Ever since I opened my shop, I have kept a ledger at home. It records every order I've received from government officials and every purchase by visiting customers, complete with dates and the names of the clerks from official residences bearing the orders. Inside each boot, there's also a slip of paper with the same serial number as that entered in the ledger.

(If the story took place today, with the way people do things now, the officers wouldn't be able to find a lead.) Sir, if you don't believe me, you need only cut open this boot and get that slip of paper to know that I'm telling the truth."

Convinced that this was indeed the truth, Inspector Wang said, "He's honest. Untie him and talk to him nicely."

Right away, they untied Ren Yilang and said, "Don't blame us, Yilang. We had to do this because our superiors so ordered."

When they showed him the slip of paper, Ren Yilang said, "Inspector, you don't have anything to worry about. Even if this boot was made four to five years ago, not to mention within the last two years, I still have the record in my ledgers at home. Please have someone go with me to get them and check the record. The truth will be out."

Thereupon two men were dispatched to follow Ren Yilang to his home. They took the ledgers and ran apace back to Inspector Wang's office, their feet hardly touching the ground. Inspector Wang personally examined the ledgers from the very first page and when he got to the fifth day of the third month of the third year of Xuanhe, he saw that the serial number exactly matched that on the slip of paper. Upon reading the rest of the entry, he gave a start and fell silent, for the boots were ordered by none other than Clerk Zhang in the employment of Preceptor Cai Jing in his residence. Without a moment's delay, Inspector Wang took Ren Yilang, the boot, and the ledger, and hurried to Prefect Teng's yamen for a report.

This being a special case which the magistrate himself had assigned them, they were immediately led into the prefect's presence. Inspector Wang related what had happened and presented the prefect with the ledger as well as the slip of paper. After checking the numbers and finding them to be identical, Prefect Teng was flabbergasted. "That explains it!" he remarked. But, still feeling skeptical, he thought for a moment before saying, "So Ren Yilang is not involved in the case. He can go now."

Ren Yilang bowed in gratitude and took off, but Prefect Teng called him back and gave him these words of admonishment: "I'm letting you go, all right, but you must not leak out a word about this. If anyone asks you, just say something non-committal and change the subject. Mark my words!"

"Yes, sir!" said Ren Yilang. With that, he went merrily on his way.

Prefect Teng took the boot and the ledger and, along with Inspector Wang and Big Ran, went to Marshal Yang's residence in his sedan-chair. The marshal had just returned home from the day's court session with the emperor. Upon the gate-keeper's announcement of the visitors, the marshal went into the main hall to receive them. Prefect Teng said, "This is not a good place to talk." The marshal then took them to a small study in the west wing, dismissed all servants, and kept only Inspector Wang and Big Ran. The prefect related everything in due order and said in conclusion, "What's to be done now? I dare not act on my own."

The marshal was dumbfounded. For a considerable time, he sat immobile and thought, "The grand preceptor is such an important official of the empire, rich and eminent. He can't have done this. But this boot is from his residence. The culprit must be someone close to him." Turning the matter over in his mind, he thought of taking the boot to the grand preceptor's mansion and confronting him with it, but he was afraid this would mean a severe loss of face on the grand preceptor's part and he would only put himself in a difficult position if the grand preceptor took offense. Then he thought of dropping the case altogether, but it was no small matter. With the involvement of two exorcists, detectives, and Ren Yilang, the case had already gone public. If he tried to keep the lid on it, he would not be able to pretend he knew nothing once it became exposed. Should the emperor fly into a rage, he would have a lot to answer for. After thinking long and hard about different options, he dismissed Inspector Wang and Big Ran. He called for his sedan-chair, had a servant tuck the boot and the ledger safely in his seat, and went at top speed with Prefect Teng to a certain place. Truly,

> You've worn out iron shoes on a long, fruitless hunt;
> But here he is; you need not have searched.

It was to Grand Preceptor Cai's residence that the marshal and the prefect went. They waited at the gate for what seemed like ages before the grand preceptor called them into his study. After an exchange of greetings and the usual serving of tea, the grand preceptor asked, "Have you got to the bottom of the case?"

The marshal replied, "We know who the criminal is, but for your sake, we dare not make an arrest."

"This is no small matter. How can I shield him?" said the grand preceptor.

"Even if you won't shield him, you'll be in for a minor shock."

"Why don't you just tell me who it is? Why all this suspense?"

"Please dismiss all the servants before I tell you."

The grand preceptor promptly dismissed all the servants. It was only then that the marshal opened his briefcase and produced the ledger. After the preceptor examined the contents, the marshal said, "You are the only one who can make a judgment in this case, Grand Preceptor. No one else can."

"How very strange! How very strange!" said the grand preceptor.

The marshal continued, "This being a case of vital importance, please do not hold me to blame."

"I won't hold it against you. I'm only wondering where this boot came from."

"The ledger says it was ordered by Clerk Zhang of your establishment. This can't be wrong."

"Zhang Qian may very well have ordered it, but he may not have had anything more to do with it. In fact, all the formal clothes, boots, shoes, and socks in my house are taken care of by different maidservants. All the items are clearly recorded, including those made by my house staff, those received as gifts, and those sent out as gifts. Every month, they make detailed reports. Everything is done in good order. Let me have someone check the in-house ledger, and then we'll know the truth."

Straightaway, he ordered that the maidservant in charge of boots be brought forth. Presently, she came with a ledger in hand.

The grand preceptor said to her, "This is a boot from this house. How did it end up with an outsider? Check this ledger for me."

The maidservant checked item by item and found that the boot had been ordered in the third month of the previous year. Soon after the pair of boots was delivered, a student of the grand preceptor's, by the name of Yang Shi, also known as Gentleman of Mount Gui, had come to bid farewell to the grand preceptor because he had just been promoted to be magistrate of a county near the capital, and he was in the grand preceptor's good graces.[6] Being a philosopher, he was unkempt in appearance. The grand preceptor therefore gave him a round-collar robe, a silver waistband, a pair of boots, and four Sichuan fans by way of farewell presents. And this was the very boot given on that occasion. (*Those giving presents, be warned!*) The record was indeed clear. The grand preceptor showed it to the marshal and the magistrate, who immediately apologized, saying, 'So this has nothing to do with members of the grand preceptor's household. Please forgive our impertinence, but we were trying to do our duty."

The grand preceptor said affably, "You did the right thing. You are not to blame. But I doubt that Mr. Yang of Mount Gui is capable of such things. There must be more to the case than what we know so far. Since his duty station is not far from here, let me have him brought here for questioning. You can go now, but don't let a word out about this." The marshal and the prefect took leave of Grand Preceptor Cai and went their separate ways home.

Right away, the grand preceptor sent for Magistrate Yang. After two days, Magistrate Yang arrived in the capital and was brought into the grand preceptor's presence.

After tea was served, the grand preceptor said, "The magistrate of a county is supposed to be like a parent to the local people. How can you commit such a heinous crime?" He then launched into a complete account of the case.

"My respects to you, my venerable teacher," said Magistrate Yang, half rising from his seat. "Last year, after I took your generous gifts, I was suddenly afflicted with an eye ailment when I was still at home, before leaving the capital to take up my post. I was told that there is in these parts a Clear Source Temple of the god Erlang, who is wonderfully responsive to prayer. So I pledged that as soon as my eye ailment was gone, I would go to the temple to offer incense and express my gratitude. So after I got well, I kept my word and went to the temple to offer incense. There, I noticed that the statue of the god Erlang was in impeccable attire, except that his black boots were torn and looked quite out of place. So I offered my boots to the god. This is the whole truth. I have never done anything dishonorable in my life. Being a student of the classics of Confucius and Mencius, how would I stoop so low? The grand preceptor will surely give the matter your fullest consideration."

Knowing the Gentleman of Mount Gui to be a great Confucian scholar averse to acts of impropriety, the grand preceptor replied, "I know your good reputation. I asked you here just to answer some questions to convince those people." He then treated Magistrate Yang to dinner, after which the magistrate took leave of him and was about to depart when the grand preceptor reminded him not to reveal any of this to anyone. Magistrate Yang then bade him good-bye and took himself off. Truly,

> He who has done nothing against his conscience by day
> Need not fear the knock on his door at night.

The grand preceptor then invited Marshal Yang and Prefect Teng over and explained everything to them, adding, "So, you see, Magistrate Yang is not our man, either." (*Clearing Mr. Yang in a light-hearted, humorous way.*) The Kaifeng Prefecture will have to keep on trying."

There was nothing Prefect Teng could say. He took back the boot, said good-bye, and returned to the yamen. Once there, he called Inspector Wang over and said to him, "Whatever clues we had have all vanished into thin air. Take the boot back. I give you an extension of five days. Be sure to bring the criminal to me."

Thus ordered, Inspector Wang returned to the detectives' office with a heavy heart. To Big Ran he said, "Luckless me! How nice it was when you tracked down Ren Yilang! Since the grand preceptor's household is involved, I thought the case was closed because one official would cover up for another. Who would have thought that they would want to pursue this case! Where am I going to start looking? Actually, since Magistrate Yang gave the boots to the god Erlang, it may indeed have been this god who indulged in a few escapades, for all we know. But how do we get evidence to show the magistrate?"

Big Ran said, "Even if you didn't say so, I just knew that Ren Yilang and Grand Preceptor Cai and Magistrate Yang had no part in this. You say this was the work of the god Erlang, but I can hardly imagine a god doing such an unconscionable thing. It must have been the work of some sorcerer living near the temple. Let's go to the area around the temple and try to find out something. If we can catch him, don't rejoice. If not, don't be upset."

"Right," conceded the inspector. He gave the boot to Big Ran, who then filled two baskets with small general merchandise and carried them on a pole across his shoulder. Brandishing a rattle-drum called Get the Housewives Out, he headed straight for the temple of the god Erlang. Once there, he put down his load, lit a joss stick, and prayed under his breath, "God, please help me, Ran Gui, catch the one who wreaked havoc in Marshal Yang's house and, in doing so, clear your name."

After he kowtowed, he drew three lots in succession and each time the divination was favorable. Big Ran thanked the god, picked up his load, and took a walk around the temple. He kept his eyes wide open, looking left and right, without closing them for an instant. (*Ran Gui was a famous detective in the Song dynasty, who often kept his eyes closed. Hence the reference to his not closing his eyes.*) Then he approached a house with a single-leaf door with a well-used speckled bamboo curtain over it and a half-window next to it. As the door was standing ajar, he heard someone cry from inside, "Peddler, over here!"

Big Ran turned around and saw a young woman. "What can I do for you, madam?"

"You buy back used items, don't you? I've got something here that I'd like to sell for a few pennies to buy candies for my boys. Will you take it?"

"My load is called 'Take'em All.' There's nothing I don't buy. Show me what you've got."

The woman told her son to bring out the item and show it to Big Ran. What did the boy bring out? Indeed,

> *The case of the deer baffled the prime minister of Zheng;*[7]
> *The dream about a butterfly confused Zhuangzi.*[8]

What the boy brought out was a black leather boot sewn with four pieces of black leather, exactly the same as the one knocked off by Priest Pan. Showing none of the joy that flooded his heart, Big Ran said, "You've got only one, so it's not worth a lot. How much do you want for it? Don't ask for too much, though."

"I just want a few pennies to buy some candies for the boys. You name the price, but be fair."

Big Ran took out one and a half strings of cash and, handing them to her, said, "Now if this is fine with you, I'm taking it. If you don't think this is enough, the deal is off. One boot out of a pair isn't worth much, you know."

"What are a few pennies to you? Give me a couple more!"

"I can't," said Big Ran as he started to walk off with his load.

The boy burst into tears. The woman had to call Big Ran back. "Just a little more, please."

Big Ran took out twenty pennies and said, "Oh well, so be it. This is more than the thing's worth." He took the boot, tossed it into one of his baskets and set off, saying to himself in exultation, "This case is as good as half solved! But I mustn't make a fuss about this. I need to find out more about that woman before I can make my move." That evening, he deposited his load in a friend's house by Tianjin Bridge and went to the detectives' office. When Inspector Wang came to inquire, he said he had nothing new to report.

After breakfast the next day, he went again to Tianjin Bridge, picked up his load from his friend, and betook himself to the woman's house, but he found the door locked. The woman must have gone out. He knitted his brows in thought and soon hit on a plan. He put down his load and went from door to door, looking around. He saw an old man sitting on a small stool in front of a house, making a rope with straw. Big Ran asked apologetically, "Uncle, could you tell me where the young lady in the house on your left is?"

The old man stopped working and, looking up at Big Ran, said, "Why do you ask about her?"

"I'm a peddler of miscellaneous goods. Yesterday I bought an old boot from her. I didn't look carefully enough at the time. It turned out that I got shortchanged in the deal. So I'm here again to get my money back."

"My advice is to let it go at that. That woman is not one to provoke. She's the mistress of Magic Powers Sun, custodian of the temple of the god Erlang. That Magic Powers Sun is quite a sorcerer and a real holy terror! This old boot must have been taken off the statue of the god and given to her to buy candies with. She's gone to see her mother today. She's known the temple custodian for quite some time now. For some reason, they got estranged for two to three months but have recently been seeing each other again. (*Estranged because he had Lady Han. After his boot was struck off, he resumed his relationship with this woman. Meticulous attention to details of the narrative.*) If you ask her for your money back, you don't have a chance. If you upset her, she'll tell her lover, and he'll use his sorcery on you. What can you do?"

"I see. Thank you for your advice."

Big Ran took leave of the old man, picked up his load, and returned to the detectives' office, all smiles. Inspector Wang asked, "Got lucky today?"

"Yes, indeed! Show me that boot."

Inspector Wang took out the boot. Big Gui compared it with the one he had bought and saw that they were identical.

"Where did you get that one?" asked Inspector Wang eagerly.

All calm and composed, Big Ran related everything to him and added, "Didn't I say that it wasn't the doing of the god Erlang? Now we know that Magic Powers Sun is the culprit! No doubt about that!"

Inspector Wang went delirious with joy. Without losing one moment, he burned incense to ask for the gods' blessings and, offering a toast to Big Ran by way of thanking him, said, "Now, how are we going to get him? If there's a leak, that swine will give us the slip, and the game will be up."

"It's easy!" said Big Ran. "Tomorrow, let's prepare the three kinds of sacrificial offerings [pig, sheep, and ox] and go to the temple. We'll say we want to thank the god and fulfill our pledges. Once we reach the temple, the custodian will surely come out to greet us. A wine cup can be flung as a signal for action. We can then easily catch him."

"Sounds good," said the inspector. "We need to report to the prefect first, to get authorization for the arrest."

Straightaway, Inspector Wang reported to the prefect. Overcome with delight, Prefect Teng said, "You've got quite a job on your hands. Be careful. Don't make any wrong moves. I heard that sorcerers can make themselves invisible and slip away. I suggest that you bring along some antidotes like pig's blood, dog's blood, garlic, and manure. Pour those on him, and he won't be able to get away."

Thus instructed, Inspector Wang left to make the preparations. Early the next morning, they went to the temple, having first secretly ordered a few men to carry the four antidotes and wait at a distance for the signal. They would go forward for action as soon as the culprit was caught. After giving all the necessary instructions, Inspector Wang and Big Ren changed their clothes and, together with all the other officers, went into the main hall to burn incense. Magic Powers Sun, the custodian, came out to greet them and read the prayer. He was into the fourth or fifth sentence when Big Ran, who was pouring out wine next to him, flung a wine cup to the floor. The others all swarmed forward and overpowered the custodian. Truly, it was like

> Black vultures pouncing on a small swallow;
> Fierce tigers devouring a lamb.

The four antidotes were then poured right over his head. The custodian knew what the antidotes could do. However immense his magic powers, he lost the use of his limbs. The officers beat him with a rod every step of the way as they brought him to the Kaifeng prefectural yamen.

When word got to him that the sorcerer had been caught, Prefect Teng assumed his bench in the court and roared in anger, "You vile scoundrel! How dare you use your sorcery to violate an imperial consort and cheat her out of her precious possessions? And right in the capital of the empire, too! Now, what do you have to say for yourself?"

Magic Powers Sun tried to deny the charges, but under torture, he confessed, knowing that he would not be able to lie his way out of this. "I began to learn sorcery since childhood from gangs. Later I became a priest at the temple to the god of Erlang and bribed my way into the position of custodian. I overheard Lady Han's prayer that she wanted to marry a husband just like the god Erlang. That gave me the evil idea of pretending to be the god. I did indeed defile her and cheat her out of her jade waistband."

Prefect Teng ordered that he be put in a big cangue and thrown into jail, and also instructed the wardens to watch him closely while waiting for the emperor's decree.[9] He then put together a file on the case and brought it to Marshal Yang. Together they went to Grand Preceptor Cai's residence, where they consulted each other and wrote a memorial to the emperor.

The emperor's decree, when it came, was found to contain these words: "For the crimes of defilement of an imperial consort and acquisition of valuable property under false pretenses, the criminal is hereby sentenced to death by multiple cuts. His wife shall render unpaid services to government yamen. The jade waistband will be returned to the palace, if yet undisposed of. Lady Han, henceforth forbidden to enter the palace on account of her debauchery, is to be married off by Marshal Yang to a law-abiding commoner."

After an initial surge of fear, Lady Han later found her longing for love gratified and her wish fulfilled, for she was married off to a merchant who was a native of a distant place but ran a government-sponsored shop in the capital. Determined not to take her to his hometown, he traveled back and forth between the two places and they lived in conjugal harmony until a ripe old age. But this happened later.

The prefect of Kaifeng brought Magic Powers Sun from jail and the verdict was read out loud in court. A notice was put up listing his crimes and announcing the sentence of death by multiple cuts. He was then taken to the marketplace and executed in public. Indeed,

> All the evil deeds he had done in the past
> Came back to haunt him in his darkest hour.

There was a jostling crowd of spectators at the execution that day. After the supervisor of executions finished reading out his crimes, the executioners shouted, "All avenging spirits, come here!" With that, they brought their knives down on Magic Powers Sun, stirring a great commotion at the marketplace.

This story used to circulate among storytellers in the capital, but has now found its way into the unofficial history of the Song dynasty. Truly,

> Be sure to observe Confucian decorum;
> Do not violate Xiao He's penal code.[10]
> The depraved deserve violent deaths;
> Magic powers are of no avail.

Over Fifteen Strings of Cash, a Jest Leads to Dire Disasters

A smart and clever mind comes with birth;
The benighted state may not be for real.
Jealousy is often caused by a narrow mind;
Wars may arise from light-hearted banter.
Like the Yellow River with its nine bends, the mind is devious;
Under the layers of armor, the face is fearsome.
Wine and lust ruin families and countries;
Poems and books never harm the virtuous.

This poem laments the perils of life. The paths of the world are narrow, and the human heart is hard to fathom. Since the great Dao is not easy to attain, human nature manifests itself in multifarious ways. In swarming multitudes, people go in pursuit of profit and gain. In mindless folly, they land themselves in trouble and disaster. To protect themselves and their families, they need to navigate through the vicissitudes of life. Therefore, the ancients said, "Know when to frown and when to laugh." Indeed, one must exercise the greatest caution as to when to frown and when to laugh.

This story is about a man whose jesting remarks after a bout of drinking led to his own death, the destruction of his family, and the loss of several other lives. But let me begin with a prologue story first.

Back in the Song dynasty, there lived a young scholar, Wei Pengju by name and Chongxiao by courtesy name. He married at eighteen years of age a young lady who was as pretty as a flower and as fair as jade. In less than one year, Scholar Wei packed for his journey to the capital to sit for the spring examinations at the national level and took leave of his wife. Before he departed, his wife said to him, "Come back as soon as possible, whether you win an official post or not. Do not abandon your loving wife."

He replied, "Scholarly honors and official rank are what lie first and foremost in my future. You shouldn't worry." So he set off on his journey and went to the capital. Sure enough, he passed the examinations on the first try and won second place. Enjoying his moment of glory in the capital, he wrote a letter to his wife and sent a servant to bring her over, as was only to be expected. After some necessary words of greeting and the announcement about his eligibility for an official post, the letter went on to say, "There being no one to look after me here, I've gotten myself a second little wife. I await your arrival in the capital to share the wealth and honor with me." (*He is actually sounding her out. This is not entirely said in jest.*)

The servant put the letter in his luggage and went back home. After congratulating the mistress, he presented her with the letter. Upon reading it, she said to the servant, "Your master is such an ingrate! The moment he becomes eligible for an official post, he gets himself a concubine."

The servant said, "I didn't know he had a concubine when I was in the capital. My master must be joking. You will know soon enough when you get there, ma'am. Don't worry about it."

"If so, I'll let the matter drop." However, a boat for the journey was not to be had on such short notice. Therefore, while packing, she looked for someone who happened to be going to the capital to deliver a letter for her to her husband. Once in the capital, the messenger asked his way to the lodgings of Scholar Wei who had just won second place in the examinations, delivered the letter, and was treated to wine and a meal before he went his way. But of this, no more.

Now, Scholar Wei opened the letter, only to see that it contained one simple statement: "While you took a second little wife in the capital, I also got myself a second little husband at home. I will go with him to the capital sooner or later." (*They must be in the habit of teasing each other.*) Dismissing this as a joke, Scholar Wei did not put the letter away immediately. (*Too lazy and careless.*)

At this point, the janitor announced, "You've got a visitor!"

The visitor went straight into Scholar Wei's room and sat down, partly because accommodations at an inn are less spacious than in one's home, partly because he was a good friend who had also just passed the examinations, and partly because he knew Mr. Wei's wife was not with him. After an exchange of amenities, Scholar Wei rose to go to the outhouse. In his absence, his friend read the letter on the table. Amused, he purposely read it aloud upon Wei's return. (*How unkind of him!*) Caught off guard, Wei said, his face flaming red, "She doesn't mean it. I teased her, so she wrote that in retaliation."

The friend said, laughing, "But this is not something to joke about." He said good-bye and took himself off. ([Illegible].)

Being a young man prone to gossip, that friend quickly spread the story about the letter all around the inns of the capital where the examination candidates were staying. Those who were jealous of Scholar Wei for having won such high honors in such youth put this rumor in a memorial to the emperor (*Rumors mostly do people injustice. A gentleman of moral uprightness should refrain from spreading them.*), claiming that Mr. Wei, in his youthful indiscretion, was fit not for important posts in the imperial court but only for lower positions outside of the capital. Scholar Wei was seized with remorse. Later, he never managed to rise higher. All too frivolously, he had forfeited a bright future. A joke had cost him a career.

Let me move on to our story proper, in which a man, as a result of a jest after a bout of drinking, lost his own life and implicated a few others, who all died unjustly. What was it all about? There is a poem in testimony:

> *The rugged roads of life sadden the heart*
> *While some flippantly joke and laugh.*
> *A white cloud is innocent and means no harm,*
> *But wild winds draw it out to wreak havoc.*

In the Southern Song dynasty, to the left of Arrow Bridge in Lin'an, the capital [present-day Hangzhou, Zhejiang], which was not any less prosperous and affluent than Bianjing, the former capital [present-day Kaifeng, Henan], there lived a man named Liu Gui, courtesy name Junjian. The Liu family used to be quite well off, but, after Liu Gui took over the family fortune, luck began to run against him. He applied himself to the books at first, but, seeing that he was not making a success of it, he tried his hand at business. Lacking training in this line of profession, like someone who turned Buddhist late in life, he felt even more inadequate. After losing even his capital, he had to sell his house and rent a smaller one with only two or three rooms. He and his wife, Wang-shi, had married young and were a loving couple. Later, because they had no son, Liu Gui took a concubine née Chen, daughter of Chen the cake peddler. They came to call her Second Sister. But this happened before they had fallen on hard times. The three of them were the only occupants of the house. The neighbors liked Liu Junjian for his friendliness. Calling him Master Liu, they said to him, "You are in this sorry condition only because you're not in luck for the time being. Everything will go well after a while." That was easily enough said. What good did it do him? As before, he stayed at home, feeling miserable and at his wits' end.

One day, as he was sitting idly at home, his father-in-law's servant, Old Wang, approaching seventy years of age, came and said to him, "It's the master's birthday. He sent me here to invite you and the mistress over."

Liu said, "I've been so down in the mouth that I forgot it's my father-in-law's birthday today!" He and his wife began to pack a few articles of clothing into a bundle, which they then gave to Old Wang to carry. Turning to Second Sister, Liu said, "Keep good watch over the house. We won't be able to return tonight, but we'll surely be back by tomorrow evening." With that, they set out.

After arriving at Squire Wang's house, more than twenty li from the city, he exchanged greetings with his father-in-law, but, in the presence of the many other guests in the house, he could not very well discuss his wretched circumstances with his father-in-law. After the guests departed, he and his wife were put up for the night in a guest room. At daybreak, his father-in-law came to talk with him. "My son-in-law," he began, "you must not go on like this. As they say, he who sits idle will eat away a mountain of a fortune. He who stands idle will eat his way into a deep hole in the ground. The gullet is as deep as the sea, and the sun and the moon shoot back and forth as fast as shuttles on a loom. You'll have to come up with a long-term plan. My daughter married you in the hope of being well provided for. You can't let things go on like this!"

With a sigh, Master Liu said, "Yes, father-in-law, you're right. But, as they say, it's easier to go up the mountain and catch a tiger than to ask for money. The ways of the world being what they are, who cares about me as you do, sir? I'll just have to put up with the poverty. Begging for help won't get me anywhere."

"I don't blame you for saying that. But this old man can't stomach anymore of this. Let me give you some money so that you can do something like open a general store and make enough money to live on. Wouldn't that be nice?"

"Of course that would be nice," said Master Liu. "Thank you so much for your kindness, sir."

After lunch, Squire Wang took out fifteen strings of cash and, giving them to Master Liu, said, "My son-in-law, take this and open up a store. After preparations for the store are ready, I'll give you another ten strings. Your wife may stay here for a few days. When you've got a date for the store to open, I'll take her to you myself and offer you my congratulations. What do you say?"

With profuse thanks, Master Liu swung the bag of money over his shoulder and went off. After arriving in Lin'an late in the afternoon, he happened to pass the house of an acquaintance who wanted to go into business. So he thought he might as well call on him for a little talk. As he knocked on the door, he heard an answering cry from inside and out came his friend. With a greeting, the man asked, "Is there anything I can do for you?"

When Liu told him about what he had in mind, the man said, "I have nothing to do at present anyway. I'll surely come to help you if you need me."

"That would be good," said Liu.

After they talked about business matters for a while, the man treated Master Liu to what wine and food he had in the house. Without much capacity for wine, Master Liu soon began to feel the effect of the drinks. He rose to go, saying, "Sorry for having imposed on your hospitality. Please come to my house tomorrow morning. We'll talk some more about the business."

The man saw Liu to the street corner, took leave of him, and returned home. So much for this man.

If this storyteller had been born in the same year as Mr. Liu and had grown up with him shoulder to shoulder, I would have held him by the waist and dragged him away by his arms, so that he would not have been struck by such misfortune. But it turned out that Mr. Liu died a death more horrible than that of

Li Cunxiao, as recorded in History of the Five Dynasties,[1]
And Peng Yue, as recorded in History of the [Western] Han dynasty.[2]

Carrying the strings of cash on his back, Mr. Liu slowly made his way home. It was already lamp-lighting time when he knocked on his door. Second Sister was home alone, without anything to occupy herself with. In the growing darkness, she had closed the door and dozed off by the lamp. It was some time before she heard Liu's raps on the door. Crying out, "Coming," she rose and opened the door to let him in. She then took the strings of cash from him and, placing them on the table, asked, "Husband, where did you get all this money? And what are you going to do with it?"

In his wine-induced excitement and his resentment at her for having taken so long to open the door, Liu decided to be playful and give her a scare. (*It's all right if he chooses not to explain. He should not go too far with his joke.*)

"You won't like it if I tell you. But if I don't tell you now, you'll have to know later on anyway. It's just that in a moment of desperation, for lack of a better way out, I pawned you off to a man, but only for fifteen strings of cash because I don't want you to be gone for good. If my circumstances improve, I'll redeem you with interest. But if I go on being as poor as I am, I'll just have to forget it."

The young woman found this hard to believe, but the fifteen strings of cash were there to prove his story. She wondered how he could be so heartless. After all, he had never had a harsh word for her before, and she and Mrs. Liu got along perfectly well. Not knowing what to make of it, she spoke up again, "If so, you should have notified my parents."

"If I had notified your parents, they wouldn't have let me go ahead with it. (*This is beginning to look real.*) After you go to that man's house tomorrow, I'll ask someone to talk to your parents in due course. They won't blame me."

"Where were you drinking today?"

"At the house of the man to whom I pawned you, after we signed the papers."

"Why isn't Elder Sister back?"

"She hates to see you go. She'll come back after you're gone tomorrow. I did this because I had no other way out, and I must keep my word." Barely able to suppress a furtive giggle after saying that, he went to bed without removing his clothes and soon fell asleep.

Her mind in turmoil, the young woman thought, "I wonder what kind of man he sold me off to. I must tell my parents first. If the man comes to get me tomorrow, he'll have to go to my parents' house to close the deal." After a few more moments of reflection, she put the fifteen strings of cash in a pile by Mr. Liu's feet and, while he was in a besotted state, she quietly put together a few articles of clothing, slowly opened the door, and went out. After pulling the door closed behind her, she turned left, to the house of Old Zhu San and his wife, neighbors whom she knew well. She asked Mrs. Zhu to put her up for the night, adding, "For no reason at all, my husband sold me today. I must tell my parents about this first. Could you please tell my husband tomorrow to go with the buyer to my parents' house, to talk it all out and close the deal?"

Mrs. Zhu said, "You're right. You go ahead. I'll relay your message to him."

After spending the night there, the young lady took herself off to her parents' home. Of this, no more for now. Truly,

> *The sea turtle freed itself from the golden hook,*
> *Shook its head, flicked its tail, and vanished for good.*

Now, back to Master Liu. Upon waking up at the third watch of the night, he found the lamp on the table still lit but Second Sister no longer there. Believing she was cleaning in the kitchen, he called out for tea. Getting no answer after he called quite a few times, he tried to struggle up, but, not having yet slept off the wine, he dozed off again.

As it turned out, an unsavory character happened to be at Master Liu's door at this time. He was out to steal under the cover of night to make up for the gambling losses he had incurred earlier in the day. Second Sister having only pulled the door to without locking it, the burglar gave it a gentle push, and the door swung open. Unobserved, he tiptoed his way inside. As he drew near the bed, he looked around by the light of the lamp and found nothing worth stealing. Groping his way to the bed, he saw a man sleeping with his face toward the wall. At his feet was a pile of copper coins. As he helped himself to a few strings, the burglar's movements woke up Master Liu. Sitting up, he said severely, "You good-for-nothing! I borrowed these few strings of cash from my father-in-law to make a living with. If you steal them, what am I going to do?"

Without saying a word in reply, the burglar struck Liu right in the face with his fist. (*This scoundrel says nothing but acts insolently enough.*) Liu dodged and got out of bed to fight him. Intimidated by Master Liu's quick moves, the man took to his heels. Liu gave chase and ran out of the room into the kitchen, ready to cry out so that the neighbors could join him in catching the thief. Growing frantic, the man caught sight of a shining firewood ax right by his hand. As the saying goes, a desperate moment drives one to act. He picked up the ax and swung it smack into Liu's face. As Liu fell, the burglar swung the ax one more time and cut him down. Master Liu died. Bless his soul! The burglar said, "As they say, once you start something, you'd better finish it off. It was you who ran after me, not the other way around." Having gotten thus far, he thought he might as well get the money. He turned back into the room and, after wrapping up the fifteen strings of cash with a bed-sheet and binding up the parcel tightly, he pulled the door to and went off. Of this, no more.

The next morning, the neighbors noticed that Master Liu's door was closed and no sound came from within. "Master Liu, you've overslept!" they cried out. Without getting a response, they made their way in, surprised to find the door unbolted. Once inside, they saw that Master Liu was lying on the floor, dead from ax wounds. The neighbors said, "Mrs. Liu went to her parents' home two days ago, but where's Second Sister?"

In the midst of the uproar, Zhu San, the old man who had put Second Sister up the night before, said, "She came to our house last evening and said that Master Liu had sold her for no reason at all. She then went to her parents' home. She wanted me to tell Master Liu to go with the buyer to her parents' house to talk it all out and close the deal. If we send someone to bring her back, we'll be able to get to the bottom of this. In the meantime, let's also bring Mrs. Liu back before doing anything further."

"You're right," the other neighbors agreed.

So they first had someone report the terrible news to Squire Wang. Squire Wang and his daughter burst into wails of grief. "He left here yesterday perfectly all right," said Squire Wang. "I gave him fifteen strings of cash for him to set up a business. How did he come to be murdered?"

The messenger said, "Sir, madam, Master Liu returned home at dusk yesterday in a half-drunken state. Well, actually, we didn't know whether he had money with him or what time he returned. What happened was that this morning, when we saw his door ajar, we pushed it open and went in, only to see him dead on the floor, murdered. We didn't see even one penny of the fifteen strings of cash that were supposed to be in the house, nor was Second Sister there. So we cried out. Mr. Zhu San from the house on the left came and said that she had stayed at his house last night. According to her, Master Liu had sold her for no reason and she wanted to tell her parents about it, so she left this morning. We decided to report to Mrs. Liu and you, sir, and we've sent people to bring the young lady back. If they don't catch up with her on the road, they'll go to her parents' house. Whatever happens, we'll make sure that she is brought back to answer questions. You, sir, and Mrs. Liu must also go there so that you can avenge Master Liu."

In haste, Squire Wang and his daughter got ready for the trip, treated the messenger to wine and a meal, and hurried into the city. Of this, more later.

Now, back to Second Sister. After leaving the neighbor's house early in the morning, she took to the road. Before she had gone two li, her feet began to ache so terribly that she could not walk another step. As she sat by the roadside, she saw a young man wearing a headscarf with zigzag patterns, a straight loose gown, and a pair of silk shoes and white socks, and carrying a shoulder bag filled with copper coins. He was coming in her direction. When he drew near her, he threw her a glance. Though she was not a ravishing beauty, she was quite attractive, with her well-marked eyebrows, white teeth, rosy cheeks, and sparkling eyes. Truly,

Wild flowers are more eye-catching;
Village wine is more intoxicating.

The young man put down his shoulder bag and said with a deep bow, "Young lady, where are you going, all by yourself?" (*Mr. Liu died from wine; this young man is going to die from lust.*)

With a curtsey, she answered, "I'm going to my parents' home. I'm taking a rest here because I'm tired. Where have you come from, brother, and where are you going?"

Respectfully keeping his hands folded across his chest, the young man said, "I'm from the country. I just sold some silk bed-nets in the city and got some money. I'm going in the direction of Chujiatang."

"My parents live near Chujiatang. It would be nice if you could take me along."

"Of course. I'd be glad to go with you."

The two of them set off. Before they had gone three li, two men were seen running behind them as fast as their legs could carry them. All sweaty and out of breath, with the fronts of their outer garments open, they cried, "Young lady, stop! We have something to say to you!"

Mystified, Second Sister and the young man came to a halt. When the two men ran up to them, one grabbed Second Sister and the other grabbed the young man before they could protest. "A fine thing you did!" they said. "Where do you think you're going?"

Startled, Second Sister saw that they were neighbors, one of whom was the very man in whose house she had stayed the previous night. "I told you last night that my husband had sold me for no reason and that I was going home to tell my parents about it. Why have you run all the way here?"

Old Zhu San said, "I don't usually poke my nose into other people's business, but there's been a murder in your family. You must go back to answer questions."

"My husband has sold me and yesterday he carried home the money he got for the sale. What murder are you talking about? I'm not going."

Zhu San said, "You are a wayward one, aren't you? If you really don't go, we'll tell the local headman and have you arrested as a murderer. Otherwise we'll all be implicated, and he's not going to have any peace, either."

Seeing that things had taken an ominous turn, the young man said to the young lady, "In this case, you go with them. I'll go on by myself."

The two neighbors cried out, "It would be all right if you were not here, but since you are traveling with her and you stopped at the same time she did, you can't go!"

"Ridiculous! I met her on the road and just happened to walk with her for a while. I have nothing to do with all this. Why make me go with you?"

Old Zhu San said, "There's been a murder in her family. If we let you go, a party in this case will be missing." He turned a deaf ear to the protests of Second

Sister and the young man. As more people gathered around to watch, some said, "Young man, you can't leave. As they say, if you didn't do anything against your conscience during the day, you shouldn't fear when there comes a knock on your door at night. Why don't you go with them? There's no harm in that!"

The neighbor who had come with Old Zhu San said, "If you don't go, it means you have a guilty conscience, and we won't call it quits." (*Not being eloquent, they don't give good reasons.*) And so the two neighbors hustled the two of them off, making a group of four.

There was a bustling scene of excitement at Master Liu's door. Upon entering, Second Sister saw that Liu was lying on the floor, dead from ax wounds. Not a penny of the fifteen strings of cash was left on the bed. Her jaw dropped open; her tongue hung out. The young man was also appalled. He said, "Luckless me! I walked with the young lady for a while in all innocence and now I've got myself involved in a murder case!"

In the midst of the commotion, with everybody talking at once, Old Squire Wang, trembling every step of the way, came with his daughter. At the sight of his son-in-law's corpse, he burst into a fit of sobbing and said to Second Sister, "How could you have killed your husband and fled with the fifteen strings of cash? Now that the truth is out by the will of heaven, what do you have to say for yourself?"

"There were indeed fifteen strings of cash," replied Second Sister. "My husband came home last night and said that for lack of a better choice, he had pawned me to another man for fifteen strings of cash. He said that I was supposed to go to that man's home today. Without knowing what kind of a man he had pawned me to, I wanted to tell my parents first. So while he was sleeping, I piled up the fifteen strings by his feet, closed the door, and spent the night at Mr. Zhu's house, and this morning I set off for my parents' house. Before I left, I asked Mr. Zhu to tell my husband to go with the buyer to my parents' house to close the deal. I have no idea why he was killed."

Mrs. Liu said, "What are you talking about? My father gave him those fifteen strings of cash yesterday so that he could set up a business and support us. How could he have told you that he got the money from pawning you? You must have had an affair the last couple of days when you were alone. And you couldn't stand the poverty of the family. Then, tempted by the sight of fifteen strings of cash, you killed him and stole the money. Then in your clever way, you spent the night at a neighbor's house and plotted with your lover to run away together. Now that you've been caught traveling with him, you're not going to lie your way out of this!"

"Mrs. Liu has got it right," commented the spectators. To the young man, they said, "Young man, didn't you plot with the young lady to murder her husband and secretly arrange to meet at a quiet spot and then run away? What exactly were your plans?"

The young man said, "My name is Cui Ning. I've never seen this young lady before. I went into the city last evening and sold some silk. The money is still with me here. I saw her on the road and asked her where she was going all by herself. Because she was going in the same direction I was, we went together. I knew nothing about what had happened."

Turning a deaf ear to his explanations, they searched his shoulder bag and found there fifteen strings of cash, not a penny more, not a penny less. (*The young man is wronged.*) Everyone cried out. One said, "As the saying goes, 'The net of heaven is of large mesh, but it lets nothing through.' You and the young woman committed a murder. You took the money and the woman and tried to flee this place with her, dragging us all into a case in which the guilty parties couldn't be found."

With Mrs. Liu holding Second Sister, Squire Wang holding Cui Ning, and the neighbors as witnesses, the whole crowd marched noisily to the Lin'an prefectural yamen. Upon hearing of a murder, the prefect immediately called a court session to order and had the parties involved brought in for statements on the case.

Squire Wang was the first one to make a deposition. He said, "Your Honor, I am from a village of this prefecture. I'm approaching sixty years of age. My only daughter has been married for some years to Liu Gui, who lived in the city. Being childless, Liu Gui took on Chen-shi as a concubine and called her Second Sister. The three of them lived together with never a harsh word for one another. The day before yesterday was my birthday, so I sent for my daughter and my son-in-law and kept them in my house for the night. The next day, because my son-in-law had no means of a livelihood and was quite unable to provide for the family, I gave him fifteen strings of cash, so that he could set up a store and make a living. Second Sister stayed at home to look after the house. After my son-in-law went home last evening, he was hacked to death, for some reason. Second Sister then fled with a young man called Cui Ning. They've been caught and brought back. Please take pity on us, Your Honor. My son-in-law died a tragic death. The adulterous couple and the stolen money are all here. Please use your wise judgment."

Having heard him out, the prefect called Chen-shi to the bench and asked, "How did you collude with your lover, kill your husband, steal the money, and run away? What do you have to say for yourself?"

Second Sister pleaded, "Although I was but a concubine to Liu Gui, he treated me well. Mrs. Liu is also a nice and kind woman. Why would I do such an evil thing? Last evening, when my husband returned home, drunk and carrying fifteen strings of cash, I asked how he had come by the money. He replied that because he could not support the family, he had pawned me to a man in exchange for fifteen strings of cash. Without informing my parents, he wanted me to go to the buyer's house the very next day. I took fright and left later that night, first to a neighbor's house to spend the night. This morning, before I left for my parents' house, I told the neighbors to say to my husband that since he had already sold me, he could go with the buyer to my parents' house to close the deal. I was on the road when the neighbor in whose house I stayed last night caught up with me and brought me back. I have no idea why my husband has been murdered."

The prefect thundered, "Nonsense! These fifteen strings of cash were all too clearly given to him by his father-in-law. Yet you say he got the money by pawning you. This is a blatant lie. Also, why would a woman walk alone in the middle of the night? You were obviously trying to escape. You are not capable of doing all this on your own. You must have had your lover help you murder your husband in order to get his money. Confess!"

The young woman was about to protest her innocence again when the neighbors fell to their knees and said to the prefect, "Your Honor, what you said is indeed the truth. She did spend the night at the second house to the left of her house and she departed this morning. When we saw that her husband had been murdered, we sent two of the neighbors to give chase. They caught up with her. Both she and the young man with her firmly refused to come back. The two neighbors had to bring them back by force. In the meantime, we sent for Mrs. Liu and her father. When they arrived, the father-in-law said that he had given fifteen strings of cash to his son-in-law the day before, so that he could start a business. And now his son-in-law is dead and the money is gone. When we questioned her time and again, the concubine said she had put the money in a pile on the bed. We searched the young man and found fifteen strings of cash on him, not a penny less. Isn't it obvious that the two of them are an adulterous couple and they plotted the murder together? With the money as evidence, how can they lie their way out of it?"

Quite convinced, the prefect called up the young man and said to him, "How can such atrocities be allowed here in this capital of the empire! You abducted Mr. Liu's concubine, took the fifteen strings of cash, and murdered Mr. Liu. How did you do that? Where were you going with her? Out with the truth!"

"I am Cui Ning, from the country. I sold some silk in the city yesterday, for which I got these fifteen strings of cash. I happened to see this young lady on the road this morning. I didn't even know her name. How would I know anything about a murder in her family?"

In a blaze of wrath, the prefect roared, "Nonsense! There can't be such a coincidence! Fifteen strings of cash disappeared from their house, and you made fifteen strings of cash from selling silk. This is all too clearly a lie! Also, as the saying goes, 'Do not covet another man's wife; do not ride another man's horse.' If you had nothing to do with her, why were you traveling with her and staying at the same inn? A brazen scoundrel like you will never confess unless you're put to the rod!"

There and then, Cui Ning and Second Sister were beaten until they were more dead than alive. With Squire Wang, Mrs. Liu, and the neighbors clamoring that those two were the culprits, the prefect could hardly wait to close the case. Unable to hold out against the torture, poor Cui Ning and the young lady confessed to the false charges. The young lady said, "Tempted by the sight of the money, I killed my husband, took the fifteen strings of cash, and fled with my lover, and this is the truth."

After each of the neighbors drew a cross with his finger on the confession by way of signature, the two accused were put in large cangues and sent to death row. The fifteen strings of cash were returned to Squire Wang, but they turned out not to be enough even for tipping the yamen lictors.

After the imperial court reviewed the file put together by the prefect, the emperor issued a decree, saying, "Cui Ning is to be executed in accordance with the law for the crimes of adultery, murder, and robbery. Chen-shi is to die by death by dismemberment in public for the heinous crime of murdering her husband in collusion with her lover."

After the confessions were read out, the two convicted were brought out of prison and taken to the marketplace, where the sentences were carried out in public. Even if they had had mouths all over their bodies, they would not have been able to defend themselves. Truly,

> *A mute tasting bitter cork-tree bark*
> *Cannot tell his disgust through words.*

Dear audience, if the young lady and Cui Ning had indeed murdered for money, they would have fled that very night. Why should she have spent the night in a neighbor's house and left for her parents' home the next morning, only to allow herself to be caught? A careful examination of the case would have identified the truth. The prefect was a fool too eager to close the case. Under torture, who would not confess to any charge? The evil things one does are all recorded in the unseen netherworld, to haunt one or one's offspring later. Those two aggrieved souls would not let go of the prefect who had inflicted such unjust deaths on them. Therefore, officials must not judge cases arbitrarily and apply torture indiscriminately. (*A motto for all officials.*) Every effort must be made to seek justice and fairness, for the dead cannot come back to life, just as a broken object cannot be made whole again. How lamentable!

Let us not encumber our story with more of such idle comments but turn our attention to Mrs. Liu, who set up a shrine to her late husband at home in observance of the period of mourning. To her father's exhortations that she remarry, she said, "I should wait at least for one year, if not the required three years." Her father agreed and left. Time sped by. After Mrs. Liu had borne the hardships of her life for nearly a year, her father thought that widowhood was too much for her. He told Old Wang the servant to bring her over, saying to him, "Tell her to pack and come back home. She can remarry after the first anniversary of Master Liu's death."

For lack of a better choice, Mrs. Liu accepted her father's advice after some solid thinking. She packed, gave her luggage to Old Wang to carry, and took leave of her neighbors, saying she would be coming back soon. After she and Old Wang were out of the city, they were caught in one of those severe rainstorms of autumn. They had to leave the road and find shelter in the woods, but they took the wrong path. Truly,

> *Like pigs and sheep on their way to the slaughterhouse,*
> *With each step they drew nearer to their deaths.*

When they were in the woods, they heard a loud cry from behind: "Stand and deliver! The king of the Jing Mountains is here!" As Mrs. Liu and Old Wang stood petrified, a man leaped out.

> *A dark red scarf over his face,*
> *An old warrior's robe on his body,*
> *A red silk band around his waist,*
> *A pair of black boots on his feet,*
> *A wood-hilted sword in his hand.*

As the man approached them, brandishing his sword, Old Wang, who was destined to die at this hour, said, "You bandit! I know your kind! Let this old man fight you to the death!" With that, he charged at the bandit, head down. The man dodged. Having lunged ahead with all his force, Old Wang lost his balance and fell flat on the ground. "You impudent old swine!" said the man in a rage. With a few quick plunges of his sword, blood flowed over the ground. Old Wang gave up the ghost.

Witnessing this savage act, Mrs. Liu knew she would not be spared, either, but hitting on a plan to save her own skin, she clapped her hands and exclaimed, "Good job!"

The man stopped and, popping wide his devilish eyes, roared, "Who was he to you?"

Mrs. Liu replied, feigning honesty, "When my husband died on me unfortunately, a matchmaker tricked me into marrying this old man, who was good at nothing but eating. Now you've gotten rid of a pest for me, sir."

Impressed by her cautiousness and her above-average looks, the man asked, "Would you be willing to marry me?"

She saw nothing for it but to say, "Yes, I would be glad to serve you, sir."

His anger turning to joy, the man sheathed his sword and dumped Old Wang's corpse into a ravine. He then took Mrs. Liu to a sprawling manor. He picked up a few clods of earth and tossed them at the roof. Immediately the gate was opened. Once in the main hall, the man ordered a sheep slaughtered and wine prepared for a wedding ceremony. The couple got along well together. Truly,

> *Knowing full well he was not the right man,*
> *She submitted in a desperate moment.*

In less than half a year after he married Mrs. Liu, the bandit got several wind-falls in a row and was now a rich man. Mrs. Liu, with her good sense, kept advising him, "As the ancients said, 'An earthen jar used for drawing water from the well will break by the well; a general fighting battles will die in a battle.' You and I now have enough to live on for the rest of our lives. You'll come to no good end if you go on doing things that defy the will of heaven. As they say, the Liang Garden may be good, but it's nothing like home.³ You'd do well to change your ways. A small business will give us enough income."

Under her pressure day and night, the bandit indeed had a change of heart and gave up his line of work. He rented a house in the city and opened a general store. On days of leisure, he went to temples to chant the Buddha's name and observe a vegetarian diet. (*He has a bad conscience.*)

One day, when sitting idly in the house, he remarked to his wife, "I may have been a bandit, but I know that for every injustice, there is a perpetrator; for every debt, there is a debtor. Every day, I robbed and stole in order to make a living. And then after I got you, I've had some plain-sailing days, and I've now turned over a new leaf. With all this time on my hands now, I often look back on the past. I've killed two men unjustly and ruined two other people. They are constantly in my thoughts. I'd like to hold a prayer service to them. This is something I've never told you before."

"You killed two men unjustly? What do you mean?"

"One of them was your husband. When he charged at me in the woods, I killed him. Actually I had nothing against that old man. And then I married his wife. He would never rest easy in his grave."

"But how else could we have gotten together? What's gone is gone. Don't bring it up again. Who was the other one?"

"Well, that was even more of a violation against divine will. And two other innocent people also died as a result. It was one year ago. I lost at gambling one day. Without a penny left, I went out at night to steal. When I passed by a door that was unbolted, I pushed it open and went in. There was no one around. When I groped my way into the inner room, I saw a man lying drunk in bed with a pile of copper coins at his feet. I stole a few strings and was about to leave when that man woke up and said, 'My father-in-law gave me this money for me to start a business. If you steal it, this whole family will starve to death.' Then he ran after me out of the room and was about to cry out for help. When I saw that things were going badly for me, I noticed a firewood ax right by my feet. This was indeed a case of 'A desperate moment drives one to act.' I picked up the ax and shouted, 'It's either you or me!' With two blows, I cut him down. Then I went back into the room and took all fifteen strings of cash. Later, I heard that his concubine and a young man called Cui Ning were accused of murder and robbery and that both were executed. In all the time I was a bandit, these two cases were the only ones that neither heaven nor humans will ever forgive. (*By knowing that he will not be forgiven by humans, this bandit at least has some sense of what divine will is.*) I should offer a prayer service for them."

Mrs. Liu groaned inwardly and thought, "So, this brute killed my husband and caused the unjust deaths of Second Sister and that young man. It was in fact all because I was the witness demanding that they pay with their lives. The two of them in the netherworld will never forgive me."

But in the bandit's presence she gave every appearance of joy, and the night passed without ado. The next day, she slipped out at the first opportunity and went straight to the Lin'an prefectural yamen. At the gate, she cried out, "Injustice! Injustice!"

It so happened that the new prefect who had been in this post for only half a month was about to call his court session to order. The lictors brought in the woman shouting "Injustice!" At the foot of the dais, Mrs. Liu burst into sobs before she launched into an account of how the bandit had killed her husband, Liu Gui, adding, "The prefect handling the case did not investigate thoroughly. He perfunctorily closed the case and unjustly sentenced Second Sister and Cui Ning to death. Later the bandit killed Old Wang and took possession of me. Now divine justice has caught up with him. He confessed everything to me. Your Honor, please redress the wrong in your wisdom." With that, she broke down again in a flood of tears.

Touched by her words, the prefect dispatched lictors to bring the "king of the Jing Mountains" to court. Under torture, he confessed. The confession tallied with Mrs. Liu's statement in every detail. There and then he was convicted of crimes punishable by death and the file was submitted to the emperor. Upon the expiration of the required sixty-day waiting period, the emperor issued a decree, saying, "It has been found that the king of the Jing Mountains committed murder for money and implicated innocent people. He is to be executed immediately rather than in the coming autumn [the season for executions], as stipulated by the law governing cases in which the accused is responsible for the killing of three or more members of one family for offenses, if any, that are not punishable by death. The prefect who handled the case is hereby stripped of all official ranks for the miscarriage of justice. Cui Ning and Chen-shi having died tragic and unjust deaths, the authorities are to visit their families and give them compensation. Since Wang-shi married the bandit under coercion and was able to bring the murderer of her husband to justice, half of the criminal's possessions will be given to her to support her for the rest of her life. The other half will be confiscated by the government."

Mrs. Liu went to the execution ground to watch the beheading of the king of the Jing Mountains. She then brought his head to the altars of her deceased husband, Second Sister, and Cui Ning for a prayer service, at which she cried with abandon. She donated to a nunnery her half of the criminal's possessions and spent her days reading the sutras and chanting Buddha's name in memory of the dead souls, until she died of old age. There is a poem in testimony:

The good and the evil alike met their end;
A simple jest led to disaster.
Be advised: speak only in good faith;
The tongue has always been a source of trouble.

Notes

The stories in this collection were selected from the following three volumes, all compiled by Feng Menglong and translated by Shuhui Yang and Yunqin Yang: *Stories Old and New: A Ming Dynasty Collection,* vol. 1 (Seattle: University of Washington Press, 2000); *Stories to Caution the World: A Ming Dynasty Collection,* vol. 2 (Seattle: University of Washington Press, 2005); and *Stories to Awaken the World: A Ming Dynasty Collection,* vol. 3 (Seattle: University of Washington Press, 2009).

Introduction

1. For a detailed discussion of the Sanyan and its influence on Chinese fiction, as well as a bibliography of relevant works, see Feng Menglong, *Stories Old and New,* xv–xxvi, 778–94.

2. Lu Shulun, "Feng Menglong," in his book *Feng Menglong sanlun* (Shanghai: Shanghai guji, 1993), 7.

3. Pi-ching Hsu, "Celebrating the Emotional Self " (PhD diss., University of Minnesota, 1994), 48.

4. Quoted in Lu Shulun, "Feng Menglong," 92.

5. The facsimile edition of *The Complete Works of Feng Menglong* (Feng Menglong quanji), published by Shanghai Guji Chubanshe in 1993, contains forty-three volumes that, when stacked, reach more than six feet high.

6. Patrick Hanan, *The Chinese Vernacular Story* (Cambridge, MA: Harvard University Press, 1981), 80–81.

7. Ibid.

8. The moralistic and didactic tone of the three Sanyan titles (*Illustrious Words to Instruct the World, Comprehensive Words to Caution the World,* and *Constant Words to Awaken the World*) can probably also be understood in the same light.

7. Y. W. Ma, "Feng Menglong," in *The Indiana Companion to Traditional Chinese Literature,* ed. William Nienhauser (Bloomington: Indiana University Press, 1986), 381.

8. The moralistic and didactic tone of the three Sanyan titles (*Illustrious Words to Instruct the World, Comprehensive Words to Caution the World,* and *Constant Words to Awaken the*

World) can probably also be understood in the same light.

9. Y. W. Ma, "Feng Menglong," in *The Indiana Companion to Traditional Chinese Literature,* ed. William Nienhauser (Bloomington: Indiana University Press, 1986), 381.

10. Hanan, *Chinese Vernacular Story,* 104, and Patrick Hanan, *The Chinese Short Story: Studies in Dating, Authorship, and Composition* (Cambridge, MA: Harvard University Press, 1973), 76–86.

11. In his "Preface to *Art Song Prosody*" (Qulü xu), Feng complains that "the most abused literary genres today are classical poetry and prose." In his preface to *Hill Songs* he also says that "although there is an abundance of false poetry and prose, there are no false folk songs." See Guo Shaoyu, *Zhongguo lidai wenlun xuan* (Shanghai: Shanghai guji, 1979), 3: 194, 231.

12. Cyril Birch, "Feng Meng-lung and the *Ku Chin Hsiao Shuo,*" in *Bulletin of the School of Oriental and African Studies* 18 (1956): 82.

13. Patrick Hanan, "The Nature of Ling Mengch'u's Fiction," in *Chinese Narrative: Critical and Theoretical Essays,* ed. Andrew Plaks (Princeton, NJ: Princeton University Press, 1977), 87.

14. Ibid.

15. David Rolston, *Traditional Chinese Fiction and Fiction Commentary* (Stanford, CA: Stanford University Press, 1997), 232. Rolston also says that the simulated storyteller can be seen "as a functional attempt to deal with the absence of the 'author' in early vernacular fiction."

16. The word *huaben* was adopted as the regular term for the traditional Chinese vernacular short story only in the twentieth century. On its early usage as simply "story," rather than "promptbook," see Charles Wivell, "The Term 'Hua-pen,'" in David Buxbaum and Frederick Mote, eds., *Transition and Permanence: Chinese History and Culture* (Hong Kong: Cathay Press, 1972), 295–306. The promptbook theory has been criticized from another angle: because professional storytellers were more likely to have relied on abstracts or notes in the classical language, the earliest extant *huaben* texts were perhaps also meant for reading, rather than reciting, as were their later imitations; see André Lévy, "*Hua-pen*," in Nienhauser, ed., *Indiana Companion*, 443.

17. See W. L. Idema, "Storytelling and the Short Story in China," in *T'oung Pao* 59 (1973): 3, 35–39.

18. W. L. Idema, "Some Remarks and Speculations Concerning *P'ing-hua*," reprinted in Idema, *Chinese Vernacular Fiction: The Formative Period* (Leiden, the Netherlands: E. J. Brill, 1974), 72.

19. See, for example, Yang Xianyi and Gladys Yang, trans., *The Courtesan's Jewel Box* (Beijing: Foreign Languages Press, 1981).

20. See Hu Wanchuan, "*Sanyan* xu ji meipi de zuozhe wenti," reprinted in his *Huaben yu caizi jiaren xiaoshuo zhi yanjiu* (Taipei: Da'an, 1994), 123–38.

21. Patrick Hanan points out in his *Chinese Vernacular Story* (1981) that twenty-two stories in *Xingshi hengyan* were probably authored by an associate of Feng Menglong's, named Langxian, including stories 6, 15, 16, 18, 20, 25, 26, 27, 28, 29, 34, 35, 36, 37, and 38 (120–39). However, in note 21 of his introduction to *Falling in Love: Stories from Ming China* (Honolulu: University of Hawai'i Press, 2006), Hanan says that "the thesis of common authorship [of stories in *Xingshi heng yan* and *Shi diantou*] is far from proven, and I think it prudent here to consider the two sets of stories as by separate authors" (xviii). Scholars generally agree that this group of stories were not authored by Feng but by a different hand. Feng, however, was still

the chief editor, and must have had a voice in these stories in the collection, just as in any other preexisting stories in the Sanyan collections. For Feng's role as the chief editor and therefore the finalizer of *Xingshi heng yan*, see Shuhui Yang, *Appropriation and Representation: Feng Menglong and the Chinese Vernacular Story* (Ann Arbor: Center for Chinese Studies, University of Michigan, 1998), 15.

1. Jiang Xingge Reencounters His Pearl Shirt

This story, no. 1 in *Stories Old and New*, has been translated as "The Pearl-Sewn Shirt" by Cyril Birch in Feng Menglong, trans. Cyril Birch, *Stories from a Ming Collection: Translations of Chinese Short Stories Published in the Seventeenth Century* (New York: Grove Weidenfeld, 1978), 39–96; and as "The Pearl Shirt Reencountered" by Jeanne Kelly in Y. W. Ma and Joseph S. M. Lau, eds., *Traditional Chinese Stories: Themes and Variations* (New York: Columbia University Press, 1978), 264–92.

1. In the Ming dynasty, Huguang consisted of what are now Hubei and Hunan Provinces. Xiangyang Prefecture was located in the northern part of what is now Hubei.

2. The six preliminaries are: giving presents to the prospective bride's family, providing written documentation of the prospective bride's name and date of birth, securing through divination by the groom's family of a good omen endorsing the marriage, sending a letter and wedding gifts to the bride's family (whose letter of acceptance confirms the marriage), requesting approval by the bride's family of an auspicious date for the wedding, and the groom's going in person to bring the bride home.

3. "Clouds and rain" is a metaphor for sexual encounters. It was first used in the prose poem "Gao tang fu," attributed to Song Yu (c. 290–c. 223 B.C.E.).

4. The seventh day of the seventh month of the lunar calendar is a festival that celebrates the annual meeting across the Milky Way of the stars Herdboy and Weaving Maiden. On the

day of the festival, women set out fruit offerings to Weaving Maiden and prayed that they would be blessed with better skills in sewing and embroidery. As the festival was known as Qiqiao (Praying for Skills), the third (*san*) daughter of the Wang family, born on that date, was thus called Sanqiao (The Third Blessed).

5. Xishi, also known as Xizi, was a legendary beauty of the state of Yue in the Warring States period (475–221 B.C.E.).

6. Nanwei was a famous beauty in the court of Duke Wen of Jin (636–628 B.C.E.) in the Spring and Autumn period (770–476 B.C.E.).

7. The bodhisattva Guanyin, the embodiment of compassion, was popularly conceived in late imperial China as a beautiful young woman.

8. A mace in the Ming dynasty equalled 3.69 grams.

9. Song Yu was a disciple of the great poet Qu Yuan (ca. 340–278 B.C.E.). See also note 3 of this story.

10. Pan Yue (265–419), courtesy name Anren, but more often known as Pan An, personifies male beauty.

11. *Hejian fu,* "debauched woman," was a term first used by Liu Zongyuan (773–819) in his "Story of Hejian." It was later used to refer to Pan Jinlian (Gold Lily), a debauched woman in the Ming novel *The Plum in the Golden Vase.*

12. Liu Bang (256–195 B.C.E.) was the founder of the Han dynasty. Xiang Yu (232–202 B.C.E.), king of Chu, was his major rival in contending for the throne. Before he became emperor, Liu Bang enlisted the service of Han Xin (d. 196 B.C.E.) and built a platform for a grand ceremony honoring him as grand marshal. Later, Han Xin proved to be instrumental in the defeat of Xiang Yu.

13. Linqing is in present-day Shandong Province.

14. Sima Xiangru (179–117 B.C.E.), one of the most celebrated *fu* (prose poem) writers in the history of Chinese literature, is also known for his romance with Zhuo Wenjun. The two eloped after their first meeting.

15. According to Song dynasty folklore, Pan Bizheng, a native of Henan, fell in love with the Taoist priestess Chen Miaochang. The two were later joined in matrimony.

16. The Lantern Festival falls on the fifteenth day of the first month. For the Clear and Bright (Qingming) Festival in April, people visit the graves of their ancestors.

17. The seven offenses by a wife that warranted divorce were: failure to produce a son, adultery, failure to serve the parents-in-law, verbal viciousness, theft, jealousy, and affliction with foul disease.

18. Jingkou is present-day Zhenjiang, Jiangsu.

19. Hepu is a pearl-producing area in present-day Guangxi Autonomous Region.

20. According to a legend from the Eastern (or Later) Han dynasty (25–220), the pearl-bearing oysters that abounded in the sea off the coast of Hepu County gradually migrated away because successive prefects were insatiably avaricious. When Meng Chang became prefect and put an end to all corruption, the oysters returned.

21. According to a legend from the Jin dynasty (265–420), Zhang Hua (232–300) saw that there was an aura over Fengcheng that bespoke of hidden precious swords. After he appointed Lei Huan as prefect of Fengcheng, Lei Huan dug up a pair of swords and presented one to Zhang Hua, keeping the other for himself. After both men died, the swords were seen at Yanping Ferry, where they joined together and changed into two dragons.

2. Yang Siwen Meets an Old Acquaintance in Yanshan

This story, no. 24 in *Stories Old and New,* has been translated as "Strange Encounter in Yanshan" by Yang Xianyi and Gladys Yang in *Chinese Literature* (December, 1961): 46–68.

1. Hu Haoran was an obscure poet of the Song dynasty. The editors of *Quan Song ci* (The complete collection of Song *ci* poems) (Beijing: Zhonghua Shuju, 1965) attribute this poem to Chao Chongzhi.

2. Felicity Pool and Five Peaks Temple were in Bianliang (present-day Kaifeng), the Eastern Capital of the Northern Song dynasty.

3. Yanshan Prefecture is in present-day Beijing.

4. The Jurchen people established their own dynasty, the Jin, between 1115 and 1122 and drove the Song dynasty south of the Huai River. The Jin was destroyed in 1234 by the Mongols.

5. Prince Su was Zhao Shu, son of Emperor Huizong.

6. During the Jingkang period (1126) Emperors Huizong and Qinzong were captured by the Jurchens, the Northern Song dynasty perished, and many residents of Kaifeng, the capital, fled to Yanshan.

7. The badge was a pass for access to the palace grounds.

8. In the Song dynasty, the Diplomacy Section was a unit in the Bureau of Military Affairs that handled correspondence and diplomatic exchanges between the imperial court and foreign peoples.

9. Su Xiaoqing was a famous courtesan from Luzhou who figured in a popular love story during the Song dynasty.

10. Mengjiangnü was a legendary figure. Her husband, Fan Xiliang, being one of the conscripted laborers building the Great Wall, she undertook a long journey to deliver winter clothes to him, but by the time she arrived there, he had already died. Her bitter wails caused the Great Wall to collapse, revealing her husband's remains. She later threw herself into the sea and drowned.

11. Jinling is present-day Nanjing.

12. Hong Mai (1123–1202) was the author of *The Records of Yijian,* a collection of nearly 2,700 stories that deal with dreams, relations between the human and supernatural worlds, the origins of poems, etc.

13. Guo Xi was a famous landscape painter of the Northern Song dynasty.

14. On Chen Miaochang, see note 15 of story 1.

15. On the Clear and Bright Festival, see note 16 of story 1.

16. When performing exorcism, a Taoist priest would draw a magic charm, burn it, and have the ashes eaten by the person believed to be possessed by a ghost.

17. Qiantang was another name for Hangzhou.

18. According to legend, Cao E, of Shangyu County in the Eastern Han dynasty, wailed with grief for seventeen days as she went along the river to find her father's drowned corpse. She then threw herself into the river. Five days later, she reemerged with her father's body.

19. Qu Yuan (ca. 340–278 B.C.E.), one of the best known figures in traditional Chinese culture, drowned himself in the Milo River.

3. Yu Boya Smashes His Zither in Gratitude to an Appreciative Friend

This story is the first in *Stories to Caution the World.*

1. For more on the friendship between Guan and Bao, see the prologue of story 8 in Feng Menglong, *Stories Old and New.*

2. During the Ming dynasty, Huguang consisted of present-day Hubei and Hunan Provinces. Yingdu was northwest of modern Jiangling, Hubei.

3. Fuxi was one of the legendary Three Sovereigns whose reign supposedly began around 2800 B.C.E.

4. The five planets are Venus, Jupiter, Mercury, Mars, and Saturn.

5. The thirty-three layers of heaven, *trayastrimsas,* is a Buddhist concept.

6. A year was divided into seventy-two units, called *hou,* with each *hou* consisting of five days.

7. The Jasper Pool is a legendary abode of the gods at the top of the Kunlun mountains in western China.

8. The eight solar terms of the year are the Beginning of Spring, the Beginning of Summer, the Beginning of Autumn, the Beginning of Winter, the Spring Equinox, the Summer Solstice, the Autumn Equinox, and the Winter Solstice.

9. Golden Boys and Jade Maidens are page boys and maids who serve Daoist immortals.

10. The dragon's pond and the phoenix's pool are the two holes at the back of the zither.

11. Yao and Shun were legendary sage-kings who ruled in antiquity.

12. "While your parents are alive, do not travel far" is from *The Analects,* 4:19.

13. Jinyang is now Jinyuanzhen, to the southwest of the city of Taiyuan, Shanxi.

14. "If you do, you should always make your whereabouts known to them" is the sentence that follows "While your parents are alive, do not travel far" in *The Analects*, 4:19.

15. "Nine Springs" is a term for the netherworld.

16. The reader will remember that they met in autumn.

17. "The phoenix's tail" is a reference to the zither.

4. Judge Bao Solves a Case through a Ghost That Appeared Thrice

This story, no. 13 in *Stories to Caution the World*, has been translated as "The Ghost Came Thrice," in *Lazy Dragon: Chinese Stories from the Ming Dynasty*, trans. Yang Xianyi and Gladys Yang (Hong Kong: Joint Publishing Company, 1981).

1. Gan Luo was a native of the state of Qin during the Warring States period. He was granted a royal title at the age of twelve for his meritorious service to the state.

Ziya is Jiang Ziya, or Lü Wang, also popularly known as Taigong Wang or Jiang Taigong. He was a Zhou dynasty military strategist who did not rise to eminence until he was about eighty years old.

2. Peng Zu was a legendary figure in the time of the sage king Yao (before 2100 B.C.E.) who was said to have lived for eight hundred years.

Yan Hui (521–490 B.C.E.) was a student of Confucius. For more about Yan Hui, see story 3.

3. Fan Dan (112–185), an erudite scholar on the classics, was also known for his poverty.

For more on Shi Chong's wealth and downfall, see story 36 in Feng Menglong, *Stories Old and New*.

4. Zhang Dun (1035–1105), courtesy name Zihou, was a court official committed to Wang Anshi's reforms.

5. The five phases are water, fire, wood, metal, and earth. The eight characters of the astrological chart are two characters for the year of birth (one for the Heavenly Stem, one for the Earthly Branch), two for the month, two for the day, and two for the hour. Phases and characters combined are used to tell one's fortune.

6. Dongfang Shuo (154–93 B.C.E.) was a great man of letters of the Western Han dynasty. Stories about his wisdom and fortune-telling skills abound.

7. The Tai'e sword is believed to have been cast by the legendary ironsmiths Ganjian and Ouyezi in the Spring and Autumn period.

8. In fortune-tellers' parlance, a white tiger symbolizes misfortune.

9. A story in *Liezi* tells of a woodsman in the state of Zheng who forgot where he had hidden the deer he had killed and thought he had dreamed about it. Another man heard about this, found the deer, and took it home. Then the woodsman dreamed he remembered the place where he had hidden the deer and also saw the man who had taken the deer. The two men brought the case to court. When asked for his judgment, the prime minister said, "I can't tell what is dream and what is not." The mention of "Qin" suggests an allusion to Prime Minister Zhao Gao of the Qin dynasty. He demanded absolute obedience by pointing at a deer, calling it a horse, and killing everyone who disagreed. Feng Menglong may have confused the two stories.

10. Zhuangzi or Zhuang Zhou (ca. 369–286 B.C.E.) was a Daoist philosopher. According to the *Zhuangzi*, he once dreamed he was a butterfly that did not know it was Zhuang Zhou. When he awoke suddenly, he found himself Zhuang Zhou again but did not know whether he was Zhuang Zhou who had dreamed he was a butterfly or a butterfly dreaming it was Zhuang Zhou.

11. "Green" (*qing*) is a homophone of the character for "clear," implying in this context that the case is to be solved.

5. Madam White Is Kept Forever under Thunder Peak Tower

This story, no. 28 in *Stories to Caution the World*, has been translated by Diana Yu as "Eternal Prisoner under the Thunder Peak Pagoda," in *Traditional Chinese Stories: Themes and Varia-*

tions, ed. Y. W. Ma and Joseph S. M. Lau (New York: Columbia University Press, 1978).

1. Bianzhou, or Bianjing, present-day Kaifeng in Henan Province, was the capital of the Song dynasty before the court moved south to Hangzhou.

2. Lin Bu (967–1029), courtesy name Junfu, was a Song dynasty poet, posthumously given the title Hejing.

3. Bai Juyi (772–846) was a well-known Tang dynasty poet.

4. Su Shi (1037–1101), also called Su Dongpo, was a famous scholar of the Song dynasty.

5. The Qingming Festival is the Clear and Bright Festival, a day on which people visit their ancestors' graves.

6. These baskets hold paper coins, paper horses, and other items for the deceased to use in the underworld.

7. Animal blood is believed to have the power to combat sorcery.

8. *Jiangxiang,* rendered here as "fragrant wood", is *Acronychia pedunculata,* a small forest tree in the Rutaceae family.

9. This is wine seasoned with *xionghuang* (realgar), which is usually drunk at the Dragon Boat Festival, the fifth day of the fifth lunar month, to detoxify the body.

10. King Yama is the ruler of hell.

6. Du Shiniang Sinks Her Jewel Box in Anger

This story, no. 32 in *Stories to Caution the World,* has been translated as "The Courtesan's Jewel Box," in *The Courtesan's Jewel Box: Chinese Stories of the Tenth–Twelfth Centuries,* trans. Yang Xianyi and Gladys Yang (Beijing: Foreign Languages Press, 1981), and as "Tu Shih-niang Sinks the Jewel Box in Anger," in *Traditional Chinese Stories: Themes and Variations,* ed. Y. W. Ma and Joseph S. M. Lau (New York: Columbia University Press, 1978).

1. Toyotomi Hideyoshi (1536–1598), *kanpaku* (prime minister) of Japan, invaded Korea during the Chinese Wanli reign period under Emperor Shenzong and was defeated by Ming troops.

2. Bo Cheng'en, deputy commander of Xixia in northwestern China, rebelled in 1592, together with his father. The rebellion was put down later in the same year.

Yang Yinglong, pacification commissioner of Bozhou (present-day Zunyi, Guizhou Province), rebelled in 1597. The rebellion was suppressed in 1600.

3. In the Ming dynasty, the "two capitals" were Beijing and Nanjing.

4. Zhuo Wenjun was renowned for her beauty, intelligence, and musical talent.

5. Fan Su was a maid employed in the household of the famous Tang dynasty poet Bai Juyi (772–846), who wrote the line "Fan Su's cherry of a mouth."

6. Zhong Kui (formerly translated as Chung Kuei) is a deity who can drive away evil spirits in Chinese folklore.

7. A white tiger symbolizes bad luck.

8. Shi Hui, courtesy name Junmei, a native of Hangzhou, is believed to be the author of the play *Bai yue ting* (Moon pavilion).

9. Gao Qi (1336–1374), courtesy name Jidi, was a poet and a historian who was put to death by the first Ming emperor, Zhu Yuanzhang.

7. The Oil-Peddler Wins the Queen of Flowers

This story, no. 3 in *Stories to Awaken the World,* has been translated as "The Oil Peddler Courts the Courtesan" by Lorraine Lieu and the editors in *Traditional Chinese Stories: Themes and Variations,* ed. Y. W. Ma and Joseph S. M. Lau (New York: Columbia University Press, 1978); by Yang Xianyi and Gladys Yang as "The Oil Vendor and the Courtesan" in *Lazy Dragon: Chinese Stories from the Ming Dynasty* (Hong Kong: Joint Publishing Co., 1981); and as "The Oil Seller" by Patrick Hanan in *Falling in Love: Stories from Ming China* (Honolulu: University of Hawai'i Press, 2006).

1. Pan Yue (247–300), courtesy name Anren, popularly known as Pan An, was a man of letters in the Western Jin dynasty and reputedly very handsome.

2. Deng Tong of the Western Han dynasty

was a fabulously rich court favorite with the authority to mint his own money. But later he lost favor with the new emperor and died of hunger in prison.

3. Zheng Yuanhe and Li Yaxian are characters in "The Story of Li Wa" by Bai Xingjian (775–826) of the Tang dynasty.

4. According to legend, Zhao Gou, Prince Kang, later to be Emperor Gaozong of Southern Song dynasty, crossed the Yangzi River on a horse he found in a temple to flee from Jurchen soldiers, but once he was out of danger, he saw that the horse was made of clay.

5. Jin Wuzhu or Wanyan Zongbi, was the fourth son of Emperor Jin Taizu (r. 1115–22) of the Jin (Jurchen) dynasty. The Jin was overthrown by the Mongols in 1234.

6. Xishi, also known as Xizi, was a famous beauty of the state of Yue in the late Spring and Autumn period.

7. A "girl of stone" (*shinü*) is a woman with a hypoplastic vagina.

8. Sui He and Lu Jia were political advisers of great eloquence in the Western Han dynasty.

9. Granny Wang is a fictional character in *Outlaws of the Marsh* (Shuihu zhuan) and is also featured in *The Plum in the Golden Vase* (Jin Ping Mei), both full-length novels published earlier in the Ming dynasty.

10. According to legend, Xiaoji, son of King Wuding of the Shang dynasty, died in exile, a victim of his stepmother's machinations.

11. Shensheng, son of Duke Xian of the state of Jin in the Spring and Autumn period, was driven to suicide by Liji, Duke Xian's beloved concubine, who planned to have her own son designated as heir.

12. Benzoin is a hard fragrant yellowish balsamic resin from trees native to Indonesia, Vietnam, and other southeastern Asian countries.

13. This is a famous line by Liu Yuxi (772–842), poet and philosopher of the Tang dynasty.

14. The Clear and Bright (Qingming) Festival falls in early April and is the time for people to visit the graves of their ancestors.

15. The four treasures of the scholar's study are brush-pen, ink slab, ink stick, and rice paper.

16. Guan Yu (160–220), courtesy name Yunchang, was a valiant warrior in the Three Kingdoms period and a central figure in the folk pantheon. A complete translation of this phrase should be: ". . . in the pose of Guan Yunchang when he went valiantly, armed with a sword, and practically all by himself, to the enemy camp to attend a meeting that was clearly devised as a trap to capture him." There has been a whole array of popular stage versions of this story.

8. *The Leather Boot as Evidence against the God Erlang's Impostor*

This story, no. 13 in *Stories to Awaken the World,* has been translated as "The Boot That Reveals the Culprit" by Lorraine Lieu and the editors in *Traditional Chinese Stories: Themes and Variations,* ed. Y. W. Ma and Joseph S.M. Lau (New York: Columbia University Press, 1978).

1. For more on Emperor Taizu of the Song dynasty, see story 21 in Feng Menglong, *Stories to Caution the World: A Ming Dynasty Collection,* trans. Shuhui Yang and Yungin Yang (Seattle: University of Washington Press, 2005).

2. Liangguang is now Guangdong and Guangxi.

3. Marshal Yang Jian was one of the Six Villains of Xuande mentioned above.

4. Lantian, in present-day Shaanxi, is famous for its jade.

5. Grand Preceptor Cai is Cai Jing, one of the Six Villains of Xuanhe mentioned at the beginning of the story.

6. Yang Shi (1053–1135), also known as Gentleman of Mount Gui, was a philosopher of the neo-Confucian school of principle.

7. According to "King Mu of Zhou, III" in *Liezi,* a woodsman in the state of Zheng forgot where he hid the deer that he had killed and thought he had dreamt about it. Another man heard about this, found the deer, and took it home. Then the woodsman remembered in a dream the place where he had hidden the deer and, in the same dream, also saw the man who got the deer. He sought out that man, and the two brought the case to court. When asked for

his judgment, the prime minister said, "I can't tell what is dream and what is not."

8. Zhuang Zhou, or Zhuangzi (ca. 369–286 B.C.E.), was a Daoist philosopher. According to the book that bears his name, he once dreamed that he was a butterfly, which did not know that it was Zhuang Zhou. When he awoke suddenly, he found himself Zhuang Zhou again, but he did not know whether he was Zhuang Zhou who had dreamed that he was a butterfly, or a butterfly dreaming that it was Zhuang Zhou.

9. A cangue is a wooden collar, usually three or four feet square, used in ancient China to confine the neck and sometimes also the hands of convicts.

10. Xiao He (d. 193 B.C.E.) was an early lawmaker. When he was prime minister under the first emperor of the Han dynasty, he formulated the larger part of the Han penal code.

9. Over Fifteen Strings of Cash, a Jest Leads to Dire Disasters

The title of the Song dynasty version of the story is "The Wrongful Execution of Cui Ning."

This story, no. 33 in *Stories to Awaken the World,* has been translated by Jeanne Kelly as "The Jest that Leads to Disaster" in *Traditional Chinese Stories: Themes and Variations,* ed. Y. W. Ma and Joseph S. M. Lau (New York: Columbia University Press, 1978); by Yang Xianyi and Gladys Yang as "Fifteen Strings of Cash" in *Lazy Dragon: Chinese Stories from the Ming Dynasty* (Hong Kong: Joint Publishing Co., 1981); and by William Dolby as "A Joke over Fifteen Strings of Cash Brings Uncanny Disaster" in *The Perfect Lady by Mistake and Other Stories by Feng Menglong* (London: Paul Elek, 1976).

1. Li Cunxiao (d. 894) was an adopted son of Li Keyong (856–908), whose birth son, Li Cunxu (885–926), founded the Later Tang dynasty. Li Cunxiao performed meritorious military service but was later framed and executed.

2. Peng Yue (d. 196 B.C.E.) helped Liu Bang found the Han dynasty but was later killed by Liu Bang. For an account of his tragic death, see story 31 in Feng Menglong, *Stories Old and New.*

3. Liu Wu (d. 144 B.C.E.), prince of Liang of the Han dynasty, had a fabulous garden located near Kaifeng in Henan.

www.ingramcontent.com/pod-product-compliance
Lightning Source LLC
Chambersburg PA
CBHW020110030726

47498CB00006B/2037